WHO PLAYED WHO IN THE MOVIES

AN A–Z

WHO PLAYED WHO IN THE MOVIES

AN A–Z

Roy Pickard

Schocken Books · New York

First published by Schocken Books 1981
10 9 8 7 6 5 4 3 2 1   81 82 83 84 85

Copyright © 1979 Roy Pickard

Library of Congress Cataloging in Publication Data

Pickard, Roy.
    Who played who in the movies.
    Reprint of the ed. published by F. Muller,
London.
    Includes index.
    1. Characters and characteristics in moving-
pictures—Dictionaries. 2. Historical films—
Dictionaries. 3. Film adaptations—Dictionaries.
I. Title.
PN1995.9.C36P5   1981   791.43′09′0927   80-26546

Manufactured in the United States of America
ISBN 0-8052-3766-6 hardcover
ISBN 0-8052-0676-0 paperback

Dedication

For Charles, for suggesting the rebirth.

Stills by courtesy of:

American International; Avco Embassy; Columbia; Commonwealth United; EMI; First Artists; GTO; Innovasions/ECA; MGM; Paramount; Rank; Twentieth Century-Fox; Universal; United Artists; Warner Bros.

Preface

This volume is the third in a quartet of reference books begun by *The Oscar Movies* and *The Hollywood Studios*. Its aim is a simple one, namely to answer questions about who *has* played who in the movies, settle long-standing arguments and provide information not readily available in existing books of its kind. Above all, it tries to delete, as much as possible, those two words most disliked in film reference works — 'includes' and 'etc'.

Set out in an A–Z format by name of character, the book provides immediate answers to such frequently asked questions as: How many times has James Bond been played on screen? Or Jack The Ripper? Or Miss Marple? Or Buddy Holly? Or Henry VIII? Or Al Capone? Or Fanny Brice? Or 'Dirty Harry' Callahan?

The net, which incorporates several hundred entries, is cast that wide.

Great care has been taken to ensure that the book contains something for everyone. Personal preference has been set aside so that The Good, The Bad and The Ugly can be included. *Who Played Who In The Movies* attempts to be a book for all seasons.

No previous book has devoted itself entirely to this one aspect of movie reference. This volume therefore fills a gap. Hopefully, it fills it in an entertaining and lively manner for although it has been compiled after months of exhaustive research at the British Film Institute and correspondence with Institutes all over the world, it is meant, on occasion to amuse as well as be a useful browse for information.

Who Played Who In The Movies concentrates on sound cinema (although it frequently mentions the silent days) and is international in scope. The main yardstick for the inclusion of each character is that he or she should have been the subject of at least one major film biography. The entries also combine fiction with fact and include many of the most famous characters in world literature. Much of the information is published here for the first time.

Each entry is prefaced by an introductory paragraph about each character, then followed by comprehensive listings detailing the number of times the character has been portrayed on film. These listings are broken down thus: name of actor, name of film, its director, country of origin and year of release.

Porn movies such as *The Erotic Adventures Of Zorro* have been omitted as they bear little or no relevance to serious screen interpretations. So too have ballet and opera films. Also, most (although not all) Made-For-TV

Movies which, for some reason, fail to hold the same attraction as old cinema films and, as a general rule, disappear after one showing, never to appear again.

Chief amongst my reference sources have been the pages of Variety, the Monthly Film Bulletin of the British Film Institute, the Catalogues of the American Film Institute and Denis Gifford's invaluable British Film Catalogue. Hundreds of other magazines and books, too numerous to mention here, were consulted and double checked.

Obviously, no film book will ever be 100% correct in the information that it provides. But this book is a serious attempt to present comprehensive facts about a hitherto frequently neglected aspect of the movies.

It is, in short, a beginning. At the moment, it is right up to date. I hope that it remains so for many years to come. Please do not hesitate to write to me, c/o my publishers Frederick Muller, if you discover any omissions or mistakes or feel that other characters should be included. All suggestions will be carefully noted and taken into account when future editions of the book are being prepared.

Happy browsing.

Roy Pickard

A

Adams, Nick

The central character in Ernest Hemingway's 1924 collection of short stories, 'In Our Time', a young man, closely modelled on the author himself, who reaches an early maturity when he leaves home in Michigan to serve as an ambulance driver in Italy in World War 1. Martin Ritt's 145-minute film of his experiences combined several of the Nick Adams stories including 'The Battler' (played by Paul Newman), 'Big Two-Hearted River' and 'Indian Camp'.

Richard Beymer   *Hemingway's Adventures Of A Young Man*   (Ritt)
USA, 62

Adamson, Joy

The wife of a senior game warden in Kenya who raised a wild lion cub (named Elsa) to maturity and then had the painful task of reconditioning it to life in the wild. Her rearing of the baby lioness was filmed in 1966 as *Born Free*, her subsequent caring for Elsa's own cubs related in the sequel *Living Free*.

Virginia McKenna   *Born Free*   (Hill)   GB, 66
Susan Hampshire   *Living Free*   (Couffer)   GB, 72

Adler, Polly

The most notorious (and successful) New York bordello madam of the 20s, known for her line-up of beautiful girls and renowned clientele which included the rich, the famous and the infamous, e.g. Mafia boss 'Lucky' Luciano. Shelley Winters played her in the 1964 biography, *A House Is Not A Home*, a film not helped by Miss Winters having to deliver such lines as 'I pin my diamonds on my loneliness and despair.' Still, as madams go, she remains one of the few to get her life story on the screen.

Shelley Winters   *A House Is Not A Home*   (Rouse)   USA, 64

Ahab, Captain

The half-crazed, vengeful sea captain of Herman Melville's 'Moby Dick' (1851), a man obsessed with his search for the great white whale that has maimed him and who takes his schooner 'Pequod' on its last doomed voyage. With its dark, symbolic overtones, one of the most difficult roles to interpret satisfactorily on screen. John Barrymore made two attempts, one silent, one sound, Gregory Peck just one in John Huston's near perfect adaptation of 1956.

John Barrymore	*Moby Dick*	(Bacon)	USA, 30
Gregory Peck	*Moby Dick*	(Huston)	USA, 56

Note: John Barrymore first appeared as Ahab in 1926 in Millard Webb's *The Sea Beast*; Gregory Peck was the final choice of John Huston who had originally wanted to make the film with his father Walter Huston in the pivotal role.

Alexander The Great

(356–323 B.C.) King Of Macedonia (educated by Aristotle) who extended the Greek civilization into the East and founded an empire that stretched through Syria and Egypt and into India. Robert Rossen's ambitious film of his conquests was not a success, but it did at least have the distinction of being the first intelligent epic at a time when the genre was dominated by slave girls, crashing temples and fatal haircuts!

Richard Burton	*Alexander The Great*	(Rossen)	USA, 56

Alexandra, Feodorovna

(1872–1918) German-born wife of Tsar Nicholas II, much hated by the Russian people and who gained notoriety when she fell under the influence of the peasant monk Rasputin. Eventually imprisoned and shot with her family in July 1918, she was portrayed with distinction by Janet Suzman in *Nicholas And Alexandra* which encompassed the events that precipitated the collapse of the dynasty.

Hermine Sterler	*Rasputin* (Trotz)		Ger, 32
Ethel Barrymore	*Rasputin And The Empress* (Boleslawsky)		
			USA, 32
Lucie Hoeffrich	*1914: The Last Days Before The War*		
		(Oswald)	Ger, 32
Marcelle Chantal	*Rasputin* (L'Herbier)		Fra, 39
Isa Miranda	*Rasputin* (Combret)		Fra, 54
Gianna Maria Canale	*The Nights Of Rasputin* (Chenal)		Fra/It, 60
Renee Asherson	*Rasputin — The Mad Monk* (Sharp)		GB, 66
Janet Suzman	*Nicholas And Alexandra* (Schaffner)		USA, 71

Note: Julia Dean in *Rasputin, The Black Monk* (USA, 17), Elinor Vanderveer in *Into Her Kingdom* (USA, 26) and Diana Karenne in *Rasputin And The Holy Devil* (Ger, 28) all appeared as Alexandra in silent productions.

Alice In Wonderland

One of literature's most enduring heroines, a little girl who experiences a remarkable series of adventures when she tumbles down a rabbit hole and discovers a world dominated by a fantastic illogicality. No film-maker has quite managed to come to terms with the fantasy elements of the tale, although Disney's animated version of 1951 continues to improve with age. Most films combine incidents from the two Lewis Carroll novels 'Alice's Adventures In Wonderland' (1865) and 'Alice Through The Looking Glass' (1872).

Ruth Gilbert	*Alice In Wonderland*	(Pollard)	USA, 31
Charlotte Henry	*Alice In Wonderland*	(McLeod)	USA, 33
Carol Marsh	*Alice In Wonderland*	(Bower)	Fra/GB, 50
Kathryn Beaumont	*Alice In Wonderland*	(Disney)	USA, 51
Fiona Fullerton	*Alice's Adventures In Wonderland*	(Sterling)	GB, 72

Note: Carol Marsh's performance was in a part puppet, part live-action version of the story, Kathryn Beaumont voiced Alice in the Disney film of 1951.

On the silent screen, May Clark appeared in a British film of 1903 and Mary Fuller in an American production of 1910.

Amundsen, Roald

(1872–1928) Norwegian explorer who became the first man to reach the South Pole when he beat Captain Scott to the objective by just a few weeks in December, 1911. Seventeen years later, he met his death whilst flying to rescue the survivors of General Nobile's disastrous airship expedition to the Arctic, an event recorded in the 1971 film *The Red Tent*.

Sean Connery	*The Red Tent* (Kalatozov)	It/USSR, 71

Anastasia

(1901–1918?) The youngest of the four daughters of Tsar Nicholas and Alexandra, supposedly murdered by the Bolsheviks in July, 1918, but later rumoured to have survived the massacre. Two films of 1956, one German, one American, investigated the possibility of Anastasia being alive. The latter starred Ingrid Bergman as an amnesiac refugee who is passed off by a group of con men as the last of the Romanovs.

Dawn O'Day	*Rasputin And The Empress* (Boleslawsky)	USA, 32
Lilli Palmer	*Is Anna Anderson Anastasia?* (Harnack)	Ger, 56
Ingrid Bergman	*Anastasia* (Litvak)	USA, 56
Fiona Fullerton	*Nicholas And Alexandra* (Schaffner)	USA, 71

Note: Dawn O'Day later changed her name to Anne Shirley.

Anastasia, Alberto

A Mafia boss, featured prominently in the recent spate of movies about organized crime in the United States. Known as the 'Lord High Executioner' for his ruthless methods of killing, he rose to power through his association with Mafia king, Lucky Luciano, and in the 50s challenged for the top spot in Murder Inc. Like most Mafia leaders he met his end in a grisly fashion — shot to death in a New York hotel barber shop in 1957. Richard Conte's performance in *My Brother Anastasia* is the most detailed screen portrait to date.

Howard I. Smith	*Murder, Inc* (Balaban/Rosenberg)	USA, 60
Fausto Tozzi	*The Valachi Papers* (Young)	Fra/It, 73
Richard Conte	*My Brother Anastasia* (Vanzina)	It, 73
Gianni Russo	*Lepke* (Golan)	USA, 75

Andersen, Hans Christian

(1805–1875) Danish poet and teller of fairy tales; the subject of a large-scale Technicolor Goldwyn musical of the 50s and an animated feature of 1972. Goldwyn's film starred Danny Kaye as the story teller in love with a ballerina and adapted several of Andersen's stories into musical numbers e.g. 'The Ugly Duckling', 'Thumbelina' and 'The King's New Clothes'.

Danny Kaye	*Hans Christian Andersen* (Charles Vidor)	USA, 52
Paul O'Keefe	*The Daydreamer* (Bass)	USA, 66
Richard Wordsworth	*Song Of Norway* (Stone)	USA, 70
Jesper Klein	*Hans Christian Andersen in Italy* (Cavaterra)	Den/It, 79

Note: Hetty Galen voiced the role in *The World Of Hans Christian Andersen*, the '72 cartoon of Chuck McCann and Al Kilgore.

Annie, Apple

Gin-soaked, derelict old street vendor, transformed by a group of Broadway mobsters into a society matron when her long lost daughter threatens a surprise visit to New York. The central character in Damon

Runyon's early short story 'Madame La Gimp' and portrayed twice on screen — both times memorably.

May Robson	*Lady For A Day* (Capra)	USA, 33
Bette Davis	*Pocketful Of Miracles* (Capra)	USA, 61

Antony, Marc

(*c.* 82–30 B.C.) Roman soldier and politician who avenged the murder of Caesar by destroying Cassius and Brutus at Philippi, then lost his influence in Rome when he became infatuated with Egyptian Queen, Cleopatra, and opted for a dissipated rather than a distinguished way of life. Marlon Brando delivered Shakespeare's 'Friends, Romans, Countrymen' speech in Mankiewicz's 1953 film; Richard Burton dallied with Elizabeth Taylor in the same director's *Cleopatra*, made a decade later. Charlton Heston has been drawn to the character on three occasions, twice in Shakespeare's *Julius Caesar* and once in *Antony And Cleopatra* which he also directed in 1972.

Henry Wilcoxon	*Cleopatra* (DeMille)	USA, 34
Charlton Heston	*Julius Caesar* (Bradley)	USA, 50
Marlon Brando	*Julius Caesar* (Mankiewicz)	USA, 53
Raymond Burr	*Serpent Of The Nile* (Castle)	USA, 53
Helmut Dantine	*The Story Of Mankind* (Allen)	USA, 57
Georges Marchal	*Legions Of The Nile* (Cottafavi)	It/Spa/Fra, 59
Bruno Tocci	*Caesar The Conqueror* (Anton)	It, 62
Richard Burton	*Cleopatra* (Mankiewicz)	USA, 63
Sidney James	*Carry On Cleo* (Thomas)	GB, 65
Charlton Heston	*Julius Caesar* (Burge)	GB, 70
Charlton Heston	*Antony And Cleopatra* (Heston)	Swi/Spa/GB, 72

Note: Philip Saville appeared as the Antony character in *An Honourable Murder* (GB, 60), a modernized version of *Julius Caesar*; Frank Benson featured in the role in a silent British production of 1911.

Aramis

The most elegant of Alexandre Dumas' Three Musketeers, a poetry-writing womaniser who is forever vowing to renounce his adventurous ways for a more pious life in a monastery. In the movies he is simply a well-bred swashbuckler, more dandyish than most but still rallying to the call, 'All For One and One For All!' Richard Chamberlain has come the closest to capturing the true Aramis on screen.

Gino Corrado	*The Iron Mask* (Dwan)	USA, 29
Onslow Stevens	*The Three Musketeers* (Lee)	USA, 35
John King	*The Three Musketeers* (Dwan)	USA, 39
Miles Mander	*The Man In The Iron Mask* (Whale)	USA, 39

Robert Coote	*The Three Musketeers* (Sidney)	USA, 48
Carlo Ninchi	*The Gay Swordsman* (Freda)	It, 50
Keith Richards	*Sword Of D'Artagnan* (Boetticher)	USA, 52
Judd Holdren	*Lady In The Iron Mask* (Murphy)	USA, 52
Jacques Francois	*The Three Musketeers* (Hunebelle)	Fra, 53
Paul Campbell	*The Knights Of The Queen* (Bolognini)	
		It, 54
Jacques Toja	*The Three Musketeers* (Borderie)	Fra, 61
Giacomo Rossi Stuart	*Zorro And The Three Musketeers* (Capuano)	
		It, 63
Roberto Risso	*Revenge Of The Musketeers* (Tulli)	It, 64
Richard Chamberlain	*The Three Musketeers* (Lester)	
		Panama/Spa, 74
Richard Chamberlain	*The Four Musketeers* (Lester)	
		Panama/Spa, 75
Lloyd Bridges	*The Fifth Musketeer* (Annakin)	Aus, 79

Note: Dan O'Herlihy starred as the son of Aramis in *At Sword's Point* (52): Eugene Pallette in *The Three Musketeers* (USA, 21) and Pierre de Guingand in the French serials, *The Three Musketeers* (22) and *Twenty Years After* (22), featured as Aramis on the silent screen.

Arrowsmith, Dr. Martin

An idealistic young doctor who struggles against public apathy, corruption and the hypocrisies of his colleagues in his search for a cure for bubonic plague. One of Sinclair Lewis' most intricate characters, created in 1925 and transferred to the screen just once — by John Ford in 1931.

Ronald Colman	*Arrowsmith* (Ford)	USA, 31

D'Artagnan

The prince of swashbucklers, brought to life in three novels by Alexandre Dumas — 'The Three Musketeers' (1844), 'Twenty Years After' (1845) and 'The Viscount of Bragelonne' (1848–50) — and then again in the 20th century when a host of actors (notably Douglas Fairbanks) recreated him for the screen. A quick-tempered young Gascon who takes up service with the King's Musketeers, he was based on a real historical personage who lived in 16th century France. Dumas' novels follow D'Artagnan's exploits from his days as a young man to his death as Comte d'Artagnan, Master of France. The films have generally concentrated on his earlier adventures.

Douglas Fairbanks	*The Iron Mask* (Dwan)	USA, 29
Walter Abel	*The Three Musketeers* (Lee)	USA, 35
Warren William	*The Man In The Iron Mask* (Whale)	USA, 39

Don Ameche	*The Three Musketeers* (Dwan)	USA, 39
Gene Kelly	*The Three Musketeers* (Sidney)	USA, 48
Robert Clarke	*Sword Of D'Artagnan* (Boetticher)	USA, 52
Louis Hayward	*Lady In The Iron Mask* (Murphy)	USA, 52
Georges Marchal	*The Three Musketeers* (Hunebelle)	USA, 53
Jeff Stone	*The Knights Of The Queen* (Bolognini)	It, 54
Gerard Philipe	*Versailles* (Guitry)	Fra, 54
Jacques Dumsenil	*Le Vicomte de Bragelonne* (Cerchio)	Fra/It, 55
Gerard Barry	*The Three Musketeers* (Borderie)	Fra, 61
Jean-Pierre Cassel	*Cyrano And D'Artagnan* (Gance)	Fra, 62
Jean Marais	*The Iron Mask* (DeCoin)	Fra, 62
George Nader	*The Secret Mark Of D'Artagnan* (Marcellini)	
		It/Fra, 62
Franco Fantasia	*Zorro And The Three Musketeers* (Capuano)	It, 63
Fernando Lamas	*Revenge Of The Musketeers* (Tulli)	It, 64
Michael York	*The Three Musketeers* (Lester)	Panama/Spa, 74
Michael York	*The Four Musketeers* (Lester)	Panama/Spa, 75
Cornel Wilde	*The Fifth Musketeer* (Annakin)	Aus, 79

Note: Louis Jourdan featured as D'Artagnan in the TV movie *The Man In The Iron Mask* (77); Cornel Wilde appeared as his son in *At Sword's Point* (52).

Douglas Fairbanks, in the 1921 version of *The Three Musketeers*, remains the most famous of the silent portrayals. Sydney Booth (USA, 11), M. Dehelly (Fra, 13), Aime Simon-Girard (Fra, 22) and Yonnel (Fra, 22) were others who featured in the role.

Artful Dodger, The

Otherwise, 'Master John Dawkins', smartest of Fagin's boy pupils in Dickens' 'Oliver Twist'. Adept in villainy, especially pickpocketing, he leads the innocent young workhouse boy into a life of crime in 19th century London. Most authoritative screen portrait: Anthony Newley in Lean's film of 1948.

Sonny Ray	*Oliver Twist* (Cowen)	USA, 33
Anthony Newley	*Oliver Twist* (Lean)	GB, 48
Jack Wild	*Oliver!* (Reed)	GB, 68

Note: Willie West (GB, 12), Charles Rogers (USA, 12), Raymond Hatton (USA, 16) and Edouard Trebaol (USA, 22) all played The Artful Dodger on the silent screen; Scott McKee appeared in the 1921 modernized verion *Oliver Twist Jr*. A Hungarian adaptation directed by Marton Garas, was released in 1919.

Arthur, King

British king, possibly legendary, who was reputed to have defeated the invading Saxons in 6th century Britain. Much better known, however, as the mythical figure who extracted the sword 'Excalibur' from the rock and presided over the famous knights of the round table. The screen has presented him in various moods — heroic, cynical and, through the song 'How To Handle A Woman' in *Camelot*, sadly embittered.

William Farnum	*A Connecticut Yankee* (Butler)	USA, 31
Cedric Hardwicke	*A Connecticut Yankee In King Arthur's*	
	Court (Garnett)	USA, 49
Brian Aherne	*Prince Valiant* (Hathaway)	USA, 54
Mel Ferrer	*Knights Of The Round Table* (Thorpe)	
		GB, 54
Anthony Bushell	*The Black Knight* (Garnett)	GB, 54
Brian Aherne	*Lancelot And Guinevere* (Wilde)	GB, 63
Mark Dignam	*Siege Of The Saxons* (Juran)	GB, 63
Richard Harris	*Camelot* (Logan)	USA, 67
Vladimir Antolek-Oresek	*Lancelot du lac* (Bresson)	Fra/It, 74
Graham Chapman	*Monty Python And The Holy Grail*	
	(Gilliam/Jones)	GB, 75
Marc Eyraud	*Perceval Le Gallois* (Rohmer)	Fra, 78
Kenneth More	*The Spaceman and King Arthur*	
	(Mayberry)	GB, 79

Note: Rickie Sorensen voiced the boy Arthur in Disney's *The Sword In The Stone* (63); Charles Clary featured as the king in the 1921 silent version of *A Connecticut Yankee At King Arthur's Court*.

Athos

The most introspective of Dumas' three musketeers, moody, embittered and forever haunted by the memory of a romance with a woman who turned out to be an unscrupulous whore. When sober, possibly the best swordsman of the three; when drunk, an irresponsible saturnine woman hater. Van Heflin admirably caught the varied moods of the character in MGM's lavish colour spectacular of 1948.

Leon Barry	*The Iron Mask* (Dwan)	USA, 29
Paul Lukas	*The Three Musketeers* (Lee)	USA, 35
Douglas Dumbrille	*The Three Musketeers* (Dwan)	USA, 39
Bert Roach	*The Man In The Iron Mask* (Whale)	USA, 39
Van Heflin	*The Three Musketeers* (Sidney)	USA, 48
Rossano Brazzi	*Milady And The Musketeers* (Cottafavi)	It, 51
John Hubbard	*Sword Of D'Artagnan* (Boetticher)	USA, 52
Steve Brodie	*Lady In The Iron Mask* (Murphy)	USA, 52
Jean Martinelli	*The Three Musketeers* (Hunebelle)	Fra, 53
Domenico Modugno	*The Knights Of The Queen* (Bolognini)	It, 54
Georges Descrieres	*The Three Musketeers* (Borderie)	Fra, 61
Gianni Rizzo	*Zorro And The Three Musketeers* (Capuano)	
		It, 63

Franco Fantasia	*Revenge Of The Musketeers* (Tulli)	It, 64
Oliver Reed	*The Three Musketeers* (Lester)	
		Panama/Spa, 74
Oliver Reed	*The Four Musketeers* (Lester)	Panama/Spa, 75
Jose Ferrer	*The Fifth Musketeer* (Annakin)	Aus, 79

Note: Maureen O'Hara featured as Claire, daughter of Athos in *At Sword's Point* (52); Leon Barry was also a silent Athos in *The Three Musketeers* (21) and Henri Rollan appeared in the role in Henri Berger's *The Three Musketeers* (22) and *Twenty Years After* (22).

Attila The Hun

(*c.* 406–453) Fifth century Hunnish king, known affectionately as the 'Scourge Of God', who overran much of Europe with his Asian hordes, creating terror and devastation in his wake. Ideal for the movies one would have thought, but until Miklos Jancso's *Young Attila*, strictly a formularised villain whose intriguing paganism was lost among the usual casts of thousands!

Jack Palance	*The Sign Of The Pagan* (Sirk)	USA, 54
Anthony Quinn	*Attila The Hun* (Fransisci)	Fra/It, 55
Jozsef Madaras	*Young Attila* (Jancso)	It, 71

Aylward, Gladys

English servant girl who assisted at a remote mission station in China in the days prior to World War II and became world famous through her best-selling book 'The Small Woman'. A victim of the Hollywood soap opera treatment in *The Inn Of The Sixth Happiness* but not, luckily, the Japanese from whom she escaped with some orphaned children on a dangerous trek over the mountains. She died in 1970, aged 68.

| Ingrid Bergman | *The Inn Of The Sixth Happiness* (Robson) | GB, 58 |

B

Bader, Douglas

(1910–   ) RAF fighter pilot who lost both legs in a flying accident in 1931 and bravely overcame his disability through the use of artificial limbs. The 1956 film with Kenneth More covered ten years in Bader's life, from the time of his accident to when he rejoined the airforce and became one of the heroic 'few'.

Kenneth More	*Reach For The Sky* (Gilbert)	GB, 56

Barabbas

The criminal condemned to death on the cross and released instead of Jesus by Pontius Pilate. A 'cameo' role in biblical epics, a major one in Richard Fleischer's 1962 film which traced Barabbas' life from the time of his release through his years as a slave and gladiator to his eventual ironic death by crucifixion.

Anthony Warde	*The Day Of Triumph* (Pichel/Coyle)	USA, 54
Harry Guardino	*King Of Kings* (Ray)	USA, 61
Livio Lorenzon	*Ponzio Pilato* (Callegari)	It/Fra, 61
Anthony Quinn	*Barabbas* (Fleischer)	It, 62
Richard Conte	*The Greatest Story Ever Told* (Stevens)	USA, 65
Stacy Keach	*Jesus Of Nazareth* (Zeffirelli)	GB, 77

Note: George Seigmann played Barabbas in DeMille's 1927 silent film, *King Of Kings*.

Barker, Kate 'Ma'

(1880–1935) Queen of the 'lady' gangsters of the 30s. Together with her four sons and Alvin Karpis, she executed several quarter-of-a-million bank jobs in Kansas, Missouri and Minnesota before coming to a bloody end in a shootout with the FBI at her Florida hideout. Shelley Winters' massive performance in Roger Corman's *Bloody Mama* is the definitive screen portrayal and likely to remain so for many years to come.

Jean Harvey	*Guns Don't Argue* (Karn/Kahn)	USA, 55
Lurene Tuttle	*Ma Barker's Killer Brood* (Karn)	USA, 60
Shelley Winters	*Bloody Mama* (Corman)	USA, 70

Note: Blanche Yurka's Ma Webster was closely based on Barker in the 1940 production, *Queen Of The Mob*; the characters of Irene Dailey in *The Grissom Gang* (71) and Angie Dickinson in *Big Bad Mama* (74) were also loosely derived from that of the notorious woman outlaw.

Barnum, Phineas Taylor

(1810–1891) Brash American showman who helped put the word razzmatazz into show business and joined with rival James Anthony Bailey in forming the famous Barnum and Bailey Circus. His efforts proved worthwhile: when he died he was worth five million dollars. Wallace Beery played him twice in the early 30s, first in *A Lady's Morals* in which he managed international singing star Jenny Lind, second in *The Mighty Barnum* in which he created his massive circus.

Wallace Beery	*A Lady's Morals* (Franklin)	USA, 30
Wallace Beery	*The Mighty Barnum* (Walter Lang)	USA, 34
Burl Ives	*Jules Verne's Rocket To The Moon* (Sharp)	GB, 67

Note: Maclyn Arbuckle featured as Barnum in J. Searle Dawley's silent film *Broadway Broke* (23).

Barrymore, John

(1882–1942) Another in the long line of great Hollywood actors who literally drank themselves into the grave. Before alcohol took control he was known as 'The Great Profile' and portrayed many famous literary characters on the screen i.e. Dr. Jekyll And Mr. Hyde, Captain Ahab, Raffles, Svengali, Arsene Lupin. In *Too Much, Too Soon*, the screen biography of Barrymore's daughter Diana, Errol Flynn stole the honours with his portrait of the once great actor in the final throes of disintegration.

Errol Flynn	*Too Much, Too Soon* (Napoleon)	USA, 58
Jack Cassidy	*W. C. Fields And Me* (Hiller)	USA, 76

Note: John Barrymore was the model for the character of Tony Cavendish, played by Fredric March in *The Royal Family Of Broadway*, directed by George Cukor and Cyril Gardner in 1930.

Batman

Masked crime fighter who, together with his young aide Robin, fought a never ending 'lone battle against the evil forces in society'. Hooded, caped and muscular, he was created by Bob Kane in a 1939 issue of Detective Comics and continued his crusades in screen serials of the 40s and a popular, long-running TV series of the 60s.

Lewis Wilson	*Batman* (Hillyer)	USA, 43
Robert Lowrey	*Batman And Robin* (Bennet)	USA, 49
Adam West	*Batman* (Martinson)	USA, 66

Note: Robin was played by Douglas Croft (43) and John Duncan (49) in the 1940 serials; by Burt Ward in Martinson's 1966 feature film.

In the 1966 production the chief members of the 'opposition' were played by Burgess Meredith (The Penguin), Cesar Romero (The Joker), Frank Gorshin (The Riddler) and Lee Meriwether (Catwoman).

Bean, Judge Roy

(1825–1903) 'Justice Of The Peace' in the town of Vinegaroon (later Langtry), Texas, during the 1880s and 90s but, in reality, a minor despot who referred to himself as the sole law 'West Of The Pecos'. Not without a sense of humour, he once acquitted a man for killing a Mexican because 'it served the deceased right for getting in front of the gun'. The fact that he lived until he was 78 proved that, for him at least, his system worked very well. Favourite hobbies: hanging horse thieves and worshipping actress Lily Langtry. Portrayed at length by Paul Newman in Huston's 1972 film *The Life And Times Of Judge Roy Bean*. An Oscar to Walter Brennan in 1940 for his portrayal in *The Westerner*.

Walter Brennan	*The Westerner* (Wyler)	USA, 40
Victor Jory	*A Time For Dying* (Boetticher)	USA, 69
Paul Newman	*The Life And Times Of Judge Roy Bean* (Huston)	USA, 72

Becket, Thomas

(1118–1170) Archbishop of Canterbury in 12th century England, murdered by soldiers in his cathedral on the orders of his former friend King Henry II. The turbulent relationship between Becket and Henry, from the time they drank and whored together, to their clash of wills over matters of state, was examined in Peter Glenville's version of Anouilh's 1959 stage play. Richard Burton and Peter O'Toole (Henry) both received Oscar nominations for their portrayals.

| Father John Groser | *Murder In The Cathedral* (Hoellering) | GB, 52 |
| Richard Burton | *Becket* (Glenville) | GB, 64 |

Note: Sir Frank Benson starred in George Ridgwell's silent biography, *Becket* (GB, 23)

Beethoven, Ludwig van

(1770–1827) German composer of outstanding genius, famous for his development of the symphony and his inspired work in many other musical forms, including chamber music, sonatas and concertos. Ewald Balser offered a sensitive portrayal of the composer in the 1949 Austrian film, *Eroica*; in 1970, the bicentennial of Beethoven's birth, Hans Conrad Fischer produced the documentary *Ludwig van Beethoven*. In 1960 Hollywood looked at episodes in the life of the young composer and referred to him as *The Magnificent Rebel*.

Harry Baur	*The Life And Loves Of Beethoven* (Gance)	Fra, 36
Auguste Boverio	*Schubert's Serenade* (Boyer)	Fra, 40
Albert Basserman	*New Wine* (Schunzel)	USA, 41
Rene Deltgen	*Whom The Gods Love* (Hartl)	Ger, 42
Memo Benassi	*Rossini* (Bonnard)	It, 46
Ewald Balser	*Eroica* (Kolm-Veltee)	Aus, 49
Erich von Stroheim	*Napoleon* (Guitry)	Fra, 54
Ewald Balser	*Das Dreimaderlhaus* (Marischka)	Aus, 58
Carl Boehm	*The Magnificent Rebel* (Tressler)	USA, 60

Bel Ami

Guy de Maupassant's unscrupulous young scoundrel who uses his power over women to reach the top in Parisian society during the 1880s. Real name: Georges Duroy. Three portrayals on film.

Willi Forst	*Bel Ami* (Forst)	Ger, 39
George Sanders	*The Private Affairs of Bel Ami* (Lewin)	USA, 47
Jean Danet	*Bel Ami* (Daquin)	Fra/Aus, 55

Bell, Alexander Graham

(1847–1922) Scottish-born American physicist whose invention of the telephone in 1876 brought him wealth, fame and a posthumous Hollywood biography starring Don Ameche!

Don Ameche	*The Story Of Alexander Graham Bell* (Cummings)	USA, 39
Jim Ameche	*The Story Of Mankind* (Allen)	USA, 57

Bernadette of Lourdes

(1844–1879). Real name, Bernadette Soubirous. The humble French peasant girl who, in 1858, saw visions of the Virgin Mary and discovered a miraculous healing spring at Lourdes. Jennifer Jones won a best actress Academy Award for her visions of 1943; Daniele Ajoret featured in a little-known French/Italian film of 1960.

Jennifer Jones	*The Song Of Bernadette* (King)	USA, 43
Daniele Ajoret	*Bernadette Of Lourdes* (Darene)	Fra/It, 60.

Bernhardt, Sarah

(1844–1923) In the words of Oscar Wilde, 'The Divine Sarah', regarded by many who saw her as the greatest of all French actresses. Eccentric (she often slept in a rosewood coffin) and energetic (she reputedly enjoyed a thousand lovers), she just managed to be recorded on film for posterity in *Camille* (10), *Queen Elizabeth* (12), *Jeanne Dore* (15). In the 1976 biography by Richard Fleischer her lovers were reduced by 997 to three!

Glenda Jackson	*The Incredible Sarah* (Fleischer)	USA, 76

Bernstein, Carl and Woodward, Bob

The young Washington Post reporters who stumbled onto the story of the Watergate burglary and then uncovered a terrifying trail of corruption that led to the Department of Justice, the FBI and finally the President of the United States. In Pakula's political thriller, *All The President's Men*, Dustin Hoffman is Carl Bernstein, Robert Redford Bob Woodward.

Dustin Hoffman & Robert Redford	*All The President's Men* (Pakula)	USA, 76

Billy The Kid

(1859–1881) Outlaw of the American West who, if legend is to be believed, might have stayed on the right side of the law had his boss, rancher John Tunstall, not been killed in the Lincoln County War. Thereafter, it was a life of crime and a final boast that he had killed one man for every day of his young life. Screen portrayals have become less romantic and more realistic with the passing of time, i.e. Michael J. Pollard in *Dirty Little Billy* and Kris Kristofferson in Peckinpah's *Pat Garrett And Billy The Kid*. Real name: William Bonney

Johnny Mack Brown	*Billy The Kid* (King Vidor)	USA, 30
Roy Rogers	*Billy The Kid Returns* (Kane)	USA, 38

Robert Taylor	*Billy The Kid* (Miller)	USA, 41
Jack Buetel	*The Outlaw* (Hughes)	USA, 43
Dean White	*Return Of The Badmen* (Enright)	USA, 48
Don Barry	*I Shot Billy The Kid* (Berke)	USA, 50
Audie Murphy	*Texas Kid Outlaw* (Neumann)	USA, 50
Scott Brady	*The Law vs Billy The Kid* (Castle)	USA, 54
Tyler MacDuff	*The Boy From Oklahoma* (Curtiz)	USA, 54
Nick Adams	*Strange Lady In Town* (LeRoy)	USA, 55
Anthony Dexter	*The Parson And The Outlaw* (Drake)	USA, 57
Paul Newman	*The Left-Handed Gun* (Penn)	USA, 58
Jack Taylor	*Billy The Kid* (Klimovsky)	Spa, 62
Johnny Ginger	*The Outlaws Is Coming* (Maurer)	USA, 65
Chuck Courtenay	*Billy The Kid vs Dracula* (Beaudine)	USA, 66
Peter Lee Lawrence	*The Man Who Killed Billy The Kid* (Buchs)	
		Spa/It, 67
Geoffrey Deuel	*Chisum* (McLaglen)	USA, 70
Jean-Pierre Leaud	*A Girl Is A Gun* (Moullet)	Fra, 71
Michael J. Pollard	*Dirty Little Billy* (Dragoti)	USA, 72
Kris Kristofferson	*Pat Garrett And Billy The Kid* (Peckinpah)	
		USA, 73

Bismarck, Otto von

(1815–1898) Prussian statesman and diplomat, a key figure in German nationalism and responsible for the unification of Germany in 1871. Not surprisingly, his achievements attracted Hitler's Third Reich and two major biographies, both featuring Emil Jannings, appeared in the early 40s. In *Royal Flash*, Oliver Reed played Bismarck in his younger years, before his rise to power.

Lyn Harding	*Spy Of Napoleon* (Elvey)	GB, 36
Emil Jannings	*Bismarck* (Liebeneiner)	Ger, 40
Emil Jannings	*Bismarck's Dismissal* (Liebeneiner)	Ger, 41
Lyn Harding	*The Prime Minister* (Dickinson)	GB, 41
Friedrich Domin	*Ludwig 11* (Kautner)	Ger, 55
Oliver Reed	*Royal Flash* (Lester)	GB, 75

Blackbeard

(Died 1718) Fierce, wild-looking English pirate (real name, Edward Teach) who operated with barbaric success in the Caribbean in the early years of the 18th century. Just one screen biography, by Raoul Walsh in 1952, a film with one of the most gruesome last scenes in movie history — Blackbeard buried up to his neck in sand and unable to prevent his drowning by the incoming tide.

Louis Bacigalupi	*Double Crossbones* (Barton)	USA, 50
Thomas Gomez	*Anne Of The Indies* (Tourneur)	USA, 51

Robert Newton	*Blackbeard The Pirate* (Walsh)	USA, 52
Murvyn Vye	*The Boy And The Pirates* (Gordon)	USA, 60
Peter Ustinov	*Blackbeard's Ghost* (Stevenson)	USA, 67

Blaise, Modesty

Female counterpart to 007, Matt Helm, etc., a voluptuous super-agent/ adventuress who runs a successful international crime network. The one film made about her exploits has her hired by the British Secret Service to protect a shipment of diamonds. Knifings, druggings, chases and general bed-hopping result. She first appeared in the 1963 Evening Standard comic strip of Peter O'Donnell and Jim Holdaway.

| Monica Vitti | *Modesty Blaise* (Losey) | GB, 66 |

Blandish, Barbara

Heroine, if that is the correct word, of the James Hadley Chase novel 'No Orchids For Miss Blandish', a beautiful young heiress who falls in love with one of her captors when she is kidnapped by a brutal mob of gangsters. The 1948 version of the book, made in England, was filmed straight; Robert Aldrich's remake, *The Grissom Gang*, was set in rural America during the early Depression years. Chase's thriller, published in 1939, remains one of the best-selling mysteries ever published.

| Linden Travers | *No Orchids For Miss Blandish* (Clowes) | GB, 48 |
| Kim Darby | *The Grissom Gang* (Aldrich) | USA, 71 |

Note: Claire, daughter of Barbara, carried on from where her mother left off in *The Flesh Of The Orchid*, made by Patrice Chereau in France in 1975. Charlotte Rampling featured as Claire.

Bligh, William

(1754–1817) Sadistic captain of HMS Bounty, relieved of his command in 1789 and, along with eighteen men, set adrift in a small boat. A master seaman, he navigated nearly 3,600 miles of open sea and succeeded in returning to England. Charles Laughton's famous leer and the accompanying 'Fifty lashes, Mr. Christian' earned him world fame and an Oscar nomination.

Mayne Lynton	*In The Wake Of The Bounty* (Chauvel)	
		Austral, 33
Charles Laughton	*Mutiny On The Bounty* (Lloyd)	USA, 35
Trevor Howard	*Mutiny On The Bounty* (Milestone)	USA, 62

Blofeld, Ernst

Supreme controller of SPECTRE, the international criminal organization bent on world domination in Ian Fleming's series of James Bond novels. A shadowy, background figure in movies (only his voice was heard and his hands seen stroking his white cat) until Donald Pleasence arrived on the scene in *You Only Live Twice*.

Donald Pleasence	*You Only Live Twice* (Gilbert)	GB, 67
Telly Savalas	*On Her Majesty's Secret Service* (Hunt)	GB, 69
Charles Gray	*Diamonds Are Forever* (Hamilton)	GB, 71

Anne Boleyn

(1507–1536) The second wife of Henry VIII and the only one of the six to be afforded a full-scale film biography i.e. *Anne Of The Thousand Days*. A lady of honour to Henry's first queen, Catherine of Aragon, she bore the king a daughter (later Queen Elizabeth I) and a still-born son. Made to stand trial for adultery and witchcraft when Henry eventually tired of her, she was executed on the scaffold.

Merle Oberon	*The Private Life of Henry VIII* (Korda)	GB, 33
Barbara Shaw	*The Pearls Of The Crown* (Guitry/Jaque)	Fra, 37
Elaine Stewart	*Young Bess* (Sidney)	USA, 53
Vanessa Redgrave	*A Man For All Seasons* (Zinnemann)	GB, 66
Genevieve Bujold	*Anne Of The Thousand Days* (Jarrott)	GB, 69
Charlotte Rampling	*Henry VIII And His Six Wives* (Hussein)	GB, 72

Note: Anne was played on the silent screen by Laura Cowie in *Henry VIII* (GB, 11) and Henny Porten in Lubitsch's *Anna Boleyn* (Ger, 20).
   The other wives have been played on screen as follows:

Catherine of Aragon (1483–1536)

Rosalie Crutchley	*The Sword And The Rose* (Annakin)	GB, 53
Irene Papas	*Anne Of The Thousand Days* (Jarrott)	GB, 69
Frances Cuka	*Henry VIII And His Six Wives* (Hussein)	GB, 72

Jane Seymour (1509–1537)

Wendy Barrie	*The Private Life Of Henry VIII* (Korda)	GB, 33
Helen Valkis	*The Prince And The Pauper* (Keighley)	USA, 37
Lesley Paterson	*Anne Of The Thousand Days* (Jarrott)	GB, 69
Jane Asher	*Henry VIII And His Six Wives* (Hussein)	GB, 72

Anne Of Cleves (1515–1557)

Elsa Lanchester	*The Private Life Of Henry VIII* (Korda)	GB, 33
Jenny Bos	*Henry VIII And His Six Wives* (Hussein)	GB, 72

Catherine Howard (*c.* 1520–1542)

Binnie Barnes	*The Private Life Of Henry VIII* (Korda)	GB, 33
Dawn Addams	*Young Bess* (Sidney)	USA, 53
Monica Dietrich	*Carry On Henry* (Thomas)	GB, 71
Lynne Frederick	*Henry VIII And His Six Wives* (Hussein)	GB, 72

Catherine Parr (1512–1548)

Everley Gregg	*The Private Life Of Henry VIII* (Korda)	GB, 33
Deborah Kerr	*Young Bess* (Sidney)	USA, 53
Barbara Leigh-Hunt	*Henry VIII And His Six Wives* (Hussein)	
		GB, 72

Bond, James

The secret agent of modern times, an indestructible operator licensed 'to kill for queen and country'. Something of a sadist in the novels of Ian Fleming, little more than a comic-strip hero in the later films in the series. Code number: 007. Favourite drink: vodka martini, very dry, shaken not stirred. First appeared in print in 'Casino Royale' in 1953.

Sean Connery	*Dr. No* (Young)	GB, 62
Sean Connery	*From Russia, With Love* (Young)	GB, 63
Sean Connery	*Goldfinger* (Hamilton)	GB, 64
Sean Connery	*Thunderball* (Young)	GB, 65
Sean Connery	*You Only Live Twice* (Gilbert)	GB, 67
George Lazenby	*On Her Majesty's Secret Service* (Hunt)	GB, 69
Sean Connery	*Diamonds Are Forever* (Hamilton)	GB, 71
Roger Moore	*Live And Let Die* (Hamilton)	GB, 73
Roger Moore	*The Man With The Golden Gun* (Hamilton)	GB, 74
Roger Moore	*The Spy Who Loved Me* (Gilbert)	GB, 77
Roger Moore	*Moonraker* (Gilbert)	GB, 79

Note: In the 1967 spoof *Casino Royale* David Niven appeared as an ageing 007 and Woody Allen as his inept nephew Jimmy Bond.

Bonney, Anne

17th century woman pirate who operated in the Caribbean with all the ruthlessness of her male counterparts. Something of an early 'women's libber', she dressed as a man, wore close-cropped hair and eventually escaped with her life after a trial in Jamaica. Jean Peters (as Captain Providence) featured as Bonney in *Anne Of The Indies*.

Binnie Barnes	*The Spanish Main* (Borzage)	USA, 45
Hope Emerson	*Double Crossbones* (Barton)	USA, 50
Jean Peters	*Anne Of The Indies* (Tourneur)	USA, 51
Hillary Brooke	*Abbott And Costello Meet Captain Kidd* (Lamont)	
		USA, 52

Bonnie And Clyde

Young gangster twosome (full names, Bonnie Parker and Clyde Barrow) who operated in the early 30s and robbed and murdered some 18 people in a three-year killing spree across the American Midwest. Finally ambushed and shot by police in May, 1934. Romanticised out of all proportion in Arthur Penn's famous 1967 film but portrayed more realistically in William Witney's earlier 'cheapie', *The Bonnie Parker Story*.

Dorothy Provine and Jack Hogan	*The Bonnie Parker Story* (Witney)	USA, 58
Faye Dunaway and Warren Beatty	*Bonnie And Clyde* (Penn)	USA, 67

Booth, John Wilkes

(1839–1965) Assassin of President Lincoln, an embittered Southerner who, in 1865, joined a conspiracy to avenge the defeat of the Confederates. The murder occurred on April 14 at Ford's Theatre in Washington. Lincoln was shot in the head and Booth escaped on horseback. A few days later, he was tracked to a barn in Virginia and shot. The event has been portrayed several times on film, in most detail in the 1977 film *The Lincoln Conspiracy*.

Ian Keith	*Abraham Lincoln* (Griffith)	USA, 30
Francis McDonald	*The Prisoner Of Shark Island* (Ford)	USA, 36
John Derek	*Prince Of Players* (Dunne)	USA, 55
Bradford Dillman	*The Lincoln Conspiracy* (Conway)	USA, 77

Note: Raoul Walsh in *Birth Of A Nation* (USA, 15) and William Moran in *Abraham Lincoln* (USA, 24) both featured as Booth in silent movies; Edwin Booth, the actor-brother of John, was played by Richard Burton in *Prince Of Players*.

Borgia, Cesare

(1475–1507) Italian prince, son of Pope Alexander VI, notorious for his ruthlessness in Renaissance Italy. He lived for only thirty-two years, but left behind him countless legends of cruelty and murder, including the killing of his own brother, and incest with his sister Lucrezia. Orson Welles relished in a brief cameo of sinister treachery in *Prince Of Foxes*, Lorenzo Berinizi in one of uncontrollable lust in Borowczyk's *Immoral Tales*.

Gabriel Gabrio	*Lucrezia Borgia* (Gance)	Fra, 35
Macdonald Carey	*Bride Of Vengeance* (Leisen)	USA, 49
Orson Welles	*Prince Of Foxes* (King)	USA, 49
Pedro Armendariz	*Lucrezia Borgia* (Christian-Jaque)	Fra, 52

Franco Fabrizi	*The Nights Of Lucrezia Borgia* (Grieco)	
		It/Fra, 59
Cameron Mitchell	*The Black Duke* (Mercanti)	It/Spa, 63
Edmund Purdom	*The Man With The Golden Mask* (Corbucci)	
		It/Fra, 65
Lou Castel	*Lucrezia* (Civirani)	It/Aus, 68
Lorenzo Berinizi	*Immoral Tales* (Borowczyk)	Fra, 74

Note: Enrico Piacentini in *The Power Of The Borgias* (It, 20), Conrad Veidt in *Lucrezia Borgia* (Ger, 22) and Warner Oland in *Don Juan* (USA, 26) were among the actors who contributed to Cesare's villainy on the silent screen.

Borgia, Lucrezia

(1480–1519) Sister of Cesare and, for many, the world's most infamous woman. Disappointingly, most of her legendary poisonings and incestuous relationships are untrue and although she worked her way through three husbands in her thirty-nine years, she was a much respected woman and patron of many artists. But for moviemakers the motto has always been, 'film the legend, not the fact'.

Edwige Feuillere	*Lucrezia Borgia* (Gance)	Fra, 35
Paulette Goddard	*Bride Of Vengeance* (Leisen)	USA, 49
Martine Carol	*Lucrezia Borgia* (Christian-Jaque)	Fra, 52
Belinda Lee	*The Nights Of Lucrezia Borgia* (Grieco)	It/Fra, 59
Lisa Gastoni	*The Man With The Golden Mask* (Corbucci)	
		It/Fra, 65
Olinka Berova	*Lucrezia* (Civirani)	It/Aus, 68
Florence Bellamy	*Immoral Tales* (Borowczyk)	Fra, 74

Boston Blackie

Wise-cracking, girl-chasing ex-jewel thief who turns his attentions to the amateur detective business but never quite convinces the police that he's going straight for good. Numerous silent screen portrayals but best remembered for Chester Morris' B movie interpretations of the 40s. Appears in only one book — 'Boston Blackie', written by Jack Boyle in 1919.

Chester Morris	*Meet Boston Blackie* (Florey)	USA, 41
Chester Morris	*Confessions Of Boston Blackie* (Dmytryk)	USA, 41
Chester Morris	*Alias Boston Blackie* (Landers)	USA, 42
Chester Morris	*Boston Blackie Goes Hollywood* (Gordon)	USA, 42
Chester Morris	*After Midnight With Boston Blackie* (Landers)	
		USA, 43
Chester Morris	*The Chance Of A Lifetime* (Castle)	USA, 43
Chester Morris	*One Mysterious Night* (Boetticher, Jr)	USA, 44

Chester Morris	*Boston Blackie Booked On Suspicion* (Dreifuss)	
		USA, 45
Chester Morris	*Boston Blackie's Rendezvous* (Dreifuss)	USA, 45
Chester Morris	*A Close Call For Boston Blackie* (Landers)	USA, 46
Chester Morris	*The Phantom Thief* (Lederman)	USA, 46
Chester Morris	*Boston Blackie And The Law* (Lederman)	USA, 46
Chester Morris	*Trapped By Boston Blackie* (Friedman)	USA, 48
Chester Morris	*Boston Blackie's Chinese Venture* (Friedman)	USA, 49

Note: The following actors also played Boston Blackie on the silent screen — Bert Lytell in *Boston Blackie's Little Pal* (18) and *Blackie's Redemption* (19), Lionel Barrymore in *The Face In The Fog* (22), David Powell in *Missing Millions* (22), William Russell in *Boston Blackie* (23), Forrest Stanley in *Through The Dark* (24) and Raymond Glenn in *The Return of Boston Blackie* (27)

The Boston Strangler

The notorious sex maniac whose activities terrified the female population of Massachussetts between June 1962 and January 1964 when he raped and murdered thirteen women. A 34-year-old former mental patient (real name, Albert DeSalvo) eventually confessed to the crimes and in 1967 was committed to a state mental institution. In 1973 he was found dead in his prison cell, stabbed through the heart. The film starring Tony Curtis was advertised with the words: 'Come In — He did, thirteen times!'

Tony Curtis	*The Boston Strangler* (Fleischer)	USA, 68

Bovary, Emma

Young doctor's tragic wife whose discontent and thirst for romance lead her to adultery, disillusionment and ultimately suicide. The central character in 'Madame Bovary' (1856), Gustave Flaubert's classic novel of mid-19th century provincial France, and a role much coveted by actresses over the years. Valentine Tessier's performance in Renoir's 1934 version remains perhaps the most satisfying screen interpretation to date.

Lila Lee	*Unholy Love* (Ray)	USA, 32
Valentine Tessier	*Madame Bovary* (Renoir)	Fra, 34
Pola Negri	*Madame Bovary* (Lamprecht)	Ger, 37
Jennifer Jones	*Madame Bovary* (Minnelli)	USA, 49
Edwige Fenech	*Madame Bovary* (Scott)	W.Ger/It, 69

Note: In the 1949 version by Vincente Minnelli, James Mason appeared as Flaubert.

Bowie, Jim

(c. 1790–1836) Inventor of the deadly Bowie knife and, like Davy Crockett, a folk hero of the American West. In 1836 he died with Crockett and 180 other heroes defending the Alamo against the might of a Mexican army totalling 4,000 men. Alan Ladd and Richard Widmark brought their star persona to the role; Sterling Hayden a more rugged realism in Frank Lloyd's *The Last Command*.

Robert Armstrong	*Man Of Conquest* (Nicholls, Jr)	USA, 39
Macdonald Carey	*Comanche Territory* (Sherman)	USA, 50
Alan Ladd	*The Iron Mistress* (Douglas)	USA, 52
Stuart Randall	*The Man From The Alamo* (Boetticher)	USA, 53
Kenneth Tobey	*Davy Crockett, King Of The Wild Frontier* (Foster)	USA, 55
Sterling Hayden	*The Last Command* (Lloyd)	USA, 55
Jeff Morrow	*The First Texan* (Haskin)	USA, 56
Richard Widmark	*The Alamo* (Wayne)	USA, 60

Bowles, Sally

Amoral but forever optimistic cabaret singer whose adventures in pre-war Berlin during the rise to power of the Nazi party were first chronicled by Christopher Isherwood in his books 'Sally Bowles' (1937) and 'Goodbye To Berlin' (1939). Later, she went on to become both a stage and film heroine in *I Am A Camera* and *Cabaret*. For her performance in the latter movie Liza Minnelli won an Academy Award as the best actress of 1972.

Julie Harris	*I Am A Camera* (Cornelius)	GB, 55
Liza Minnelli	*Cabaret* (Fosse)	USA, 72

Bradley, General Omar N.

(1893–) American general of World War II, chosen by Eisenhower to command the US First Army during the D-Day landings of June, 1944. A quiet, calm man, the very opposite to General Patton, with whom his career was closely linked during the war. Portrayed in most depth and with quiet effectiveness by Karl Malden in the Award-winning *Patton*.

Nicholas Stuart	*The Longest Day* (Marton/Annakin/Wicki)	USA, 62
Glenn Ford	*Is Paris Burning?* (Clement)	Fra/USA, 66
Karl Malden	*Patton* (Schaffner)	USA, 70
Fred Stuthman	*MacArthur* (Sargent)	USA, 77

Braun, Wernher von

(1912–1977) German scientist who designed wartime rockets for Hitler, including the V-2 which could travel over a distance of 200 miles and land on target. He surrendered to the Americans in 1945 who used his knowledge and expertise in the development of their space programme. Von Braun's story was chronicled in the 1960 production, *I Aim At The Stars*.

Curt Jurgens	*I Aim At The Stars*	(Lee Thompson)	USA, 60

Breck, Alan

Jacobite adventurer who helps the young David Balfour secure his rightful inheritance in Robert Louis Stevenson's 'Kidnapped' (1886). On screen, usually no more than a straightforward swashbuckler, although Michael Caine provided a less than romantic portrait of a sometimes ruthless man dogged by weariness and disillusionment.

Warner Baxter	*Kidnapped*	(Werker)	USA, 38
Daniel O'Herlihy	*Kidnapped*	(Beaudine)	USA, 48
Peter Finch	*Kidnapped*	(Stevenson)	GB, 60
Thomas Weisgerber	*Kidnapped*	(Seemann)	E.Ger, 68
Michael Caine	*Kidnapped*	(Delbert Mann)	GB, 71

Note: David Balfour has been played by Freddie Bartholomew (38), Roddy McDowall (48), James MacArthur (60), Werner Kanitz (68) and Lawrence Douglas (71).

Breckinridge, Myra

The end result of a sex change operation, a shapely man-eater whom, sadly, 'no man can ever possess'. Before the change: a dedicated young film critic named Myron. Created by Gore Vidal in his 1968 novel and played before and after by Rex Reed and Raquel Welch, respectively.

Raquel Welch	*Myra Breckinridge*	(Sarne)	USA, 70

Brice, Fanny

(1891–1951) American singer-comedienne whose success on the Broadway stage contrasted sharply with the unhappiness of her private life, which included two tortuous marriages, to gambler Nick Arnstein and showman Billy Rose. A star in just a handful of movies, she remains best-known for her appearances for Ziegfeld and the introduction of the songs, 'Second Hand Rose', 'My Man' and 'Rose Of Washington Square'. Twice portrayed on screen by Barbra Streisand (one marriage per film), who won an Oscar for her performance in the first picture, *Funny Girl.*

| Barbra Streisand | *Funny Girl* (Wyler) | USA, 68 |
| Barbra Streisand | *Funny Lady* (Ross) | USA, 75 |

Brown, Father

The meekest of all amateur detectives, a gentle little Essex priest who detects crimes by using a psychological and humane approach to his mysteries. Frequently more interested in a criminal's redemption than his arrest. Most notable adversary: arch criminal Flambeau. The creation of G. K. Chesterton, he first appeared in print in the short story collection, 'The Innocence Of Father Brown' (1911).

Walter Connolly	*Father Brown, Detective* (Sedgwick)	USA, 34
Alec Guinness	*Father Brown* (Hamer)	GB, 54
Heinz Rühmann	*Das Schwarze Schaf* (Ashley)	W.Ger, 60
Heinz Rühmann	*Er Kanns Nicht Lassen* (Ambesser)	W.Ger, 62

Browning, Lt. General Frederick 'Boy'

(1896–1966) British general who pioneered the use of airborne troops and commanded the First Airborne Corps at Arnhem during the ill-fated 'Operation Market Garden' of 1944. Recently given wide exposure on film in Richard Attenborough's Arnhem epic, *A Bridge Too Far.*

| Dirk Bogarde | *A Bridge Too Far* (Attenborough) | GB, 77 |

Bruce, Lenny

For some, a brilliantly inventive American comic who was one of the precursors of social upheaval and change; for others, a dangerous, obscene performer whose use of four-letter words and scathing material made him a figure to despise. Either way, a prominent figure on the night club circuit of the 60s and a man whose tortured, self-destructive life (which ended from a drug overdose in 1966) was recreated with great skill by Bob Fosse in his 1974 biography.

| Dustin Hoffman | *Lenny* (Fosse) | USA, 74 |

Brummell, George Bryan ('Beau')

(1778–1840) Handsome English dandy who won the friendship of the Prince of Wales in Regency England and led a colourful bachelor's life until his indiscretions with the ladies and eventual quarrel with the

Prince led to his downfall. Forced to leave England to escape his creditors, he died in poverty in France. Two major interpretations on screen, one by John Barrymore in the silent era, one by Stewart Granger in MGM's swashbuckling period of the early 50s.

Barry Morse	*Mrs. Fitzherbert* (Tully)	GB, 47
Stewart Granger	*Beau Brummell* (Bernhardt)	GB, 54

Note: John Barrymore appeared in Harry Beaumont's silent *Beau Brummell* in 1924.

Brutus

(*c.* 85–42 B.C.) The last to plunge his sword into Caesar in Shakespeare's play of conspiracy and political power in Ancient Rome, 'Julius Caesar'. The 'noblest Roman of them all', he agonizes over the morality of the murder and eventually commits suicide after the battle of Philippi. Given a quiet sincerity and dignity by James Mason in the 1953 version of Shakespeare's play; only a minor figure in the two spectacles made about Cleopatra.

Arthur Hohl	*Cleopatra* (DeMille)	USA, 34
David Bradley	*Julius Caesar* (Bradley)	USA, 50
James Mason	*Julius Caesar* (Mankiewicz)	USA, 53
Kenneth Haig	*Cleopatra* (Mankiewicz)	USA, 63
Jason Robards	*Julius Caesar* (Burge)	GB, 70

Note: Norman Wooland played the Brutus character in *An Honourable Murder* (GB, 60), a modern business drama based on Shakespeare's stage play; Murray Carrington featured as a silent Brutus in a 1911 British *Julius Caesar*.

Bullitt, Frank

Honest San Francisco cop who outwits a politically ambitious D.A. as he investigates the details of an intricate Mafia plot. Arguably Steve McQueen's most famous role, although stunt co-ordinator Carey Loftin and driver Bud Ekins lent considerable assistance during the car chase sequence.

Steve McQueen	*Bullitt* (Yates)	USA, 68

Bumble, Mr.

Officious, arrogant and self-important beadle of the Parish workhouse in Dickens' 'Oliver Twist'. A portly figure, he is painted by Dickens as an odious tyrant who finishes his days a pauper inmate of the establishment he once ruled with such power. Less viciously portrayed on screen than on the printed page; even has a song or two in the musical version of the novel.

Lionel Belmore	*Oliver Twist* (Cowen)	USA, 33
Francis L. Sullivan	*Oliver Twist* (Lean)	GB, 48
Harry Secombe	*Oliver!* (Reed)	GB, 68

Note: Henry Ruttenberg (USA, 16) and James Marcus (USA, 22) were among the silent screen Bumbles.

Buntline, Ned

(1823–1886) Prolific American dime novelist who turned Buffalo Bill into a hero of legendary proportions with a long series of exaggerated adventure stories. Generally overlooked in films about Cody but allowed his proper place in Western mythology in movies by Wellman and Altman. Real name: Edward Zane Carroll Judson.

Thomas Mitchell	*Buffalo Bill* (Wellman)	USA, 44
Burt Lancaster	*Buffalo Bill And The Indians, Or Sitting Bull's History Lesson* (Altman)	USA, 76

Burke And Hare

A pair of 19th century scoundrels who enjoyed a lucrative grave-robbing career in Edinburgh in the 1820s, often providing corpses for the medical dissecting table just 24 hours after burial! Carried away by success, they finally overstepped the mark when they turned to murder and tried to up the rate of sale. Burke was hanged in 1829, Hare turned king's evidence and finished his days a blind beggar in London. All screen portrayals have been suitably black and enjoyable.

George Rose & Donald Pleasence	*The Flesh And The Fiends* (Gilling)	GB, 60
Ivor Dean & Tony Calvin	*Dr. Jekyll and Sister Hyde* (Baker)	GB, 71
Derren Nesbitt & Glynn Edwards	*Burke And Hare* (Sewell)	GB, 72

Note: The characters of Boris Karloff and Bela Lugosi in the Robert Wise horror film, *The Body Snatcher* (USA, 45) were modelled on Burke and Hare.

Byron, Lord George

(1788–1824) English poet and satirist, the darling of early 19th century society, not only for his prose but also for his debauchery and dissipated life. A short, somewhat stout man who limped as the result of a club foot, he was turned by cinema magic into Richard Chamberlain in Robert Bolt's soap opera *Lady Caroline Lamb*. Noel Willman, in a minor role in *Beau Brummell*, has come the closest to a realistic screen interpretation.

Malcolm Graham	*The Last Rose Of Summer* (Fitzpatrick)	
		GB, 37
Dennis Price	*The Bad Lord Byron* (Macdonald)	GB, 49
Noel Willman	*Beau Brummell* (Bernhardt)	GB, 54
Richard Chamberlain	*Lady Caroline Lamb* (Bolt)	GB/It, 72

Note: Howard Gaye in *A Prince Of Lovers* (GB, 22) and Andre de Beranger in *Beau Brummell* (USA, 24) both featured as Byron on the silent screen; Lady Caroline Lamb, who enjoyed a brief two month love affair with Byron, has been played by Mary Clare in *A Prince Of Lovers*, Joan Greenwood in *The Bad Lord Byron*, and Sarah Miles in *Lady Caroline Lamb*.

C

Caesar, Julius

(101–44 B.C.) Roman general, statesman and dictator; one of the foremost orators of his age whose career changed the course of Roman history. Kubrick sketched in his youth via the performance of John Gavin in *Spartacus*, Claude Rains and Rex Harrison lingered with Cleopatra, and Louis Calhern and John Gielgud acted out Caesar's last days just prior to his assassination on the Ides of March.

Warren William	*Cleopatra* (DeMille)	USA, 34
Claude Rains	*Caesar And Cleopatra* (Pascal)	GB, 46
Harold Tasker	*Julius Caesar* (Bradley)	USA, 50
Louis Calhern	*Julius Caesar* (Mankiewicz)	USA, 53
William Lundigan	*Serpent Of The Nile* (Castle)	USA, 53
Reginald Sheffield	*The Story Of Mankind* (Allen)	USA, 57
John Gavin	*Spartacus* (Kubrick)	USA, 60
Cameron Mitchell	*Caesar The Conqueror* (Anton)	It, 62
Ivo Garrani	*Son Of Spartacus* (Corbucci)	It, 62
Rex Harrison	*Cleopatra* (Mankiewicz)	USA, 63
Kenneth Williams	*Carry On Cleo* (Thomas)	GB, 65
John Gielgud	*Julius Caesar* (Burge)	GB, 70

Note: John Longden played the equivalent of the Caesar role in the modern updating of Shakespeare's play, *An Honourable Murder* (GB, 60).

Guy Rathbone featured as Caesar in a silent British production of *Julius Caesar* (11).

Caligari, Dr.

After Dr. Jekyll, the most famous doctor in movies, a frightening figure who creates a reign of terror in a German town by hypnotizing a somnambulist into committing a series of murders. At the final count, however, revealed to be a kindly doctor and no more than a figment of the insane narrator's imagination. In the 1962 remake, Caligari is a bearded sadist who subjects his patients to a series of tortures inside a mysterious mansion. Again, in the final scenes, he is revealed as a kindly specialist, and the narrator, a woman undergoing psychiatric treatment.

| Werner Krauss | *The Cabinet Of Dr. Caligari* | (Wiene) | Ger, 19 |
| Dan O'Herlihy | *The Cabinet Of Dr. Caligari* | (Kay) | USA, 62 |

Callahan, Harry

Hard-hitting cop ('Dirty Harry'), isolated from his colleagues because of his strong arm methods, but constantly coming out ahead in his war against psychotic killers and revolutionary thugs. Too many fascist impulses for some, just right for others. Three movies to date.

Clint Eastwood	*Dirty Harry* (Siegel)	USA, 71
Clint Eastwood	*Magnum Force* (Post)	USA, 73
Clint Eastwood	*The Enforcer* (Fargo)	USA, 76

Camille

Notorious courtesan of 19th century Paris, a tragic heroine who enjoys an idyllic interlude with a young lover before returning to her pleasure-seeking ways and a lingering death from consumption. Garbo's Camille, with her long death scene in the arms of Robert Taylor, is regarded by many as her finest achievement; Daniele Gaubert brought the melodramatics up-to-date in *Camille 2000* which incorporated drugs, sex and a background of modern day Rome. Dumas' novel 'La Dame aux Camelias' introduced Camille and was published in 1848.

Yvonne Printemps	*La Dame aux Camelias* (Rivers/Gance)	Fra, 34
Greta Garbo	*Camille* (Cukor)	USA, 37
Lina Montes	*La Dama de las Camelias* (Soria)	Mex, 44
Micheline Presle	*La Dame aux Camelias* (Bernard)	Fra, 52
Maria Felix	*Camelia* (Gavaldon)	Mex, 52
Sarita Montiel	*La Belle Lola, Une Dame aux Camelias*	
	(Balcazar)	Spa/It/Fra, 62
Daniele Gaubert	*Camille 2000* (Metzger)	USA, 69

Note: Camille was perhaps the most popular female role of the silent cinema. The following actresses all portrayed the tragic courtesan on screen: Oda Alstrup (Den, 07), Vittoria Lepanto (It, 09), Sarah Bernhardt (Fra, 11), Gertrude Shipman (USA, 12), Clara Kimball Young (USA, 15), Francesca Bertini (It, 15), Theda Bara (USA, 17), Erna Morena (Ger, 17), Nazimova (USA, 21), Tora Teje (Swe, 25) and Norma Talmadge (USA, 27).

Cantor, Eddie

(1892–1964) Eye-popping American comedian who rose to fame by playing the small man who always triumphs over adversity. His rags to riches story, from New York's Lower East Side to Broadway and then the movies, was related in Warners' biography of 1954. Cantor's films for Goldwyn, with whom he enjoyed a fruitful relationship in the early 30s, included *Palmy Days* (31), *The Kid From Spain* (32), *Roman Scandals* (33) and *Kid Millions* (34).

Buddy Doyle	*The Great Ziegfeld* (Leonard)	USA, 36
Keefe Brasselle	*The Eddie Cantor Story* (Green)	USA, 54

Note: Cantor appeared as himself in *Thank Your Lucky Stars* (43) and *Hollywood Canteen* (44); Jimmie Quinn played him on the silent screen in *Pretty Ladies* (USA, 25).

Capone, Al

Two parallel scars on his left cheek earned this Italian-born gangster the name of Scarface; the deaths of a thousand people in Chicago's gang wars of the 20s established him as the undisputed 'Public Enemy Number One'. The statistics duly impressed Hollywood who began painting Capone's bloody career on celluloid as early as 1932, when Howard Hawks cast Paul Muni as *Scarface*. Since then the films and performances have ranged from the good to the indifferent. Tops in the former category: Rod Steiger in Richard Wilson's documentary-styled 1959 film *Al Capone*.

Paul Muni	*Scarface* (Hawks)		USA, 32
Rod Steiger	*Al Capone* (Wilson)		USA, 59
Neville Brand	*The Scarface Mob* (Karlson)		USA, 59
Neville Brand	*Spin Of A Coin* (Newman)		USA, 62
Jason Robards	*The St. Valentine's Day Massacre* (Corman)	USA, 67
Ben Gazzara	*Capone* (Carver)		USA, 75

Note: The character of Rico Bandello in *Little Caesar* (31) was supposedly based on Capone.

Capone was never convicted for any of his gangland crimes, not even the St. Valentine's Day Massacre. Instead, he was arrested in 1931 for tax evasion and sentenced to 11 years imprisonment. He was paroled in 1939 for 'good behaviour' and died in 1947, aged 48, either of bronchial pneumonia or a brain haemorrhage or syphilis — or a bit of all three.

Carella, Steve

The most prominent member of Ed McBain's famous 87th Precinct and among the best-known cops in modern fiction. Despite appearing in over thirty novels since 1956, his screen career has been spasmodic, ranging from the low budget *Cop Hater* in 1958 (in which he was renamed Carelli) to the semi-humorous *Fuzz* with Burt Reynolds. In 1978 Claude Chabrol turned his eyes in his direction with the thriller *Blood Relatives*, set in Montreal.

Robert Loggia	*Cop Hater* (Berke)	USA, 58
Jean-Louis Trintignant	*Without Apparent Motive* (Labro)	Fra, 71
Burt Reynolds	*Fuzz* (Colla)	USA, 72
Donald Sutherland	*Blood Relatives* (Chabrol)	Can/Fra, 78

Note: *The Mugger* (58) was based on an 87th Precinct novel but did not feature Carella; Kurosawa's *High And Low* (63) was adapted from 'King's Ransom' and again did not feature the detective.

Robert Lansing played Carella in a 1961/2 TV series.

Carmen

Lustful gypsy tigress of Prosper Merimee, the ultimate *femme fatale* who wrecks the career of a young Spanish officer and eventually pays for her fickle ways with her life. Her amorous escapades inspired the Bizet opera of 1875 and also several films which have told her story, both in its original form and in updated versions. Rita Hayworth, at her peak in the 1948 film, *The Loves Of Carmen*, remains the most beautiful of screen Carmens; Dorothy Dandridge in the all black *Carmen Jones*, the most seductive.

Imperio Argentina	*Andalusische Nachte* (Maisch)	Ger/Spa, 38
Viviane Romance	*Carmen* (Christian-Jaque)	Fra, 43
Rita Hayworth	*The Loves Of Carmen* (Charles Vidor)	USA, 48
Dorothy Dandridge	*Carmen Jones* (Preminger)	USA, 54
Sara Montiel	*Carmen, de la Ronda* (Demicheli)	Spa, 59
Giovanna Ralli	*Carmen Di Trastevere* (Gallone)	It, 62
Uta Levka	*Carmen, Baby* (Metzger)	USA, 67

Note: Grace Bumbry appeared in a Swiss film of Bizet's opera, directed by Herbert von Karajan in 1967; the following actresses all flirted successfully as Carmen on the silent screen — Marguerite Snow (USA, 13), Geraldine Farrar (USA, 15), Theda Bara (USA, 15), Pola Negri (Ger, 18), Annie Bos (Holl, 19), Raquel Meller (Fra, 26) and Dolores Del Rio (USA, 27).

Carter, Nick

Dime novel American detective who has figured in literally thousands of stories since making his debut in the 'New York Weekly' in 1886. In the late 30s appeared set for a flourishing career at MGM, but his traditional methods were found wanting when compared with the wily oriental talents of Charlie Chan, Mr. Moto, etc. Resurrected briefly by Eddie Constantine in France in the 60s. First created by John R. Coryell.

| Walter Pidgeon | *Nick Carter, Master Detective* (Tourneur) | USA, 39 |
| Walter Pidgeon | *Phantom Raiders* (Tourneur) | USA, 40 |

Walter Pidgeon	*Sky Murder* (Seitz)	USA, 40
Eddie Constantine	*Nick Carter Va Tout Casser* (Decoin)	Fra, 64
Eddie Constantine	*Nick Carter Et Le Trefle Rouge* (Savignac)	
		Fra, 66
Michael Docolomansky	*Nick Carter in Prague* (Lipsky)	Czech, 77

Note: Lyle Talbot starred as the son of Nick Carter in the 15-episode Columbia serial, *Chick Carter, Detective* (46); Carter himself appeared on the silent screen in four French serials between 1909 and 1912 and was played by both Thomas Carrigan and Edmund Lowe in a series of short films in 1922.

Carton, Sydney

Dissolute, drunken lawyer who sacrifices his life for the woman he loves in Dickens' stirring novel of the French Revolution, 'A Tale Of Two Cities' (1859). An early anti-hero, famous for his 'Far, far better thing" speech as he meets his death on the guillotine and incomparably played by Ronald Colman in the MGM production of 1935.

| Ronald Colman | *A Tale Of Two Cities*   (Conway) | USA, 35 |
| Dirk Bogarde | *A Tale Of Two Cities*   (Thomas) | GB, 58 |

Note: On the silent screen Carton was played by Maurice Costello (USA, 11), William Farnum (USA, 17) and John Martin Harvey in Herbert Wilcox's 1925 British production, *The Only Way*.

Caruso, Enrico

(1873–1921) One of the greatest operatic tenors of all time, born in Naples and especially famous for his lead roles in 'Aida', 'Pagliacci', 'La Bohème' and 'Tosca'. Mario Lanza reached star status with his portrayal of Caruso in MGM's 1951 biography; Caruso himself appeared in a few films just prior to his death in 1921 – *My Cousin, The Splendid Romance*, etc.

Mario Lanza	*The Great Caruso* (Thorpe)	USA, 51
Ermanno Randi	*Enrico Caruso, Legend Of A Voice* (Gentilomo)	
		It, 51
Howard Caine	*Pay Or Die* (Wilson)	USA, 60

Note: Peter Edward Price played Caruso as a boy in *The Great Caruso*; Maurizio Di Nardo in *Enrico Caruso, Legend Of A Voice*.

Casanova, Giovanni

(1725–1798) 18th century Italian profligate and ardent amorist whose lively career as a charlatan and lecher took him to all the capitals of Europe. A run-of-the-mill screen romantic, until Fellini's three-hour spectacular stripped away the glamour and presented Casanova's story as a pathetic saga of a wasted life and Casanova himself as an adventurer with a need to declare undying love to a succession of women.

Gustav Waldau	*Munchhausen* (von Baky)	Ger, 43
Georges Guetary	*Les Adventures de Casanova* (Boyer)	Fra, 46
Arturo de Cordova	*The Adventures Of Casanova* (Gavaldon)	USA, 48
Gabriele Ferzetti	*Casanova* (Vanzina)	It/Fra, 55
Marcello Mastroianni	*Casanova 70* (Monicelli)	It/Fra, 65
Felix Le Breux	*Les Dernieres Roses De Casanova* (Krska)	Czech, 66
Leonard Whiting	*The Youth, Vocation And Early Experiences Of Casanova, The Venetian* (Comencini)	It, 69
Tony Curtis	*The Rise And Rise Of Casanova* (Legrand)	Aus/It/Fra/W.Ger, 77
Donald Sutherland	*Fellini's Casanova* (Fellini)	It, 77
Giulio Boseti	*The Return Of Casanova* (Campanile)	It, 78

Note: Bob Hope appeared as a servant impersonator in *Casanova's Big Night* (USA, 54); Ivan Mosjoukine starred in a 1928 French silent film directed by Alexander Volkoff.

Cassidy, Butch

(1866–1908?) The last of the Western gang leaders; an engaging train robber who operated with his 'Wild Bunch' in Wyoming and Nevada before fleeing with the Sundance Kid to South America at the turn of the century. George Roy Hill's 1969 film had them both die at the hands of the Bolivian cavalry. Rumour has it, however, that Cassidy and possibly Sundance escaped and returned to live peacefully in America under assumed names.

John Doucette	*The Texas Rangers* (Karlson)	USA, 51
Gene Evans	*Wyoming Renegades* (Sears)	USA, 55
Howard Petrie	*The Maverick Queen* (Kane)	USA, 56
Neville Brand	*The Three Outlaws* (Newfield)	USA, 56
Neville Brand	*Badman's Country* (Sears)	USA, 58
Arthur Hunnicutt	*Cat Ballou* (Silverstein)	USA, 65
Tex Gates	*Ride A Wild Stud* (Ekard)	USA, 69
Paul Newman	*Butch Cassidy And The Sundance Kid* (Hill)	USA, 69
Tom Berenger	*Butch And Sundance – The Early Days* (Lester)	USA, 79

Note: Paul Newman's famous bicycle ride was not a film invention. It happened in real life, even down to the bowler hat perched jauntily on the side of Newman's head.

Cassius

The chief conspirator in the plot to kill Julius Caesar, the man with the 'lean and hungry look' who persuades the reluctant Brutus to join the assassination on the Ides of March. John Gielgud led the conspirators in Joe Mankiewicz's 1953 film and completed an unusual double 17 years later when he played Caesar and finished up on the receiving end of the assassins' swords!

Ian MacLaren	*Cleopatra* (DeMille)	USA, 34
Grosvenor Glenn	*Julius Caesar* (Bradley)	USA, 50
John Gielgud	*Julius Caesar* (Mankiewicz)	USA, 53
John Hoyt	*Cleopatra* (Mankiewicz)	USA, 63
Richard Johnson	*Julius Caesar* (Burge)	GB, 70

Note: Douglas Wilmer played the equivalent of Cassius in the modern drama, *An Honourable Murder* (60); Eric Maxon featured in the role in a silent British version of 1911.

Catherine The Great

(1729–1796) German-born Russian empress whose 34-year reign was marked by great territorial expansion. Like Elizabeth I of England, she has attracted many distinguished screen actresses, including Bette Davis who offered a fiery cameo in *John Paul Jones*. None, however, has quite matched Marlene Dietrich stomping around the palace in hussar's outfit in *The Scarlet Empress*, a lavish Paramount extravaganza climaxed by horsemen charging the palace steps to the accompaniment of bells and 'The Ride Of The Valkyries' on the soundtrack!

Walka Stenermann	*Seven Faces* (Viertel)	USA, 29
Marlene Dietrich	*The Scarlet Empress* (von Sternberg)	USA, 34
Elisabeth Bergner	*Catherine The Great* (Czinner)	GB, 34
Suzy Prim	*Betrayal* (Ozep)	Fra, 37
Francoise Rosay	*The Devil Is An Empress* (Dreville)	Fra, 39
Brigitte Horney	*Munchhausen* (von Baky)	Ger, 43
Tallulah Bankhead	*A Royal Scandal* (Preminger)	USA, 45
Binnie Barnes	*Shadow Of The Eagle* (Salkow)	GB, 50
Olga Zhizneva	*Admiral Ushakov* (Romm)	USSR, 53
Viveca Lindfors	*Tempest* (Lattuada)	USA/It, 58
Bette Davis	*John Paul Jones* (Farrow)	USA, 59
Hildegarde Neff	*Catherine Of Russia* (Lenzi)	It/Fra, 62
Jeanne Moreau	*Great Catherine* (Flemyng)	GB, 68

Note: Pola Negri in Lubitsch's *Forbidden Paradise* (USA, 24) and Louise

Dresser in *The Eagle* (USA, 25) both featured in the role on the silent screen.

Cavell, Nurse Edith

(1865–1915) Just one of Anna Neagle's many true-life screen heroines (they ranged from Nell Gwynn to Queen Victoria, Florence Nightingale to Amy Johnson), a gallant English nurse who served in Belgium in World War I and was finally executed by the Germans for her part in the escape of Allied and Belgian prisoners.

Anna Neagle	*Nurse Edith Cavell* (Wilcox)	GB, 39

Note: Sybil Thorndike played Edith Cavell in an earlier, silent Herbert Wilcox film, *Dawn* (28).

Cervantes, Miguel de

(1547–1616) Spanish author of 'Don Quixote' (1605), prior to his writing career as adventurous a swashbuckler as any created by Dumas or Sabatini — fighting the Moors in Spain, falling prisoner to Barbary pirates and being taken as a slave to Algiers. Horst Buchholz played the young Cervantes in a 1968 European co-production; Peter O'Toole doubled as Don Quixote and the ageing author in the musical *Man Of La Mancha*.

Horst Buchholz	*Cervantes* (Sherman)	Fra/It/Spa, 68
Peter O'Toole	*Man Of La Mancha* (Hiller)	It, 72

Challenger, Professor

Explorer-scientist of Conan Doyle's 'The Lost World' (1912). In view of his adventures in South America where he discovers a prehistoric land of animals and ape-men, something of an under-exposed figure on screen, only two versions (one silent) having been made of 'The Lost World' to date.

Claude Rains	*The Lost World* (Allen)	USA, 60

Note: Challenger was played by Wallace Beery in the 1925 silent version, directed by Harry Hoyt.

Chan, Charlie

Wily Chinese sleuth who became the screen's most prolific investigator of the 40s and 50s. Solved nearly fifty cases, making frequent use of aphorisms whenever the occasion demanded, i.e. 'Alibi, like dead fish, cannot stand test of time' and 'When player cannot see man who deal cards, much wiser to stay out of game'. Once wrapped up a scene with the words, 'Please inform me whenever any other incidents permit themselves the luxury of occurring'. Films usually second features of 65–70 minutes. Most famous interpreter: Warner Oland. First appeared in print in 'House Without A Key' (1925), a Saturday Evening Post serial by Earl Derr Biggers.

E. L. Park	*Behind That Curtain* (Cummings)	USA, 29
Warner Oland	*Charlie Chan Carries On* (MacFadden)	USA, 31
Warner Oland	*Black Camel* (MacFadden)	USA, 31
Warner Oland	*Charlie Chan's Chance* (Blystone)	USA, 32
Warner Oland	*Charlie Chan's Greatest Case* (MacFadden)	USA, 33
Warner Oland	*Charlie Chan's Courage* (Hadden/Forde)	USA, 34
Warner Oland	*Charlie Chan In London* (Forde)	USA, 34
Warner Oland	*Charlie Chan In Paris* (Seiler)	USA, 35
Warner Oland	*Charlie Chan In Egypt* (King)	USA, 35
Warner Oland	*Charlie Chan In Shanghai* (Tinling)	USA, 35
Warner Oland	*Charlie Chan's Secret* (Wiles)	USA, 36
Warner Oland	*Charlie Chan At The Circus* (Lachman)	USA, 36
Warner Oland	*Charlie Chan at the Racetrack* (Humberstone)	USA, 36
Warner Oland	*Charlie Chan At The Opera* (Humberstone)	USA, 36
Warner Oland	*Charlie Chan At The Olympics* (Humberstone)	USA, 37
Warner Oland	*Charlie Chan On Broadway* (Forde)	USA, 37
Warner Oland	*Charlie Chan At Monte Carlo* (Forde)	USA, 38
Sidney Toler	*Charlie Chan In Honolulu* (Humberstone)	USA, 38
Sidney Toler	*Charlie Chan In Reno* (Foster)	USA, 39
Sidney Toler	*Charlie Chan At Treasure Island* (Foster)	USA, 39
Sidney Toler	*Charlie Chan In The City Of Darkness* (Leeds)	USA, 39
Sidney Toler	*Charlie Chan In Panama* (Foster)	USA, 40
Sidney Toler	*Charlie Chan's Murder Cruise* (Forde)	USA, 40
Sidney Toler	*Charlie Chan At The Wax Museum* (Shores)	USA, 40
Sidney Toler	*Murder Over New York* (Lachman)	USA, 40
Sidney Toler	*Dead Men Tell* (Lachman)	USA, 41
Sidney Toler	*Charlie Chan In Rio* (Lachman)	USA, 41
Sidney Toler	*Castle In The Desert* (Lachman)	USA, 42
Sidney Toler	*Charlie Chan In The Secret Service* (Rosen)	USA, 44
Sidney Toler	*The Chinese Cat* (Rosen)	USA, 44
Sidney Toler	*Charlie Chan In Black Magic* (Rosen)	USA, 44
Sidney Toler	*The Jade Mask* (Rosen)	USA, 45
Sidney Toler	*The Scarlet Clue* (Rosen)	USA, 45
Sidney Toler	*The Shanghai Cobra* (Karlson)	USA, 45
Sidney Toler	*The Red Dragon* (Rosen)	USA, 45
Sidney Toler	*Dark Alibi* (Karlson)	USA, 46
Sidney Toler	*Shadows Over Chinatown* (Morse)	USA, 46

Sidney Toler	*Dangerous Money* (Morse)	USA, 46
Sidney Toler	*The Trap* (Bretherton)	USA, 47
Roland Winters	*The Chinese Ring* (Beaudine)	USA, 47
Roland Winters	*Docks Of New Orleans* (Abrahams)	USA, 48
Roland Winters	*The Shanghai Chest* (Beaudine)	USA, 48
Roland Winters	*The Mystery Of The Golden Eye* (Beaudine)	USA, 48
Roland Winters	*The Feathered Serpent* (Beaudine)	USA, 48
Roland Winters	*Sky Dragon* (Selander)	USA, 49

Note: Both George Kuwa, in the 1926 serial *The House Without A Key*, and Kamiyama Sojin in Paul Leni's *The Chinese Parrot*, played Chan on the silent screen; Fox produced all the sound films up until *Castle In The Desert* (1942), thereafter they were made by Monogram.

Chaney, Lon

(1883–1930) American actor (the son of deaf mute parents) who scared a whole generation with his horror roles of the 20s: *The Miracle Man* (19), *The Hunchback Of Notre Dame* (23), *The Phantom Of The Opera* (25), etc. Known as 'The Man Of A Thousand Faces', he was responsible for his own make-up and often suffered extreme pain during the course of his roles. Died of throat cancer just as he was preparing to play the vampire Count Dracula and embark on a sound career. Cagney's bio-pic remains one of the most detailed of a film personality.

| James Cagney | *Man Of A Thousand Faces* (Pevney) | USA, 57 |

Chapman, Eddie

British safecracker who performed one of the most difficult and dangerous acts of double espionage of the Second World War — pretending to spy for the Germans whilst all the time working for the Allies. Awarded the Iron Cross by Hitler, his freedom by the British.

| Christopher Plummer | *Triple Cross* (Young) | Fra/GB, 67 |

Charles I

(1600–1649) Stuart king whose disputes with Parliament over matters of finance, religion and foreign policy led to the only civil war in British history and also his own execution for treason. Alec Guinness' dandified yet stubborn and devious monarch in Ken Hughes' *Cromwell* is the only major screen portrait to date.

Hugh Miller	*The Vicar Of Bray* (Edwards)	GB, 37
Robert Rietty	*The Scarlet Blade* (Gilling)	GB, 63
Alec Guinness	*Cromwell* (Hughes)	GB, 70

Charles, Nick

The lazy half of the most refreshing husband and wife team ever to grace the detective scene, a wealthy San Francisco playboy who quipped his way through some hundred martinis and six Thin Man films during the 30s and 40s. Always ready with the throwaway wisecrack, both he and his wife Nora ignored the Depression and proved that wedded life — and crime — could be fun. William Powell and Myrna Loy featured in all the films; Asta, their wire-haired terrier was constantly in attendance. In the first film, adapted from Dashiell Hammett's novel of 1932, The Thin Man of the title was one of the subsidiary characters, an eccentric inventor who is finally murdered. Thereafter, he became the alias of Powell's reluctant private-eye.

William Powell	*The Thin Man* (Van Dyke II)	USA, 34
William Powell	*After The Thin Man* (Van Dyke II)	USA, 36
William Powell	*Another Thin Man* (Van Dyke II)	USA, 39
William Powell	*Shadow Of The Thin Man* (Van Dyke II)	USA, 41
William Powell	*The Thin Man Goes Home* (Thorpe)	USA, 44
William Powell	*Song Of The Thin Man* (Buzzell)	USA, 47

Chauvelin

Arch enemy of Sir Percy Blakeney in Baroness Orczy's French Revolution adventure, 'The Scarlet Pimpernel' (1905). Known as Citizen Chauvelin and modelled after several real-life revolutionary leaders, he features in numerous Scarlet Pimpernel films.

Raymond Massey	*The Scarlet Pimpernel* (Young)	GB, 34
Francis Lister	*The Return Of The Scarlet Pimpernel* (Schwartz)	GB, 38
Cyril Cusack	*The Elusive Pimpernel* (Powell/Pressburger)	GB, 50

Note: Norman Page featured as Chauvelin in Maurice Elvey's film of 1919, *The Elusive Pimpernel*.

Chessman, Caryl

American sex offender, tried for rape and murder in 1948, who spent twelve years in the condemned cell, studying law and delaying his execution with a succession of appeals. In 1960 his luck ran out and he was put to death at San Quentin after eight stays of execution. His life story was filmed in 1955.

William Campbell	*Cell 2455, Death Row* (Sears)	USA, 55

Cheyney, Fay

A scheming lady Raffles who travels in British high society, her eager eyes always firmly fixed on the expensive jewellery worn by her vulnerable companions. A seemingly indestructable character, first created by Frederick Lonsdale in his 1926 London play 'The Last Of Mrs. Cheyney' and still proving attractive to stage actresses in the 70s.

Norma Shearer	*The Last Of Mrs. Cheyney*	(Franklin)	USA, 29
Joan Crawford	*The Last Of Mrs. Cheyney*	(Boleslawski)	USA, 37
Greer Garson	*The Law And The Lady*	(Knopf)	USA, 51
Lilli Palmer	*Frau Cheney's Ende*	(Josef Wild)	W.Ger, 61

Chopin, Frederic

(1810–1849) Polish composer and master pianist whose brilliant career was marred by an ill-fated love affair with novelist George Sand and a losing fight against tuberculosis. Jose Iturbi played the nocturnes and preludes for Cornel Wilde in the extravagant *A Song To Remember*; Alexander Ford took a more respectful look at the composer's youth in the 1951 production, *The Young Chopin*.

Jean Servais	*Un Amour de Frederic Chopin* (Bolvary)	
		Fra, 35
Cornel Wilde	*A Song To Remember* (Charles Vidor)	
		USA, 45
Vaclay Voska	*Bohemian Rapture* (Krska)	Czech, 48
Czeslaw Wollejko	*The Young Chopin* (Ford)	Pol, 51
Alex Davion	*Song Without End* (Charles Vidor)	USA, 60
Christopher Sandford	*Jutrzenka: A Winter In Majorca* (Camino)	
		Spa, 71
Ken Colley	*Lisztomania* (Russell)	GB, 75

Christian, Fletcher

Leader of the mutineers on board HMS Bounty during the ill-fated voyage to Tahiti in 1787–9. A muscular, traditional hero in the Oscar-winning 1935 version, a fop in the controversial remake of 1962. The Flynn portrayal was in a little-known Australian production made before he began his Hollywood career.

Errol Flynn	*In The Wake Of The Bounty*	(Chauvel)	Austral, 33
Clark Gable	*Mutiny On The Bounty*	(Lloyd)	USA, 35
Marlon Brando	*Mutiny On The Bounty*	(Milestone)	USA, 62

Christie, Agatha

(1891–1976) The most celebrated British mystery writer of the 20th century. Many works filmed (*Witness For The Prosecution, Murder On The Orient Express, Death On The Nile*, etc) and herself the central subject of a film thriller about her unexplained ten day disappearance in December, 1926.

Vanessa Redgrave   *Agatha*   (Apted)   GB, 79

Christie, Anna

Waterfront tramp of Eugene O'Neill who returns home to her drunken father's river barge to find eventual happiness with an honest young sailor. The leading character in O'Neill's Pulitzer Prize-winning play of 1922; also Greta Garbo's first talking role in movies.

Greta Garbo   *Anna Christie*   (Brown)   USA, 30

Note: Blanche Sweet appeared in a 1923 silent version directed by John Griffith Wray.

Christie, John Reginald

(1898–1953) Rapist-murderer, known as 'The Strangler of Notting Hill', whose unsavoury activities at 10 Rillington Place created a sensation when brought to light in 1953. Christie's notorious career included the slaying of six women (among them his wife) whom he buried in various parts of his house. His story was told in clinical, almost documentary fashion by Richard Fleischer in 1971.

Richard Attenborough   *10 Rillington Place*   (Fleischer)   GB, 71

Note: Timothy Evans, a near mental defective who lodged in Christie's house and was hanged for the murder of his wife and baby daughter, was played by John Hurt in Fleischer's film. Later evidence revealed that both crimes were committed by Christie and Evans was granted a pardon.

Christina, Queen

(1626–1689) 17th century Queen of Sweden (contrary to legend an unattractive woman with a deformed shoulder) who, in 1654, renounced her powerful Protestant kingdom to become a convert to the Catholic Church. Romanticised out of all proportion in the two films made about her life, the first with Garbo in which she indulges in a hopeless love affair with Spanish envoy John Gilbert, the second with Liv Ullmann in which she embraces not only catholicism but the flesh that goes with it, i.e. the handsome figure of Peter Finch's Cardinal Azzolino!

Greta Garbo	*Queen Christina* (Mamoulian)	USA, 33
Liv Ullmann	*The Abdication* (Harvey)	GB, 74

Churchill, Sir Winston

(1874–1965) Ebullient English statesman and Prime Minister whose fighting spirit and eloquent speech-making did much to help Britain survive the darkest days of World War II. His role in the war has yet to be examined on screen, although his early life, from his schooldays to his military exploits in India and South Africa and his election to Parliament, were chronicled at length in the 157-minute biography, *Young Winston*.

Dudley Field Malone	*Mission To Moscow* (Curtiz)	USA, 43
Victor Stanitsine	*The Fall Of Berlin* (Chiaureli)	USSR, 49
Victor Stanitsine	*The Unforgettable Year: 1919* (Chiaureli)	USSR, 52
Jimmy Sangster	*The Siege Of Sidney Street* (Baker)	GB, 60
Patrick Wymark	*Operation Crossbow* (Anderson)	GB, 65
Yuri Durov	*The Great Battle* (Ozerov)	USSR/Pol/Yug/E.Ger/It, 69
Simon Ward	*Young Winston* (Attenborough)	GB, 72
Leigh Dilley	*The Eagle Has Landed* (Sturges)	GB, 77

Note: Patrick Wymark also voiced Churchill in the two documentaries, *The Finest Hours* (64) and *A King's Story* (65); Peter Sellers voiced the role in the spy thriller *The Man Who Never Was* (56).

In *Young Winston*, Russell Lewis played Churchill aged 7, Michael Anderson the 13-year-old Churchill.

Cicero

(1904–1970) Code name for the Albanian spy Elyesa Bazna who served as valet to the British Ambassador in Ankara in World War II and sold 35 top secrets to the Germans, including the plans for the invasion of Europe. The Nazis, believing the plans to be false, failed to act on his information and paid him in forged bank notes. Bazna subsequently disappeared from the international scene and died in poverty. Rumour has it that he once turned up on the set of Mankiewicz's *Five Fingers* and, for a fee, offered his services to the production company!

James Mason	*Five Fingers* (Mankiewicz)	USA, 52

Cinderella

Fairy tale girl heroine who finds romance and happiness with a handsome prince after losing her magic slipper at the ball. The story, which is assumed to be of Eastern origin and mentioned in 16th century German literature, has been animated by Disney, adapted into two glossy musicals by Charles Walters and Bryan Forbes, and even updated into a male fable of the 60s with Jerry Lewis.

Ilene Woods	*Cinderella* (Disney)	USA, 50
Leslie Caron	*The Glass Slipper* (Walters)	USA, 55
Jerry Lewis	*Cinderfella* (Tashlin)	USA, 60
Gemma Craven	*The Slipper And The Rose* (Forbes)	GB, 76

Note: Ilene Woods voiced the role in Disney's 1950 version; Laura Bayley appeared as Cinderella as far back as 1898 in the British film, *Cinderella And The Fairy Godmother*. Dolly Lupone (GB, 07), Gertie Potter (GB, 13), Mary Pickford (USA, 14) and Mady Christians (Ger, 23) were other silent actresses who featured in the part.

Cleopatra

(68–30 B.C.) Egyptian queen of great beauty whose years as mistress of both Caesar (whom she bore two sons) and Antony, have been chronicled many times on screen. Vivien Leigh in Shaw's *Caesar And Cleopatra* and Hildegard Neil in Shakespeare's *Antony And Cleopatra* offered classical interpretations, Elizabeth Taylor a more earthy, sensual and controversial portrait. Miss Taylor's entry into Rome in the Mankiewicz production of 1963 remains one of the most spectacular moments in epic cinema.

Claudette Colbert	*Cleopatra* (DeMille)	USA, 34
Vivien Leigh	*Caesar And Cleopatra* (Pascal)	GB, 46
Rhonda Fleming	*Serpent Of The Nile* (Castle)	USA, 53
Sophia Loren	*Due Notti con Cleopatra* (Mattoli)	It, 54
Virginia Mayo	*The Story Of Mankind* (Allen)	USA, 57
Linda Cristal	*Legions Of The Nile* (Cottafavi)	It/Spa/Fra, 59
Elizabeth Taylor	*Cleopatra* (Mankiewicz)	USA, 63
Amanda Barrie	*Carry On Cleo* (Thomas)	GB, 65
Hildegard Neil	*Antony and Cleopatra* (Heston)	Swi/Spa/GB, 72

Note: Debra Paget appeared as *Cleopatra's Daughter* (Fra/It, 60); Helen Gardner (USA, 13) and Theda Bara (USA, 17) both appeared as the Egyptian queen on the silent screen.

Clouseau, Inspector Jacques

The most accident-prone policeman in screen history, a Jacques Tati of the Paris Sûreté, forever losing battles with revolving doors, swimming pools, vacuum cleaners, etc. but always managing to come up smiling. Not so his superior, Inspector Dreyfus, who totters on the edge of insanity in every film!

Peter Sellers	*The Pink Panther* (Edwards)	USA, 64
Peter Sellers	*A Shot In The Dark* (Edwards)	USA, 64
Alan Arkin	*Inspector Clouseau* (Yorkin)	GB, 68
Peter Sellers	*The Return Of The Pink Panther* (Edwards)	GB, 75
Peter Sellers	*The Pink Panther Strikes Again* (Edwards)	GB, 76
Peter Sellers	*Revenge Of The Pink Panther* (Edwards)	GB, 78

Note: Herbert Lom has featured as Dreyfus in four of the films starring Peter Sellers; the character did not appear in *The Pink Panther* or *Inspector Clouseau*.

Cochise

(*c.*1820–1874) Chief of the Chiricahua Apaches whose long, full-scale war with the American government was finally resolved when frontiersman Tom Jeffords rode alone into the Indian camp and pleaded for a safe passage for mail riders through Apache territory. The relationship between Jeffords and Cochise was examined in Delmer Daves' classic western *Broken Arrow*. For his portrayal of Cochise, Jeff Chandler received a supporting Oscar nomination. He later played the role on two subsequent occasions.

Antonio Moreno	*Valley Of The Sun* (Marshall)	USA, 42
Miguel Inclan	*Fort Apache* (Ford)	USA, 48
Jeff Chandler	*Broken Arrow* (Daves)	USA, 50
Chief Yowlachie	*The Last Outpost* (Foster)	USA, 51
Jeff Chandler	*The Battle At Apache Pass* (Sherman)	USA, 52
John Hodiak	*Conquest Of Cochise* (Castle)	USA, 53
Jeff Chandler	*Taza, Son Of Cochise* (Sirk)	USA, 54
Michael Keep	*Forty Guns To Apache Pass* (Witney)	USA, 67

Cody, William Frederick

(1846–1917) Heroic figure of the American West whose adventures as a Pony Express rider, Indian scout and buffalo hunter became legendary through the stories of dime novelist Ned Buntline. Only William Wellman's *Buffalo Bill* has dealt with his full career; many movies have preferred to concentrate on his later years when he founded his famous Wild West Show. Robert Altman's *Buffalo Bill And The Indians* starring Paul Newman portrayed Cody as no more than a hollow fake.

| Douglas Dumbrille | *The World Changes* (LeRoy) | USA, 33 |

Moroni Olsen	*Annie Oakley* (Stevens)	USA, 35
James Ellison	*The Plainsman* (DeMille)	USA, 37
Carlyle Moore	*Outlaw Express* (Waggner)	USA, 38
Roy Rogers	*Young Buffalo Bill* (Kane)	USA, 40
Joel McCrea	*Buffalo Bill* (Wellman)	USA, 44
Richard Arlen	*Buffalo Bill Rides Again* (Ray)	USA, 47
Monte Hale	*Law Of The Golden West* (Ford)	USA, 49
Louis Calhern	*Annie Get Your Gun* (Sidney)	USA, 50
Tex Cooper	*King Of The Bullwhip* (Ormond)	USA, 50
Clayton Moore	*Buffalo Bill In Tomahawk Territory* (Ray)	USA, 52
Charlton Heston	*Pony Express* (Hopper)	USA, 53
Malcolm Atterbury	*Badman's Country* (Sears)	USA, 58
James McMullan	*The Raiders* (Daugherty)	USA, 64
Rick van Nutter	*Seven Hours Of Gunfire* (Marchent)	
		Spa/It/W.Ger, 64
Gordon Scott	*Buffalo Bill* (Costa)	It/W.Ger/Fra, 65
Guy Stockwell	*The Plainsman* (Rich)	USA, 66
Michel Piccoli	*Touche Pas La Femme Blanche* (Ferreri)	Fra, 74
Paul Newman	*Buffalo Bill And The Indians, Or Sitting Bull's*	
	History Lesson (Altman)	USA, 76

Note: George Waggner in *The Iron Horse* (USA, 24), John Fox, Jr. in *The Pony Express* (USA, 25), Jack Hoxie in *The Last Frontier* (USA, 26) and William Fairbanks in *Wyoming* (USA, 27) were among the actors who appeared as Cody on the silent screen.

Cogburn, Rooster

John Wayne's most famous Western role and the one for which he won his Academy Award; a one-eyed, hard-drinking U.S. Marshal who is hired by a 14-year old ranch girl to track down the murderer of her father. Created by Charles Portis in his 1968 novel 'True Grit'.

John Wayne	*True Grit* (Hathaway)	USA, 69
John Wayne	*Rooster Cogburn* (Millar)	USA, 75

Cohan, George M.

(1878–1942) Multi-talented song and dance man whose dynamic show-biz career was celebrated (and told in flashback to President Roosevelt) in the Warner biography *Yankee Doodle Dandy*. James Cagney repeated his Oscar-winning portrayal in a guest spot in the subsequent Eddie Foy bio-pic *The Seven Little Foys*. Among Cohan's song compositions: 'Over There', 'The Yankee Doodle Boy' and 'Give My Regards To Broadway'.

James Cagney	*Yankee Doodle Dandy* (Curtiz)	USA, 42
James Cagney	*The Seven Little Foys* (Shavelson)	USA, 55
Mark Baker	*After The Ball* (Bennett)	GB, 57

A Connecticut Yankee In King Arthur's Court

Mark Twain hero who is transported back from 19th century America to the court of King Arthur where he is branded a wizard because of his modern ingenuity and know-how. Twain's 1889 novel satirized the world of chivalry, king and church; Paramount's 1949 musical version was less ambitious and allowed Bing Crosby, William Bendix and Cedric Hardwicke to whoop it up 'Busily Doing Nothing!'

Will Rogers	*A Connecticut Yankee* (Butler)	USA, 31
Bing Crosby	*A Connecticut Yankee In King Arthur's Court* (Garnett)	
		USA, 49

Note: Harry Myers starred in a 1921 silent production, directed by Emmett J. Flynn.

Copperfield, David

Along with Oliver Twist, the best-known of Charles Dickens' boy heroes, a partly autobiographical figure who encounters cruelty in the form of his stepfather Mr. Murdstone, kindness with Yarmouth fisherman Dan Peggotty and bizarre friendship with the ever-hopeful Mr. Micawber. Played on screen by two actors, first as a small boy, second as a young man. 'David Copperfield' was published in 1849–50.

The boy David

Freddie Bartholomew	*David Copperfield* (Cukor)	USA, 35
Alistair Mackenzie	*David Copperfield* (Delbert Mann)	GB, 70

The adult David

Frank Lawton	*David Copperfield* (Cukor)	USA, 35
Robin Phillips	*David Copperfield* (Delbert Mann)	GB, 70

Note: Eric Desmond and Kenneth Ware (GB, 13) and Martin Herzberg and Gorm Schmidt (Den, 23) played the child and adult Copperfield in silent productions.

Corbett, James J.

(1866–1933) Or, as he was better known, 'Gentleman Jim', the first official heavyweight champion under the Marquis of Queensbury rules. A boxer of style, he introduced 'science' into his sport and gained the title after a 21-round epic with John L. Sullivan in New Orleans in 1892. Errol Flynn's dashing portrait in 1942 was one of the actor's own favourite performances.

Errol Flynn	*Gentleman Jim* (Walsh)	USA, 42

The Corsican Brothers

Siamese twin heroes of Alexandre Dumas, vastly different in character
— one is a Parisian gentleman, the other a Corsican bandit — but both
linked by their resolve to avenge the murder of their family. Engagingly
played by Douglas Fairbanks Jr. in Gregory Ratoff's 1942 swashbuckler;
created by Dumas in his novel of 1845.

Pierre Brasseur &			
Jacques Erwin	*The Corsican Brothers*	(Kelber)	Fra, 38
Douglas Fairbanks, Jr.	*The Corsican Brothers*	(Ratoff)	USA, 42
Richard Greene	*Return Of The Corsican Brothers*		
		(Nazarro)	USA, 53
Antonio Vilar	*The Corsican Brothers*	(Fleider)	Arg, 55
Geoffrey Horne	*The Corsican Brothers*	(Majano)	Fra/It, 60

Note: The 1938 film is the only sound version in which two actors
played the brothers Mario and Lucien; on the silent screen, King
Baggot (USA, 15), Henry Krauss (Fra, 17) and Dustin Farnum (USA, 19)
all featured in the dual role.

The Count of Monte Cristo

Swashbuckling hero of Alexandre Dumas; a young ship's officer named
Edmond Dantes who is condemned to life imprisonment on a false
political charge and then escapes from the notorious Chateau d'If to
wreak vengeance on the three men who sent him there. Robert Donat,
in the 1934 film of Rowland V. Lee, remains the definitive screen
Dantes; the character first appeared in print in 1844.

Robert Donat	*The Count Of Monte Cristo*	(Lee)	USA, 34
Arturo de Cordova	*The Count Of Monte Cristo*	(Urueta)	Mex, 41
Pierre Richard-Willm	*The Count Of Monte Cristo*	(Vernay/Cerio)	
			Fra/It, 43
Ramon Delgado	*The Sword Of The Avenger*	(Salkow)	USA, 48
Jorge Mistral	*Le Testament de Monte Cristo*	(Klimovski)	
			Arg/Mex, 53
Jean Marais	*The Count Of Monte Cristo*	(Vernay)	
			Fra/It, 54
Louis Jourdan	*The Story Of The Count Of Monte Cristo*		
		(Autant-Lara)	Fra/It, 61
Paul Barge	*The Count Of Monte Cristo*	(Hunebelle)	
			Fra/It, 68
Richard Chamberlain	*The Count Of Monte Cristo*	(Greene)	GB, 74

Note: *The Sword Of The Avenger* was a loose adaptation of the story with
the names of the characters changed; the Count spawned several
offspring, all of whom received the chance to swashbuckle like their

illustrious father — Louis Hayward (son) in *The Son Of Monte Cristo* (USA, 40) and (grand-nephew) in *Monte Cristo's Revenge* (USA, 46), and Robert Clarke (son) in *Island Of Monte Cristo* (52). Lenore Aubert featured as *The Wife Of Monte Cristo* (46).

Hobart Bosworth (USA, 12), James O'Neill (USA, 13), Leon Mathot (Fra, 17), John Gilbert (USA, 22) and Jean Angelo (Fra, 29) were among the silent actors who played the avenging count.

Coward, Noel

(1899–1973) The most successful multi-talented artist in the history of the British theatre. A writer of operettas, revues and straight plays ('Bitter Sweet', 'Cavalcade', 'Blithe Spirit', etc), he wrote and starred in several of his own films and was portrayed on celluloid in *Star!* as the young friend and confidant of British stage actress Gertrude Lawrence. Not yet the subject of a major screen biography.

Daniel Massey	*Star!* (Wise)	USA, 68

Crazy Horse

Sioux chief who, together with Sitting Bull, led the tribal uprising that culminated in the massacre of Custer's 7th Cavalry at the Little Big Horn. His triumph was short lived, however. Shortly after the battle he was captured and bayoneted to death by the cavalry. Mostly a subsidiary character in westerns, although Universal afforded him a full-scale biography in 1955 with Victor Mature.

Anthony Quinn	*They Died With Their Boots On* (Walsh)	USA, 42
Iron Eyes Cody	*Sitting Bull* (Salkow)	USA, 54
Victor Mature	*Chief Crazy Horse* (Sherman)	USA, 55
Murray Alper	*The Outlaws Is Coming* (Maurer)	USA, 65
Iron Eyes Cody	*The Great Sioux Massacre* (Salkow)	USA, 65
Will Sampson	*The White Buffalo* (Lee Thompson)	USA, 77

Note: Crazy Horse was renamed Dull Knife and played by Kieron Moore in Siodmak's 1967 film, *Custer Of The West*; the Indian chief was portrayed by High Eagle in the 1936 serial, *Custer's Last Stand*.

Crime Doctor

American radio sleuth, equally popular when portrayed in the movies by Warner Baxter in the 40s. An ex-gangster turned criminologist, he is always a cut above his fellow detectives in that he solves most of his cases through psychiatry. Ray Collins created the role on radio in 1940; the first film appeared three years later. Creator: Max Marcin.

Warner Baxter	*Crime Doctor* (Gordon)		USA, 43
Warner Baxter	*Crime Doctor's Strangest Case* (Forde)		USA, 43
Warner Baxter	*Shadows In The Night* (Forde)		USA, 44
Warner Baxter	*Crime Doctor's Courage* (Sherman)		USA, 45
Warner Baxter	*Crime Doctor's Warning* (Castle)		USA, 45
Warner Baxter	*Crime Doctor's Man Hunt* (Castle)		USA, 46
Warner Baxter	*Just Before Dawn* (Castle)		USA, 46
Warner Baxter	*The Millerson Case* (Archainbaud)		USA, 47
Warner Baxter	*Crime Doctor's Gamble* (Castle)		USA, 47
Warner Baxter	*Crime Doctor's Diary* (Friedman)		USA, 49

Crippen, Dr.

(1862–1910) Something of an enigma in the annals of crime. Either a mild-mannered little doctor driven to the murder of his overbearing wife because of his love for a young girl or, in the view of one noted criminologist, 'one of the most dangerous criminals of his century'. The 1962 film proffered the former view. The facts, however, remain. Mrs. Crippen was poisoned, her body mutilated and buried in various parts of the cellar and Crippen arrested in Canada whilst trying to make his escape.

Donald Pleasence	*Dr. Crippen* (Lynn)	GB, 62

Note: *The Suspect* (44) in which Charles Laughton played a middle-aged London shop-keeper who murders his intolerably spiteful wife for the love of a younger woman, had strong hints of the Crippen case. Samantha Eggar played the young girl, Ethel Le Neve in the 1962 film, Ella Raines her equivalent in 1944.

Crockett, Davy

(1786–1836) American frontiersman, an expert rifleman and bear hunter who served as a scout for Andrew Jackson and was elected three times to Congress before dying a hero's death defending the Alamo. Fess Parker (who played the part twice for Disney) and John Wayne rate as the best-known screen Crocketts; grizzled character actor Arthur Hunnicutt as the most accurate.

Lane Chandler	*Heroes Of The Alamo* (Fraser)	USA, 37
Robert Barrat	*Man Of Conquest* (Nichols, Jr.)	USA, 39
George Montgomery	*Davy Crockett, Indian Scout* (Landers)	USA, 49
Trevor Bardette	*The Man From The Alamo* (Boetticher)	USA, 53
Arthur Hunnicutt	*The Last Command* (Lloyd)	USA, 55
Fess Parker	*Davy Crockett, King Of The Wild Frontier* (Foster)	USA, 55

Fess Parker	*Davy Crockett And The River Pirates* (Foster)	
		USA, 56
Fess Parker	*Alias Jesse James* (McLeod)	USA, 59
John Wayne	*The Alamo* (Wayne)	USA, 60

Note: Dustin Farnum in *Davy Crockett* (USA, 16) and Cullen Landis in *Davy Crockett At The Fall Of The Alamo* (USA, 26) both featured in the role on the silent screen.

Cromwell, Oliver

(1599–1658) Puritan squire and Member of Parliament who led England into a Civil War to rid her of injustice and oppression. Commanded the famous cavalry regiment known as the 'Ironsides' and reigned as Lord Protector of England from 1653 to 1658. Generally regarded in films as a ruthless tyrant. Not so in Ken Hughes' full-scale biography in which his rise from humble beginnings to a national leader caught up in political intrigue was movingly and realistically conveyed.

George Merritt	*The Vicar Of Bray* (Edwards)	GB, 37
Edmund Willard	*Cardboard Cavalier* (Forde)	GB, 49
John Le Mesurier	*The Moonraker* (MacDonald)	GB, 58
Patrick Wymark	*Witchfinder General* (Reeves)	GB, 68
Richard Harris	*Cromwell* (Hughes)	GB, 70

Note: Booth Conway in *The Tavern Knight* (GB, 20), Henry Ainley in *The Royal Oak* (GB, 23) and Frederick Burton in *The Fighting Blade* (USA, 23) all featured as Cromwell on the silent screen.

Cromwell, Thomas

(1485–1540) Chief minister to Henry VIII who rose quickly to power after the fall from royal favour of Cardinal Wolsey and Sir Thomas More. A prominent figure during Henry's reign (but only recently on film), he advised on ecclesiastical matters and helped fake the evidence of adultery against Anne Boleyn. He eventually meddled once too often — in Henry's marriage to Anne Of Cleves — and was himself executed for treason. The scheming ambition and rough, peasant origins of the man were given full rein by Leo McKern in Zinnemann's *A Man For All Seasons*.

Leo McKern	*A Man For All Seasons* (Zinnemann)	GB, 66
John Colicos	*Anne Of The Thousand Days* (Jarrott)	GB, 69
Kenneth Williams	*Carry On Henry* (Thomas)	GB, 71
Donald Pleasence	*Henry VIII And His Six Wives* (Hussein)	GB, 72

Note: Reginald Owen appeared as Cromwell in a 1911 British silent film, *Henry VIII*.

Curie, Marie

(1867–1934) Polish-born French physicist who worked with her husband Pierre on radioactivity and magnetism and, in 1903, made the vital discovery of radium. The first person to be awarded two Nobel Prizes, she was portrayed on screen by Greer Garson in a 1943 MGM film which, despite the usual glossy Hollywood production values, still managed to capture some of the zeal and integrity of the tireless woman scientist.

Greer Garson	*Madame Curie* (LeRoy)	USA, 43

Custer, George Armstrong

(1839–1876) Vain, glory-seeking Cavalry officer (a general at 26) who tried to emulate his heroic feats of the Civil War in his subsequent campaigns against the Indians. His ambition to secure a place in the history books was satisfied when he and his 264 men of the 7th Cavalry were massacred by the Sioux and Cheyenne at the Little Big Horn in June, 1876. The picture of him standing defiant, pistol raised, against hordes of charging Indians, remains one of the classic images of Hollywood westerns. Errol Flynn expressed Custer's gallantry, Robert Shaw his flamboyance, Henry Fonda his stubborness.

Clay Clement	*The World Changes* (LeRoy)	USA, 33
John Miljan	*The Plainsman* (DeMille)	USA, 37
Paul Kelly	*Wyoming* (Thorpe)	USA, 40
Addison Richards	*Badlands Of Dakota* (Green)	USA, 41
Ronald Reagan	*Santa Fe Trail* (Curtiz)	USA, 40
Errol Flynn	*They Died With Their Boots On* (Walsh)	
		USA, 42
James Millican	*Warpath* (Haskin)	USA, 51
Sheb Wooley	*Bugles In The Afternoon* (Rowland)	USA, 52
Douglas Kennedy	*Sitting Bull* (Salkow)	USA, 54
Britt Lomond	*Tonka* (Foster)	USA, 58
Philip Carey	*The Great Sioux Massacre* (Salkow)	USA, 65
Leslie Nielsen	*The Plainsman* (Rich)	USA, 66
Robert Shaw	*Custer Of The West* (Siodmak)	USA/Spa, 67
Richard Mulligan	*Little Big Man* (Penn)	USA, 70
Marcello Mastroianni	*Touche Pas La Femme Blanche* (Ferreri)	
		Fra, 74

Note: Henry Fonda (as Colonel Thursday) in John Ford's *Fort Apache* (USA, 48) and Andrew Duggan (as General McCabe) in *The Glory Guys* (USA, 65) also appeared as the Custer character on screen; Dustin Farnum in *The Flaming Frontier* (USA, 26) and John Beck in *General Custer at the Little Big Horn* (USA, 26) were among the silent actors who portrayed him.

Cyrano de Bergerac

Owner of the longest nose in literature, a soulful poet-swordsman of 17th century France whose flamboyant ways with a rapier somewhat overshadowed his wooing of the ladies. Jose Ferrer (Academy Award, 1950) has portrayed him twice; Edmond Rostand's play, based on a real-life French playwright, was first performed in 1897.

Claude Dauphin	*Cyrano de Bergerac* (Rivers)	Fra, 45
Jose Ferrer	*Cyrano de Bergerac* (Gordon)	USA, 50
Karel Hoger	*Munchhausen* (Zeman)	Czech, 61
Jose Ferrer	*Cyrano and D'Artagnan* (Gance)	Fra/It/Spa, 62

Note: Coquelin Aine (France, 1900), Henry Krauss in Capellani's French adaptation of 1909 and Pierre Magnier in a 1923 Italian version all featured as silent Cyranos.

D

Darrow, Clarence

(1857–1938) American lawyer, famed for his liberal views and never ending crusade for the abolition of capital punishment. Two of his most famous cases — the defence of Leopold and Loeb and the schoolteacher accused of teaching Darwin's theory of evolution in a Tennessee school — were filmed in *Compulsion* and *Inherit The Wind*, respectively. Darrow was not named in either film, appearing as Jonathan Wilk in the Richard Fleischer movie and Henry Drummond in the Kramer production.

Orson Welles	*Compulsion* (Fleischer)	USA, 59
Spencer Tracy	*Inherit The Wind* (Kramer)	USA, 60

Darwin, Charles

(1809–1882) British naturalist who revolutionized 19th century thinking with his theory of the evolution of man and later authored the famous 'Origin Of The Species' (1859). Not the most entertaining subject for a film, although Jack Couffer's 1972 movie which included Darwin's journeys to South America and New Zealand, made an honest attempt to recreate his life and work.

Nicholas Clay	*The Darwin Adventure* (Couffer)	GB, 72

DeSylva, Brown and Henderson

An unusual combination, a songwriting *trio* who wrote the scores for several Broadway musicals ('George White's Scandals', 'Good News', 'Flying High'), all of which reflected the madcap mood of the Jazz Age. Their rise from Tin Pan Alley to Hollywood was the subject of the 1956 biography by Michael Curtiz. Among their hit songs: 'The Birth of The Blues', 'Button Up Your Overcoat', 'It All Depends On You', 'The Varsity Drag.'

Gordon MacRae (DeSylva)		
Ernest Borgnine (Brown)		
Dan Dailey (Henderson)	*The Best Things In Life Are Free* (Curtiz)	USA, 56

Note: Buddy DeSylva (1895–1950) was also played by Eddie Marr in *Rhapsody In Blue* (45): Lew Brown died in 1958, aged 65, Ray Henderson in 1970, aged 74.

The Devil

Satan, Beezlebub, Mephistopheles, Old Nick — call him what you will, but God's opposite number has positively thrived on the screen and even, on occasion, displayed a humorous side to his dark, forbidding nature. Walter Huston, Laird Cregar, Burgess Meredith and Peter Cook are among those who have chuckled with manic delight; in more recent years the Devil has been slightly more reticent about making personal appearances and been content to rest snugly within the frames of unsuspecting children, e.g. Linda Blair in *The Exorcist* and Harvey Stephens in *The Omen*.

Walter Huston	*All That Money Can Buy* (Dieterle)	USA, 41
Alan Mowbray	*The Devil With Hitler* (Douglas)	USA, 42
Jules Berry	*Les Visiteurs du Soir* (Carne)	Fra, 42
Rex Ingram	*Cabin In The Sky* (Minnelli)	USA, 43
Laird Cregar	*Heaven Can Wait* (Lubitsch)	USA, 43
Emil Fjellstrom	*The Heavenly Play* (Sjoberg)	Swe, 44
Claude Rains	*Angel On My Shoulder* (Mayo)	USA, 46
Ray Milland	*Alias Nick Beal* (Farrow)	USA, 49
Michel Simon	*La Beaute du Diable* (Clair)	Fra, 49
Italo Tajo	*Faust And The Devil* (Gallone)	It, 50
Stanley Holloway	*Meet Mr. Lucifer* (Pelissier)	GB, 53
Cedric Hardwicke	*Bait* (Haas)	USA, 54
Yves Montand	*Marguerite of the Night* (Autant-Lara)	Fra, 56
Fernando Gomez	*Faustina* (de Heredia)	Spa, 57
Mel Welles	*The Undead* (Corman)	USA, 57
Vincent Price	*The Story Of Mankind* (Allen)	USA, 57
Ray Walston	*Damn Yankees* (Donen)	USA, 58
Jose Galvez	*Macario* (Gavaldon)	Mex, 60
Gustaf Gruendgens	*Faust* (Gorski)	W.Ger, 60
Stig Jarrel	*The Devil's Eye* (Bergman)	Swe, 60
Georgiy Millyar	*A Night Before Christmas* (Rou)	USSR, 61
Lon Chaney, Jr.	*The Devil's Messenger* (Strock)	USA/Swe, 62
Roban Cody	*Faust* (Suman)	USA, 64
Robert Helpmann	*The Soldier's Tale* (Birkett)	GB, 64
Donald Pleasence	*The Greatest Story Ever Told* (Stevens)	USA, 65
Vittorio Gassman	*The Devil In Love* (Scola)	It, 66

Andreas Teuber	*Doctor Faustus* (Burton/Coghill)	GB/It, 67
Peter Cook	*Bedazzled* (Donen)	GB, 67
Burgess Meredith	*Torture Garden* (Francis)	GB, 67
Jorj Voicu	*Faust* (Popescu-Gopo)	Rum, 67
Pierre Clementi	*The Milky Way* (Bunuel)	Fra/It, 69
Mio Domani	*Scratch Harry* (Matter)	USA, 70
Christopher Stone	*The Joys Of Jezebel* (Stootsberry)	USA, 70
Alain Cuny	*The Master & Margarita* (Petrovic)	
		Yug/It, 72
Ralph Richardson	*Tales From The Crypt* (Francis)	GB, 72
Linda Blair	*The Exorcist* (Friedkin)	USA, 73
Juliet Mills	*The Devil Within Her* (Hellman)	It, 74
Carla Gravina	*The Antichrist* (de Martino)	It, 74
Ernest Borgnine	*The Devil's Rain* (Fuest)	USA, 76
Harvey Stephens	*The Omen* (Donner)	USA, 76
Burgess Meredith	*The Sentinel* (Winner)	USA, 77
Linda Blair	*Exorcist II: The Heretic* (Boorman)	USA, 77
Simon Ward	*Holocaust 2000* (de Martino)	It/GB, 78
Victor Buono	*The Evil* (Trikonis)	USA, 78
Jonathan Scott-Taylor	*Damien: Omen II* (Taylor)	USA, 78

Diamond, Jack 'Legs'

(–1931) The gangster they couldn't kill — almost! A racketeer and bootlegger, he was riddled with bullets on at least three occasions and still managed to live to tell the tale. The only sure way to dispose of him was to murder him in his sleep which some unknown gangsters finally accomplished in December, 1931. Strictly an also ran compared with Dillinger, Capone and the rest, but vividly portrayed in Boetticher's *The Rise And Fall Of Legs Diamond*.

Ray Danton	*The Rise And Fall Of Legs Diamond* (Boetticher)	
		USA, 60
Ray Danton	*Portrait Of A Mobster* (Pevney)	USA, 61

Dillinger, John

(1903–1934) A Public Enemy Number One before being betrayed by a prostitute and shot down outside a Chicago movie theatre in July, 1934 — an event re-enacted many times on screen. Despite his reputation, Dillinger was not one of the most vicious of American gangsters and seldom injured people during his meticulously planned bank raids. Warren Oates' portrait in John Milius' 1973 film is the most efficient screen portrayal, although Lawrence Tierney's performance in the low-budget thriller of 1945 is not without merit.

| Lawrence Tierney | *Dillinger* (Nosseck) | USA, 45 |
| Leo Gordon | *Baby Face Nelson* (Siegel) | USA, 57 |

Scott Peters	*The FBI Story* (LeRoy)	USA, 59
Nick Adams	*Young Dillinger* (Morse)	USA, 65
Warren Oates	*Dillinger* (Milius)	USA, 73
Robert Conrad	*The Lady In Red* (Teague)	USA, 79

Note: The prostitute (known as 'The Lady In Red') who helped the FBI was named Anna Sage. She was played by Cloris Leachman in the Milius film and Anne Jeffreys in the 1945 version. Jean Willes also made a fleeting appearance as the character in *The FBI Story*.

Disraeli, Benjamin

(1804–1881) British statesman and Prime Minister (1868 and 1874–1880), responsible for acquiring the Suez Canal and proclaiming Queen Victoria Empress of India. Portrayed on screen more than any other British premier with George Arliss appearing twice in the role — once on the silent screen, once in the early years of sound — and Alec Guinness rendering the definitive portrait of Disraeli as a wily opportunist in the underrated *The Mudlark*.

George Arliss	*Disraeli* (Green)	USA, 29
Derrick de Marney &		
Hugh Miller	*Victoria The Great* (Wilcox)	GB, 37
Derrick de Marney	*Sixty Glorious Years* (Wilcox)	GB, 38
Miles Mander	*Suez* (Dwan)	USA, 38
John Gielgud	*The Prime Minister* (Dickinson)	GB, 41
Abraham Sofaer	*The Ghosts Of Berkeley Square* (Sewell)	GB, 47
Alec Guinness	*The Mudlark* (Negulesco)	GB, 50

Note: Arliss first played the role in the 1921 silent film, *Disraeli* (USA); Dennis Eadie in *Disraeli* (GB, 16) and Douglas Munro in *The Life Story Of Lloyd George* (GB, 18) also featured in the part.

Doolittle, Eliza

George Bernard Shaw's cockney flower girl, turned into an elegant lady of society by a teacher of phonetics. The 'straight' screen Eliza was played by Wendy Hiller in 1938, the musical fair lady by Audrey Hepburn whose songs — 'I Could Have Danced All Night', 'Show Me', 'Wouldn't It Be Luverly' — were dubbed by Marni Dixon. Two earlier screen versions of 'Pygmalion' were produced in Germany and Holland. Shaw's play originally opened in London in 1913.

Jenny Jugo	*Pygmalion* (Engel)	Ger, 35
Lily Bouwmeester	*Pygmalion* (Berger)	Hol, 36
Wendy Hiller	*Pygmalion* (Pascal)	GB, 38
Audrey Hepburn	*My Fair Lady* (Cukor)	USA, 64

Note: Henry Higgins, the conceited, chauvinistic professor of dialects, has been played by Gustaf Grundgens (35), Johan de Meester (36), Leslie Howard (38) and Rex Harrison (64). Harrison played the stage role on Broadway (56) and in London (58) and won an Academy Award for best screen actor of 1964.

The Dolly Sisters

Dancing headliners who began in US vaudeville and then scored their first Broadway hit in the 1911 production 'Ziegfeld Follies'. Subsequently became 'the toast of two continents' with their famous sister act. In the 1945 film biography Jennie (1892–1941) was played by Betty Grable, and Rosie (1892–1970) by June Haver.

Betty Grable and June Haver	*The Dolly Sisters*	(Cummings)	
			USA, 45

Dominici, Gaston

Patriarchal French farmer who belongs in the annals of crime as one of the 'was he innocent' variety. His confessions, retractions, counter-accusations and attempted suicide when charged with the murder of the British Drummond family in the south of France in 1952, led to confusion and doubt. Eventually convicted, he was sentenced to life imprisonment but released in 1960. He died five years later, aged 88. Jean Gabin, in one of his final screen roles, portrayed him on screen in 1973.

Jean Gabin	*L'Affaire Dominici*	(Bernard-Aubert)	Fra, 73

Don Juan

Legendary rake whose dissolute life in 17th century Spain attracted two major Hollywood stars, Douglas Fairbanks and Errol Flynn, during their final swashbuckling years. His romantic escapades were also the subject of the 1926 John Barrymore costumer, *Don Juan*, the first movie to incorporate sound effects — bells, the clashing of swords, etc. — onto a synchronized soundtrack.

John Barrymore	*Don Juan* (Crosland)		USA, 26
Douglas Fairbanks	*The Private Life Of Don Juan*	(Korda)	GB, 34
Adriano Rimoldi	*The Loves Of Don Juan*	(Falconi)	It, 48
Errol Flynn	*The Adventures Of Don Juan*	(Sherman)	USA, 49
Antonio Vilar	*The Loves Of Don Juan*	(de Heredia)	Spa, 50
Jean-Marie Amato	*Men Think Only Of That*	(Robert)	Fra, 54
Erno Crisa	*Don Juan* (Berry)		Fra/It, 56
Jarl Kulle	*The Devil's Eye* (Bergman)		Swe, 60
Brigitte Bardot	*Don Juan or If Don Juan Were A Woman*		
		(Vadim)	Fra/It, 73

Note: In John Berry's 1956 film, Fernandel (as the servant of Don Juan who impersonates his master) had the starring role; Vadim's picture revamped the legend and centred on Don Juan reincarnated as a woman.

Don Quixote

Gallant 16th century knight of novelist Cervantes, an idealistic hero who takes to the road with his squire Sancho Panza in an attempt to restore the age of chivalry. The Russian version with Nikolai Cherkassov remains one of the most assured screen adaptations of a classic novel; *Man Of La Mancha*, the musical version with Peter O'Toole doubling as both Cervantes and Quixote, ranks as one of the most dismal.

Feodor Chaliapin	*Don Quixote* (Pabst)	GB, 33
Rafael Rivelles	*Don Quixote* (Gil)	Spa, 47
Nikolai Cherkassov	*Don Quixote* (Kozintsev)	USSR, 57
Peter O'Toole	*Man Of La Mancha* (Hiller)	It, 72

Note: De Wolf Hopper (USA, 16) and Jerrold Robertshaw (GB, 24) both played Quixote on the silent screen and there were French and Danish versions of the story produced in 1909 and 1926 respectively; George Robey (in 24 and 33), Juan Calvo (Spa, 47), Yuri Tolubeyev (USSR, 57), Folco Lulli (Spa, 62) and James Coco (It, 72) have all featured as Sancho Panza.

Don Quixote did not feature in the 1962 production, titled *Dulcinea*, other than in one brief scene on his death bed. And even then he was photographed from behind.

Doolittle, Lt. General James

(1896–) American general, famous for leading the 1942 bomber raid on Japan in which squadrons of B-25s were launched from aircraft carriers, bombed the Japanese capital and then landed on airfields in China. The events leading up to the raid and the raid itself were described in meticulous, often semi-documentary fashion in Mervyn LeRoy's film of 1944.

Spencer Tracy	*Thirty Seconds Over Tokyo* (LeRoy)	USA, 44

Doone, Lorna

Heroine of R. D. Blackmore's novel of 17th century Devonshire, the kidnapped daughter of a Scottish nobleman who is raised by the Doone outlaw clan on the wilds of Exmoor. Somewhat out of screen favour in recent years, no version of her story having been made since Phil Karlson's low budget production of 1951. More popular in the less demanding silent era.

Victoria Hopper	*Lorna Doone*	(Dean)	GB, 35
Barbara Hale	*Lorna Doone*	(Karlson)	USA, 51

Note: Silent performances were given by Dorothy Bellew (GB, 12), Bertie Gordon (GB, 20) and Madge Bellamy (USA, 22).

Dorsey, Jimmy

(1904–1957) Saxophone player/band leader of the 30s and 40s who made several screen appearances with his orchestra — *The Fleet's In, I Dood It, Four Jills And A Jeep, Hollywood Canteen* — before achieving the unique distinction of portraying himself in the 1947 biography, *The Fabulous Dorseys*.

As himself	*The Fabulous Dorseys*	(Green)	USA, 47
Ray Anthony	*The Five Pennies*	(Shavelson)	USA, 59

Dorsey, Tommy

(1905–1956) Like his brother, a top bandleader of the pre-war and war periods, featuring with his trombone and orchestra in several top movies at MGM — *Du Barry Was A Lady, Presenting Lily Mars, Girl Crazy, Broadway Rhythm*. Played himself in *The Fabulous Dorseys*, a minor, uninspired little biography redeemed by several of the Dorseys' most popular hits i.e. 'Green Eyes', 'Marie', 'Never Say Never', 'The Object Of My Affections'.

As himself	*The Fabulous Dorseys*	(Green)	USA, 47
Bobby Troup	*Drum Crazy*	(Weis)	USA, 59

Dowding, Air Chief Marshal Sir Hugh

(1882–1970) The leader of RAF Fighter Command during the critical months of July, August and September 1940, when the Luftwaffe made a massive air assault on the British Isles. A man of single-minded determination and rather humourless character, played with quiet authority by Olivier in Guy Hamilton's *Battle Of Britain*.

Charles Carson	*Reach For The Sky*	(Gilbert)	GB, 56
Laurence Olivier	*Battle of Britain*	(Hamilton)	GB, 69

Doyle, Jimmy 'Popeye'

Fanatical American cop, a member of the New York narcotics squad, obsessed with tracking down a French dope syndicate smuggling heroin into the USA. A 'Lock 'em up and throw away the key' personality, a

Barbra Streisand as singer-comedienne Fanny Brice in Columbia's *Funny Lady* (1975).

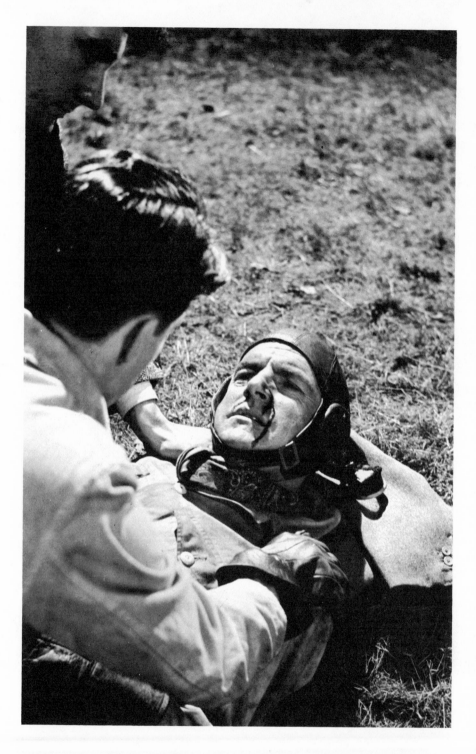

RAF pilot Douglas Bader (Kenneth More) receives injuries in a plane crash that result in his legs being amputated. A scene from the 1956 Rank movie, *Reach For The Sky*.

The hanging judge, Roy Bean, played by an impassive Paul Newman in John Huston's *The Life And Times Of Judge Roy Bean* (First Artists, 1972).

Kris Kristofferson as notorious outlaw William Bonney in Sam Peckinpah's western *Pat Garrett And Billy The Kid* (MGM, 1973).

007 (Sean Connery) in action for the first time in United Artists' *Dr. No* (1962).

Bond's deadliest adversary, Ernst Blofeld, played here by Telly Savalas in the sixth 007 adventure, *On Her Majesty's Secret Service* (United Artists, 1969).

Dustin Hoffman (as Lenny Bruce) and Valerie Perrine, stars of Bob Fosse's biography of the notorious nightclub entertainer, *Lenny* (United Artists, 1974).

Richard Chamberlain as Lord Byron in Robert Bolt's 1972 production, *Lady Caroline Lamb* (EMI).

The most beautiful Cleopatra of them all! Elizabeth Taylor about to take her life in Fox's 37 million dollar epic, *Cleopatra* (1963).

Temptress Dorothy Dandridge about to lead Harry Belafonte from the straight and narrow in Otto Preminger's all black musical *Carmen Jones* (Twentieth Century-Fox, 1954).

A less than romantic Casanova. Donald Sutherland as the legendary Italian philanderer in *Fellini's Casanova* (Twentieth Century-Fox, 1977).

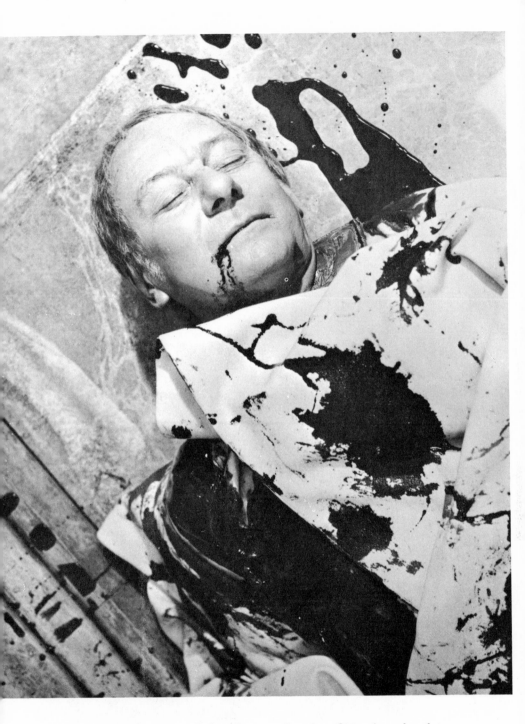

John Gielgud's Julius Caesar fails to beware the Ides of March and ends his life beneath Pompey's statue. A scene from the 1970 Commonwealth United production, *Julius Caesar*.

Richard Attenborough as mass murderer John Reginald Christie in *10 Rillington Place* (Columbia, 1971).

The toughest movie cop of the 70s. Clint Eastwood as Dirty Harry Callahan in *Magnum Force* (Warners, 1973).

Al Capone (Jason Robards, Jr.) survives an attempted assassination by Bugs Moran in Roger Corman's *The St. Valentine's Day Massacre* (Twentieth Century-Fox, 1967).

Vanessa Redgrave as celebrated detective writer Agatha Christie in the real-life thriller, *Agatha* (First Artists, 1979).

One of the most popular movie couples of all time. William Powell and Myrna Loy (and Asta), stars of MGM's *Thin Man* films.

Audrey Hepburn, dressed to perfection by Cecil Beaton, as the new look
Eliza Doolittle in the Oscar winning *My Fair Lady* (Warners, 1964). On her
left: Wilfrid Hyde White.

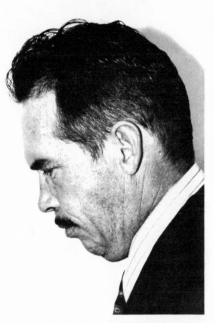

The real John Dillinger (left) photographed in 1933; the screen equivalent, Warren Oates (right) in John Milius' 1973 biography, *Dillinger* (American International).

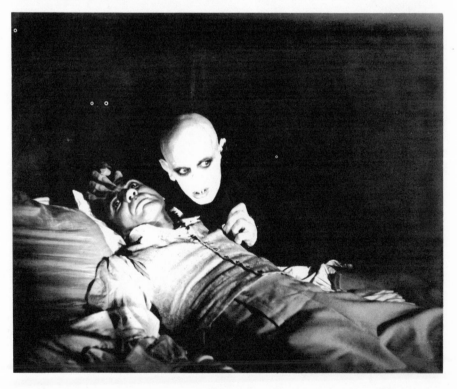

A recent reworking of Bram Stoker's Dracula story. Klaus Kinski about to satisfy his appetite in *Nosferatu— The Vampyre* (Twentieth Century-Fox, 1979).

Tony Curtis as Albert DeSalvo with just one of his thirteen victims in
The Boston Strangler (Twentieth Century-Fox, 1968).

The young Elizabeth. Jean Simmons as *Young Bess* in MGM's 1953 costume romance, directed by George Sidney.

shabby determination, and a better than average skill behind the wheel of a car, eventually see him through, although it takes him two movies to nail criminal kingpin Fernando Rey. Gene Hackman won an Oscar for the first of his two characterizations.

Gene Hackman	*The French Connection*	(Friedkin)	USA, 71
Gene Hackman	*The French Connection II*	(Frankenheimer)	USA, 75

Dr. Jekyll And Mr. Hyde

Victorian doctor who tampers with the laws of nature and experiments with a potion that transforms him from good to evil (the bestial Mr. Hyde) in a matter of seconds. A serious challenge for any actor, whether he be required to turn into a hairy creature of monstrous strength as in Mamoulian's 1932 film, or a more subtle but equally malignant sadist in Victor Fleming's remake. Robert Louis Stevenson's story, based, not surprisingly, on a nightmare, was published in 1886.

Fredric March	*Dr. Jekyll And Mr. Hyde*	(Mamoulian)	USA, 32
Spencer Tracy	*Dr. Jekyll And Mr. Hyde*	(Fleming)	USA, 41
Louis Hayward	*Son Of Dr. Jekyll*	(Friedman)	USA, 51
Boris Karloff	*Abbott & Costello Meet Dr. Jekyll And Mr. Hyde*	(Lamont)	USA, 53
Gloria Talbot	*Daughter Of Dr. Jekyll*	(Ulmer)	USA, 57
Jean-Louis Barrault	*Le Testament du Dr. Cordelier*	(Renoir)	Fra, 59
Paul Massie	*Two Faces Of Dr. Jekyll*	(Fisher)	GB, 60
Christopher Lee	*I, Monster*	(Weeks)	GB, 70
Ralph Bates & Martine Beswick	*Dr. Jekyll And Sister Hyde*	(Baker)	GB, 71
Bernie Casey	*Dr. Black, Mr. Hyde*	(Crain)	USA, 76

Note: In 1963 Jerry Lewis starred in *The Nutty Professor* (USA), a modern updating of Stevenson's story, with Lewis as a campus college professor who turns into a ladykilling hero; the 1970 film with Christopher Lee renamed the characters Dr. Marlowe and Edward Blake, and in *Dr. Jekyll And Sister Hyde*, Ralph Bates achieved the ultimate personality change by becoming Martine Beswick.

Silent actors who appeared in the dual role included Alwin Neuss (USA, 10), King Baggot (USA, 13), Sheldon Lewis (USA, 20), John Barrymore (USA, 20) and Conrad Veidt (20) who starred in a German variation of the theme, *Janus-Faced*, directed by F. W. Murnau.

In a 1912 version, directed by Lucius Henderson, James Cruze played Jekyll, Harry Benham appeared as Hyde.

Dracula

The most enduring horror figure in all cinema, a Transylvanian count who sleeps in a coffin by day and drinks human blood to sustain him in working hours. Bela Lugosi brought Dracula worldwide fame in Tod Browning's 1931 film; Christopher Lee enhanced the vampire's popularity still further in the post-war years and to date has played the count on at least nine occasions. Bram Stoker's novel was published in 1897 and derived from the unsavoury activities of a certain Vlad Dracula who operated in the Carpathian mountains in the 15th century. A checklist of the major screen Draculas is shown below:

Bela Lugosi	*Dracula* (Browning)	USA, 31
Carlos Villarias	*Dracula* (Melford)	Mex, 31
Lon Chaney, Jr.	*Son Of Dracula* (Siodmak)	USA, 43
John Carradine	*House Of Frankenstein* (Kenton)	USA, 44
John Carradine	*House Of Dracula* (Kenton)	USA, 45
Bela Lugosi	*Abbott & Costello Meet Frankenstein* (Barton)	USA, 48
Atif Kaptan	*Drakula Istanbulda* (Muhtat)	Turk, 53
Christopher Lee	*Dracula* (Fisher)	GB, 58
Francis Lederer	*The Return Of Dracula* (Landres)	USA, 58
Yechoon Lee	*Ahkea Khots* (Lee)	S.Korea, 61
John Carradine	*Billy The Kid vs Dracula* (Beaudine)	USA, 66
Christopher Lee	*Dracula — Prince Of Darkness* (Fisher)	GB, 66
Pluto Felix	*The Worst Crime Of All!* (Lamb)	USA, 66
Mitch Evans	*Dr. Terror's Gallery Of Horrors* (Hewitt)	USA, 67
Christopher Lee	*Dracula Has Risen From The Grave* (Francis)	GB, 68
John Carradine	*Blood Of Dracula's Castle* (Adamson)	USA, 69
Vince Kelly	*Dracula (The Dirty Old Man)* (Edwards)	USA, 69
Des Roberts	*Guess What Happened To Count Dracula* (Merrick)	USA, 70
Christopher Lee	*The Scars Of Dracula* (Baker)	GB, 70
Christopher Lee	*Taste The Blood Of Dracula* (Sasdy)	GB, 70
Christopher Lee	*El Conde Dracula* (Franco)	Spa, 70
Zandor Vorkov	*Blood Of Frankenstein* (Adamson)	USA, 70
Paul Albert Krumm	*Jonathan, Vampire Sterben Nicht* (Gissendorfer)	W.Ger, 70
Howard Vernon	*Dracula Contra El Doctor Frankenstein* (Franco)	Spa, 71
Christopher Lee	*Dracula A.D. 1972* (Gibson)	GB, 72
Mori Kishida	*Lake Of Dracula* (Yamamoto)	Jap, 72
Paul Naschy	*Count Dracula's Great Love* (Aguirre)	Spa, 72
Howard Vernon	*La Hija De Dracula* (Franco)	Spa, 72
Narciso Ibanez Menta	*The Dracula Saga* (Klimovsky)	Spa, 73
Christopher Lee	*The Satanic Rites Of Dracula* (Gibson)	GB, 73

Jack Palance	*Dracula* (Cohen)	USA, 73
Udo Kier	*Blood For Dracula* (Morrissey)	USA, 74
John Forbes Robertson	*The Legend Of The Seven Golden Vampires*	
	(Baker)	GB/Hong Kong, 74
David Niven	*Vampira* (Donner)	GB, 75
Christopher Lee	*Dracula, Pere Et Fils* (Molinaro)	Fra, 76
Michael Pataki	*Zoltan : Hound of Dracula* (Band)	USA, 77
Klaus Kinski	*Nosferatu, The Vampyre* (Herzog)	
		W.Ger, 79
Frank Langella	*Dracula* (Badham)	USA, 79
George Hamilton	*Love At First Bite* (Dragoti)	USA, 79
John Carradine	*Nocturna* (Tampa)	USA, 79
Stefan Sileanu	*The True Life of Dracula* (Nastase)	
		Rum, 79

Note: Gloria Holden appeared as *Dracula's Daughter* in 1936; Bela Lugosi (as Armand Tesla) in *The Return Of The Vampire* (USA, 43) and David Peel (as Baron Meinster) in *Brides Of Dracula* (GB, 60) both featured as the Dracula character under another name.

Max Schreck (as Count Orlock) appeared for F. W. Murnau in the German silent production, *Nosferatu* (22).

Drake, Sir Francis

(1540–1596) English naval adventurer who sailed as a privateer against the ships of Spain and helped defeat the Armada in 1588. An under-exposed figure on screen despite being portrayed by Matheson Lang in a little-known British biography of the 30s and Rod Taylor (as a heroic swashbuckler) in *Seven Seas To Calais*.

Matheson Lang	*Drake Of England* (Woods)	GB, 35
Rod Taylor	*Seven Seas To Calais* (Mate)	It/USA, 62
Philip Stearns	*Winstanley* (Brownlow/Mollo)	GB, 76

Note: Hay Plumb appeared in the role in the British silent production, *Drake's Love Story* (13).

Dreyfus, Alfred

(1859–1935) Jewish officer of the French artillery who was unjustly accused of betraying military secrets and, in 1894, sentenced to life imprisonment on Devil's Island. Only through the untiring efforts of novelist Emile Zola who uncovered anti-semitism and corruption in the establishment in his letter 'J'Accuse', was he eventually pardoned. The case has been the subject of four different films. Joseph Schildkraut won a supporting actor Academy Award for his performance in *The Life Of Emile Zola*.

Fritz Kortner	*The Dreyfus Case* (Oswald)	Ger, 30
Cedric Hardwicke	*Dreyfus* (Kraemer/Rosmer)	GB, 31
Joseph Schildkraut	*The Life Of Emile Zola* (Dieterle)	USA, 37
Jose Ferrer	*I Accuse!* (Jose Ferrer)	GB, 58

Drummond, Bulldog

On the printed page an ex-World War I officer who is little more than an upper-class fascist thug seeking an outlet for his latent violence. On screen the epitome of the gallant English adventurer, especially when portrayed by Ronald Colman in his two films for Goldwyn. Unsatisfactorily updated in the 60s to become a womanising super-hero. First appeared in print in 1920 in H. C. McNeile's 'Bulldog Drummond'.

Ronald Colman	*Bulldog Drummond* (Jones)	USA, 29
Kenneth MacKenna	*Temple Tower* (Gallagher)	USA, 30
Ralph Richardson	*The Return Of Bulldog Drummond* (Summers)	
		GB, 34
Ronald Colman	*Bulldog Drummond Strikes Back* (Del Ruth)	
		USA, 34
Athol Fleming	*Bulldog Jack* (Forde)	GB, 35
John Lodge	*Bulldog Drummond At Bay* (Lee)	GB, 37
Ray Milland	*Bulldog Drummond Escapes* (Hogan)	USA, 37
John Howard	*Bulldog Drummond Comes Back* (Louis King)	
		USA, 37
John Howard	*Bulldog Drummond's Revenge* (Louis King)	
		USA, 37
John Howard	*Bulldog Drummond's Peril* (Hogan)	USA, 38
John Howard	*Bulldog Drummond In Africa* (Louis King)	
		USA, 38
John Howard	*Arrest Bulldog Drummond* (Hogan)	USA, 38
John Howard	*Bulldog Drummond's Secret Police* (Hogan)	
		USA, 39
John Howard	*Bulldog Drummond's Bride* (Hogan)	USA, 39
Ron Randell	*Bulldog Drummond At Bay* (Salkow)	USA, 47
Ron Randell	*Bulldog Drummond Strikes Back* (McDonald)	
		USA, 47
Tom Conway	*The Challenge* (Yarbrough)	USA, 48
Tom Conway	*Thirteen Lead Soldiers* (McDonald)	USA, 48
Walter Pidgeon	*Calling Bulldog Drummond* (Saville)	GB, 51
Richard Johnson	*Deadlier Than The Male* (Thomas)	GB, 67
Richard Johnson	*Some Girls Do* (Thomas)	GB, 69

Note: Carlyle Blackwell in Oscar Apfel's *Bulldog Drummond* (22) and Jack Buchanan in *Bulldog Drummond's Third Round* (25) both played the role on the British silent screen.

Duchin, Eddy

(1909–1951) Boston pianist-bandleader, a society favourite of the 30s, whose show-biz career and ill-fated private life were sentimentally recounted by George Sidney in Columbia's 1956 biography. Duchin and his band appeared on screen in person in *Mr. Broadway* (32), *Coronado* (35), *1937 Hit Parade* (37).

Tyrone Power   *The Eddy Duchin Story*   (Sidney)   USA, 56

Note: Carmen Cavallaro played the piano music for Power in Sidney's film.

Duncan, Isadora

(1878–1927) San Francisco-born dancer who created 'headlines' wherever she went, both in her scandalous private life and through her revolutionary interpretations of classical Greek dancing. Scarves were frequently used to bring expression to her dances; ironically, it was a scarf that caused her untimely end, catching in the wheel of her fast-moving car and choking her to death. Vanessa Redgrave starred for Karel Reisz in his detailed 138-minute biography, based on Duncan's 'Life' and the memoirs by Sewell Stokes.

Vanessa Redgrave   *Isadora*   (Reisz)   GB, 69

E

Eagels, Jeanne

(1894–1929) One of Hollywood's most unhappy figures, a high-living, tempestuous Broadway actress who rose quickly to the top in the 20s and then became a victim of alcohol and narcotics. Her rise and fall were the subject of a 1957 biography by George Sidney. Film appearances in *The World And The Woman* (16), *Under False Colours* (17), *Man, Woman And Sin* (27), *The Letter* (29), *Jealousy* (29).

| Kim Novak | *Jeanne Eagels* (Sidney) | USA, 57 |

Earp, Wyatt

(1848–1929) The most famous lawman of the American West, not, in reality, a 'whiter than white' good guy but an often merciless character equally as tough as some of the gunmen he disposed of in Wichita and Dodge City. Best known for his part in the Gunfight At The O.K. Corral (1881) when, along with his brothers Virgil and Morgan and Doc Holliday, he wiped out the Clanton gang. Romanticised, lengthy portrayals by Fonda and Lancaster; more three-dimensional portraits by James Garner and Harris Yulin.

Randolph Scott	*Frontier Marshal* (Dwan)	USA, 39
Richard Dix	*Tombstone, The Town Too Tough To Die* (McGann)	
		USA, 42
Henry Fonda	*My Darling Clementine* (Ford)	USA, 46
Will Geer	*Winchester 73* (Anthony Mann)	USA, 50
James Millican	*Gun Belt* (Nazarro)	USA, 53
Bruce Cowling	*Masterson Of Kansas* (Castle)	USA, 54
Joel McCrea	*Wichita* (Tourneur)	USA, 55
Burt Lancaster	*Gunfight At The O.K. Corral* (Sturges)	USA, 57
Buster Crabbe	*Badman's Country* (Sears)	USA, 58
Hugh O'Brian	*Alias Jesse James* (McLeod)	USA, 59
James Stewart	*Cheyenne Autumn* (Ford)	USA, 64
Guy Madison	*Gunmen Of The Rio Grande* (DeMicheli)	
		Fra/It/Spa, 65
Bill Camfield	*The Outlaws Is Coming* (Maurer)	USA, 65

| James Garner | *Hour Of The Gun*   (Sturges) | USA, 67 |
| Harris Yulin | *Doc*   (Perry) | USA, 71 |

Note: Walter Huston (as Frame Johnson) featured as the Wyatt Earp character in Edward L. Cahn's 1932 production *Law And Order*.

Edison, Thomas A.

(1847–1931) In real life, the inventive genius of the incandescent electric lamp, microphone, phonograph and over a thousand other inventions. On screen a man who changed from Mickey Rooney into Spencer Tracy in the course of one year. Between inventions took time out to describe genius as '2% inspiration, 98% perspiration.'

| Mickey Rooney | *Young Tom Edison*   (Taurog) | USA, 40 |
| Spencer Tracy | *Edison, The Man*   (Brown) | USA, 40 |

Note: Frank Glendon featured as Edison in the 1925 silent production, *Lights Of Old Broadway*.

Ehrlich, Dr. Paul

(1854–1915) German scientist, 1908 Nobel prizewinner, who discovered one of the first cures for syphilis and forced an unwilling medical profession to take notice of the disease. Portrayed by Edward G. Robinson in one of the last of William Dieterle's biographies for Warner Bros.

| Edward G. Robinson | *Dr. Ehrlich's Magic Bullet*   (Dieterle)   USA, 40 |

Eichmann, Adolf

(1906–1962) Nazi war criminal, condemned to death and executed in Israel for his part in the extermination of six million Jews. His reign of terror and post-war life were recreated in the 1961 film *Operation Eichmann*; his trial in *The Man In The Glass Booth*, in which Maximilian Schell starred as a confessed Nazi commandant of a World War II concentration camp.

| Werner Klemperer | *Operation Eichmann*   (Springsteen) | USA, 61 |
| Maximilian Schell | *The Man In The Glass Booth*   (Hiller) | USA, 75 |

El Cid

(*c.* 1043–1099) Spanish warrior (real name Rodrigo Diaz de Vivar), famous for his heroic exploits against the Moors in 11th century Spain.

Earned the name 'Cid' or 'Cid Campeador' (Lord or Lord Conqueror) and achieved his greatest success when capturing Valencia in 1094. A major figure in Spanish history, given due legendary status in Anthony Mann's superior epic of 1961.

Charlton Heston	*El Cid* (Mann)	USA, 61

Elizabeth I

(1533–1603) Powerful British monarch, daughter of Henry VIII and Anne Boleyn, whose often ruthless personality and ill-fated love affairs have attracted actresses of the calibre of Bette Davis, Glenda Jackson and Flora Robson. Davis provided portraits of a middle-aged Elizabeth in love with first Essex and then Raleigh; Glenda Jackson's performance centred on the queen's feud with Mary, Queen Of Scots whom she executed for her complicity in a Catholic plot to seize the throne. Elizabeth's reign lasted for 45 years and heralded the beginning of Britain's great colonial empire.

Athene Seyler	*Drake Of England* (Woods)	GB, 35
Florence Eldridge	*Mary Of Scotland* (Ford)	USA, 36
Yvette Pienne	*The Pearls Of The Crown* (Guitry/Jaque)	
		Fra, 37
Flora Robson	*Fire Over England* (Howard)	GB, 37
Bette Davis	*The Private Lives Of Elizabeth And Essex*	
	(Curtiz)	USA, 39
Maria Koppenhofer	*Heart Of A Queen* (Froelich)	Ger, 40
Flora Robson	*The Sea Hawk* (Curtiz)	USA, 40
Jean Simmons	*Young Bess* (Sidney)	USA, 53
Bette Davis	*The Virgin Queen* (Koster)	USA, 55
Agnes Moorehead	*The Story Of Mankind* (Allen)	USA, 57
Irene Worth	*Seven Seas To Calais* (Mate)	It, 62
Catherine Lacey	*The Fighting Prince Of Donegal* (O'Herlihy)	
		GB, 66
Glenda Jackson	*Mary, Queen Of Scots* (Jarrott)	GB, 71
Lalla Ward	*The Prince And The Pauper* (Fleischer)	GB, 77
Jenny Runacre	*Jubilee* (Jarman)	GB, 77

Note: The following actresses played Elizabeth in silent movies: Sarah Bernhardt in *Queen Elizabeth* (Fra, 12), Miriam Nesbitt in *Mary Stuart* (USA, 13), Lady Diana Manners in *The Virgin Queen* (GB, 23), Ellen Compton in *Loves Of Mary, Queen Of Scots* (GB, 23) and Dagny Servaes in *Carlos And Elizabeth* (Ger, 24).

Emmanuelle

70s softcore heroine of novelist Emmanuelle Arsan, a free-liver whose slim, sexual frame and deceivingly innocent good looks allowed her to be seduced with consummate ease. In her first film she falls for a lesbian anthropologist, masturbates with a young girl and is raped in an opium den. From then on, the wonders of sex hold no fear for her, and she goes on to bigger and better things.

Sylvia Kristel	*Emmanuelle* (Jaeckin)	Fra, 74
Sylvia Kristel	*Emmanuelle II* (Giacobetti)	Fra, 75
Sylvia Kristel	*Goodbye, Emmanuelle* (Leterrier)	Fra, 78

Etting, Ruth

(1896–1978) Actress-singer who rose from humble beginnings in the chorus of a Chicago revue to starring roles in the Ziegfeld Follies and several Hollywood movies. Made famous such songs as 'Ten Cents A Dance', 'Shine On Harvest Moon' and 'Love Me Or Leave Me', the last named being used as the title for the 1955 biography with Doris Day as Etting and James Cagney as Martin Snyder, the racketeer whose influence helped her to the top.

Doris Day	*Love Me Or Leave Me* (Charles Vidor)	USA, 55

Eyre, Jane

Charlotte Bronte's young orphan girl who takes up a post of governess in the mysterious household of Thornfield where she experiences fear, love and ultimately the only real happiness in her young life. A shy, intense heroine whose early experiences at a harsh Yorkshire orphanage are vividly created, both in print and in the numerous screen versions of her story.

Virginia Bruce	*Jane Eyre* (Cabanne)	USA, 34
Joan Fontaine	*Jane Eyre* (Stevenson)	USA, 44
Susannah York	*Jane Eyre* (Delbert Mann)	GB, 71

Note: The 1943 horror picture *I Walked With A Zombie* was an updated version of the 'Jane Eyre' story, transferred to a West Indies setting. Frances Dee featured in the Eyre role.

At least eight silent versions of the story were produced, including a little-known Hungarian production, *The Orphan Of Lowood* (20). Ethel Grandin (14), Louise Vale (15) and Mabel Ballin (21) were among the American silent actresses who appeared in the role; Evelyn Holt featured in Kurt Bernhardt's 1926 German version.

F

Fagin

One of Charles Dickens' most memorable creations, a villainous old Jewish fence who trains a gang of youthful thieves in the art of pickpocketing in the slums of 19th century London. Little more than a merry old gentleman in Lionel Bart's musical *Oliver!* but a grasping figure, full of cruelty and malice, in Alec Guinness' brilliant portrait of 1948. Features in Dickens' 1837–39 novel 'Oliver Twist.'

Irving Pichel	*Oliver Twist* (Cowen)	USA, 33
Alec Guinness	*Oliver Twist* (Lean)	GB, 48
Ron Moody	*Oliver!* (Reed)	GB, 68

Note: John McMahon (GB, 12), Nat C. Goodwin (USA, 12), Tully Marshall (USA, 16) and Lon Chaney (USA, 22) all starred as Fagin in silent productions; Wilson Hummell appeared in a modernized 1921 adaptation, *Oliver Twist Jr.* A Hungarian version of the novel, directed by Marton Garas, was released in 1919.

The Falcon

Another suave detective adventurer of the 40s; most at home 'in society' with champagne and a bevy of witty girls, but invariably drawn out on a case by the distress signals of a beautiful female. Net result: 65 minutes of RKO crime. The third movie in the series, *The Falcon Takes Over*, is an adaptation of Chandler's 'Farewell My Lovely.'

George Sanders	*The Gay Falcon* (Reis)	USA, 41
George Sanders	*A Date With The Falcon* (Reis)	USA, 41
George Sanders	*The Falcon Takes Over* (Reis)	USA, 42
George Sanders	*The Falcon's Brother* (Logan)	USA, 42
Tom Conway	*The Falcon Strikes Back* (Dmytryk)	USA, 43
Tom Conway	*The Falcon And The Co-Eds* (Clemens)	USA, 43
Tom Conway	*The Falcon In Danger* (Clemens)	USA, 43
Tom Conway	*The Falcon In Hollywood* (Douglas)	USA, 44
Tom Conway	*The Falcon In Mexico* (Berke)	USA, 44
Tom Conway	*The Falcon Out West* (Clemens)	USA, 44

Tom Conway	*The Falcon In San Francisco* (Lewis)	USA, 45
Tom Conway	*The Falcon's Alibi* (McCarrey)	USA, 46
Tom Conway	*The Falcon's Adventure* (Berke)	USA, 46
John Calvert	*The Devil's Cargo* (Link)	USA, 48
John Calvert	*Appointment With Murder* (Bernhard)	USA, 48
John Calvert	*Search For Danger* (Martin)	USA, 49

Falstaff, Sir John

Shakespeare's portly, lecherous lover of life, invariably to be found in the company of his fellow scoundrels, Bardolph, Pistol and company, at the tavern of Mistress Quickly. Orson Welles' *Chimes At Midnight*, which included scenes from 'Richard II', 'Henry IV Parts I & II', 'Henry V' and 'The Merry Wives Of Windsor', centred on Falstaff's friendship with the young Prince Hal and his rejection when the prince becomes King Henry V of England.

Leo Slezak	*The Merry Wives Of Windsor* (Hoffmann)	Ger, 35
George Robey	*Henry V* (Olivier)	GB, 45
Orson Welles	*Chimes At Midnight* (Welles)	Spa/Swi, 66

Fanny

A central figure in Marcel Pagnol's delightful trilogy of life in the old port of Marseilles; a young fish seller who is deserted by her adventurous lover, marries an elderly sailmaker to provide a father for her unborn child and is finally reunited with her lover after the death of her husband. The characters who surround her in Marseilles — Cesar, the proprietor of the quayside bistro, Panisse, the warm-hearted widower she marries, and Marius, her seafaring lover — helped turn the three films made in France in the early 30s into film classics. The three stories were subsequently combined into one film, first in *Port Of Seven Seas* and then in *Fanny*.

Fanny

Orane Demazis	*Marius* (Korda)	Fra, 31
Orane Demazis	*Fanny* (Allegret)	Fra, 32
Orane Demazis	*Cesar* (Pagnol)	Fra, 36
Maureen O'Sullivan	*Port Of Seven Seas* (Whale)	USA, 38
Leslie Caron	*Fanny* (Logan)	USA, 61

Marius

Pierre Fresnay	*Marius* (Korda)	Fra, 31
Pierre Fresnay	*Fanny* (Allegret)	Fra, 32
Pierre Fresnay	*Cesar* (Pagnol)	Fra, 36
John Beal	*Port Of Seven Seas* (Whale)	USA, 38
Horst Buchholz	*Fanny* (Logan)	USA, 61

Cesar

Raimu	*Marius* (Korda)	Fra, 31
Raimu	*Fanny* (Allegret)	Fra, 32
Raimu	*Cesar* (Pagnol)	Fra, 36
Wallace Beery	*Port Of Seven Seas* (Whale)	USA, 38
Charles Boyer	*Fanny* (Logan)	USA, 61

Panisse

Fernand Charpin	*Marius* (Korda)	Fra, 31
Fernand Charpin	*Fanny* (Allegret)	Fra, 32
Fernand Charpin	*Cesar* (Pagnol)	Fra, 36
Frank Morgan	*Port Of Seven Seas* (Whale)	USA, 38
Maurice Chevalier	*Fanny* (Logan)	USA, 61

Faust

Legendary figure who sells his soul to the Devil in exchange for all knowledge and experience. Based on a 15th century necromancer named George Faust, he was developed by Goethe (1808) and has been revamped many times on screen, appearing as a New Hampshire farmer in *All That Money Can Buy*, an ambitious politician in *Alias Nick Beal*, a young baseball player in *Damn Yankees* and even a hamburger chef in *Bedazzled*.

James Craig	*All That Money Can Buy* (Dieterle) USA, 41
Thomas Mitchell	*Alias Nick Beal* (Farrow) USA, 49
Gerard Philipe and Michel Simon	*La Beaute du Diable* (Clair) Fra, 49
Gino Mattera	*Faust & The Devil* (Gallone) It, 50
Jean François and Calve Palau	*Marguerite of the Night* (Autant-Lara) Fra, 56
Will Quadflieg	*Faust* (Gorski) Ger, 56
Maria Felix	*Faustina* (de Heredia) Spa, 57
Tab Hunter	*Damn Yankees* (Donen) USA, 58
Robert Towner	*Faust* (Suman) USA, 64
Emil Botta	*Faust* (Popescu-Gopo) Rum, 67
Dudley Moore	*Bedazzled* (Donen) GB, 67
Richard Burton	*Doctor Faustus* (Burton/Coghill) GB/It, 67

Note: Michel Simon played the ageing Faust (and also Mephistopheles) and Gerard Philipe the young Faust in Rene Clair's *La Beaute du Diable*. Palau (old) and Jean François Calve (young) also divided the role in *Marguerite of the Night*. Maria Felix is the only female Faust to appear on screen.

   Gosta Ekmann appeared for F. W. Murnau in the silent German *Faust* of 1926.

Feversham, Harry

'The Four Feathers' hero; a young British officer who is branded a coward by his fiancée then sets out for the Sudan to perform fantastic feats of endurance in order to prove his courage. If ever a movie hero seems passé it is this one, yet, as recently as 1978, a film has been made about his exploits. Somehow, against all the odds, he seems to have survived such lunatic ravings as 'You're a Feversham and the army expects every Feversham to be a hero!' John Clements starred in the definitive screen version of 1939; A. E. W. Mason's novel was first published in 1902.

Richard Arlen	*The Four Feathers*	(Cooper/Schoedsack/Mendes)	USA, 29
John Clements	*The Four Feathers*	(Zoltan Korda)	GB, 39
Anthony Steel	*Storm Over The Nile*	(Young/Zoltan Korda)	GB, 55
Beau Bridges	*The Four Feathers*	(Sharp)	GB, 78

Note: Harry Ham starred as Feversham in a 1921 British adaptation directed by Rene Plaissetty.

Fields, W. C.

(1879–1946) Bulbous-nosed, rasping ex-vaudevillian who played swindlers, pool hustlers, card sharks and salesmen in over 40 films, endowing each with an acid sense of humour. A sample: 'If at first you don't succeed, try, try again. Then quit. No use being a damn fool about it.' The author of many of his own scripts, he brought about his own self-destruction through an excess in just about everything, especially alcohol.

Rod Steiger	*W. C. Fields And Me*	(Hiller)	USA, 76

Finn, Huckleberry

Orphan boy hero of Mark Twain's 1884 classic, 'The Adventures Of Huckleberry Finn.' A carefree, pipe-smoking rebel, he lives on the river banks of the Old South, enjoying the company of fellow adventurer Tom Sawyer and the runaway slave Jim, with whom he adventures on a raft down the Mississippi. Many times played on screen, Jeff East appearing in the two musicals of the 70s, *Tom Sawyer* and *Huckleberry Finn*.

Junior Durkin	*Tom Sawyer*	(Cromwell)	USA, 30
Junior Durkin	*Huckleberry Finn*	(Taurog)	USA, 31
Donald O'Connor	*Tom Sawyer, Detective*	(Louis King)	USA, 38
Mickey Rooney	*The Adventures Of Huckleberry Finn*	(Thorpe)	USA, 39

Eddie Hodges	*The Adventures Of Huckleberry Finn* (Curtiz)	
		USA, 60
Marc Dinapoli	*Tom Sawyer* (Iacob)	Fra/Rum, 69
Jeff East	*Tom Sawyer* (Taylor)	USA, 73
Jeff East	*Huckleberry Finn* (Lee-Thompson)	USA, 74
Roman Madianov	*Huckleberry Finn* (Daniela)	USSR, 74

Note: Robert Gordon in *Tom Sawyer* (USA, 17) and *Huck And Tom* (USA, 18), and Lewis Sargent in *Huckleberry Finn* (USA, 20) all played Huck in silent movies.

Fitzgerald, F. Scott

(1896–1940) Distinguished American author who enjoyed phenomenal success with a series of novels about the jazz age, then declined into obscurity in Hollywood during the 30s. Gregory Peck played him on screen in *Beloved Infidel*, which concentrated on the final months of Fitzgerald's life when he embarked on a turbulent romance with gossip columnist Sheilah Graham. Among the Fitzgerald novels: 'This Side Of Paradise' (1920), 'The Beautiful And The Damned' (1921), 'The Great Gatsby' (1925) and 'Tender Is The Night.' (1934).

Gregory Peck	*Beloved Infidel* (Henry King)	USA, 59

Note: Sheilah Graham was portrayed by Deborah Kerr in *Beloved Infidel*.

Flambeau

A French colossus of crime and master of disguise, who reforms and starts his own private detective agency after losing a battle of wits with Chesterton's amateur sleuth, Father Brown. Generally portrayed on screen *before* his reformation, most notably by Peter Finch in Hamer's *Father Brown* in which he attempts to steal a priceless, diamond-studded church cross.

Paul Lukas	*Father Brown, Detective* (Sedgwick)	USA, 34
Peter Finch	*Father Brown* (Hamer)	GB, 54
Siegfried Lowitz	*Das Schwarze Schaf* (Ashley)	W.Ger, 60

Flashman, Harry

The cheating 'bounder' from Thomas Hughes' 'Tom Brown's Schooldays' (1857), and a character who has continued to thrive, thanks to the best-selling novels of George MacDonald Fraser who has taken Flashman into young adulthood and turned him into a popular anti-hero. Only one screen version to date of Flashman's latter-day activities — as a captain in the 11th Hussars in *Royal Flash* — but several of him in his younger days as chief bully at Rugby school.

Billy Halop	*Tom Brown's Schooldays*	(Stevenson)	USA, 40
John Forrest	*Tom Brown's Schooldays*	(Parry)	GB, 51
Malcolm McDowell	*Royal Flash* (Lester)		GB, 75

Note: Laurie Leslie played Flashman in a British silent version of *Tom Brown's Schooldays* (16).

Floyd, Charles 'Pretty Boy'

Oklahoma farm boy turned gangster who earned himself a prominent place on the FBI's wanted list when he committed a series of bank robberies in the early 30s. Different from his fellow gangsters in that he only robbed the rich, he also brought a new term into the English language when he shouted at the FBI, 'Don't shoot, G-men!' One detailed film biography with John Ericson.

Doug Wilson	*Guns Don't Argue* (Karn/Kahn)	USA, 55
John Ericson	*Pretty Boy Floyd* (Leder)	USA, 59
Robert Conrad	*Young Dillinger* (Morse)	USA, 64
Fabian Forte	*A Bullet For Pretty Boy* (Buchanan)	USA, 71

Fogg, Phileas

Intrepid, never-say-die English gentleman who wagers £20,000 with members of the Reform Club that he can journey round the world in eighty days. Eventually succeeds in his aim after experiencing numerous hazardous adventures with his French servant Passepartout. The gallant, elegant hero of Verne's 1873 novel 'Around The World In Eighty Days.'

| David Niven | *Around The World In 80 Days* (Anderson) | USA, 56 |

Note: Conrad Veidt portrayed Fogg in Richard Oswald's silent German version of 1919.

Ford, Bob

(–1893) Cousin and assassin of Jesse James, notorious for shooting the famous outlaw in the back when he was straightening a picture on a wall in his home. Subsequently became a wanderer and stage actor, appearing in 'The Outlaws Of Missouri' in which he related (incorrectly) how he had shot down his outlaw chief. He was finally killed in a barroom fight but not, as shown in *The Return of Frank James*, by the vengeful Frank.

| John Carradine | *Jesse James* (Henry King) | USA, 39 |
| John Carradine | *The Return Of Frank James* (Fritz Lang) | USA, 40 |

John Ireland	*I Shot Jesse James* (Fuller)	USA, 49
Clifton Young	*The Return Of Jesse James* (Hilton)	USA, 50
Whit Bissell	*The Great Missouri Raid* (Douglas)	USA, 51
Jim Bannon	*The Great Jesse James Raid* (Le Borg)	USA, 53
Rory Mallinson	*Jesse James v The Daltons* (Castle)	USA, 54
Carl Thayler	*The True Story of Jesse James* (Ray)	USA, 56
Robert Vaughn	*Hell's Crossroads* (Andreon)	USA, 57

Note: Harry Woods played the role in a 1927 version of *Jesse James*, directed by Lloyd Ingraham.

Foy, Eddie

(1854–1928) The subject of one of Bob Hope's more serious performances of the 50s, an American vaudeville comic and dancer who trained his large family to join him on stage in an act which became famous as 'Eddie Foy And The Seven Little Foys.' Eddie Foy, Jr, later went on to portray his father several times on screen e.g. in *Lillian Russell* (40), *Yankee Doodle Dandy* (42), *Wilson* (44).

| Bob Hope | *The Seven Little Foys* (Shavelson) | USA, 55 |

Francis Of Assisi

(1181–1226) 13th century Italian monk who devoted himself to the sick and poor and founded the monastic order of the Franciscans. Hollywood thought him a suitable case for screen treatment in the 60s; so too did the Italian cinema with Liliana Cavani's controversial production of 1966. Predictably, Hollywood lost and Italy won!

Jose Luis Jiminez	*St. Francis Of Assisi* (Gout)	Mex, 47
Bradford Dillman	*Francis Of Assisi* (Curtiz)	USA, 61
Lou Castel	*Francis Of Assisi* (Cavani)	It, 66
Graham Faulkner	*Brother Sun, Sister Moon* (Zeffirelli)	It/GB, 72

Frank, Anne

(1929–1945) German Jewish girl who hid with her family and four other people in an Amsterdam attic in a futile attempt to escape the Nazi holocaust of World War II. Her deeply moving diary, discovered after her death in Belsen and published in 1947, records the daily lives of the hideaways from 1942 until August 1944 when they were eventually betrayed. George Stevens' film was an adaptation of the stage play by Frances Goodrich and Albert Hackett which, in turn, was based on the diary.

| Millie Perkins | *The Diary Of Anne Frank* (Stevens) | USA, 59 |

Note: Anne Frank's father, Otto, who discovered the diary after the war, was played by Joseph Schildkraut.

Frankenstein, Baron

The longest-serving mad scientist in the business, dating back over 160 years to when he first startled an unprepared reading public by making a monster from the organs of dead bodies. Mary Shelley's novel (published in 1818) has been filmed by James Whale in 1931, Terence Fisher in 1957 and Jack Smight in 1974, but ever since Karloff escaped from the burning mill in *Bride Of Frankenstein*, a host of the baron's relatives — sons, nephews, grandsons, etc — have been trying to emulate their illustrious predecessor by creating bigger and better monsters. In the 30s, Colin Clive was the best known Baron Frankenstein; for post-war audiences no-one can hold a scalpel to Peter Cushing!

Colin Clive	*Frankenstein* (Whale)	USA, 31
Colin Clive	*Bride Of Frankenstein* (Whale)	USA, 35
Basil Rathbone	*Son Of Frankenstein* (Lee)	USA, 39
Cedric Hardwicke	*The Ghost Of Frankenstein* (Kenton)	USA, 42
Ilona Massey	*Frankenstein Meets The Wolf Man* (Neill)	USA, 43
Boris Karloff	*House Of Frankenstein* (Kenton)	USA, 44
Peter Cushing	*The Curse Of Frankenstein* (Fisher)	GB, 57
Whit Bissell	*I Was A Teenage Frankenstein* (Strock)	USA, 57
Peter Cushing	*The Revenge Of Frankenstein* (Fisher)	USA, 58
Boris Karloff	*Frankenstein — 1970* (Koch)	USA, 58
Peter Cushing	*The Evil Of Frankenstein* (Francis)	GB, 64
Robert Reilly	*Frankenstein Meets The Space Monster* (Gaffney)	USA, 66
Peter Cushing	*Frankenstein Created Woman* (Fisher)	GB, 67
Peter Cushing	*Frankenstein Must Be Destroyed* (Fisher)	GB, 69
Robin Ward	*Dr. Frankenstein On Campus* (Taylor)	Can, 70
J. Carrol Naish	*Blood Of Frankenstein* (Adamson)	USA, 70
Ralph Bates	*The Horror Of Frankenstein* (Sangster)	GB, 70
Joseph Cotten	*Lady Frankenstein* (Mel Welles)	It, 71
Peter Cushing	*Frankenstein And The Monster From Hell* (Fisher)	GB, 73
Gene Wilder	*Young Frankenstein* (Mel Brooks)	USA, 74
Leonard Whiting	*Frankenstein: The True Story* (Smight)	USA, 74
Leon Vitali	*Victor Frankenstein* (Floyd)	Swe/Ire, 77
Gianrico Tedeschi	*Frankenstein — Italian Style* (Crispino)	It, 77

Note: Narda Onyx and Steven Geray played the grandchildren of Frankenstein in *Jesse James Meets Frankenstein's Daughter* (USA, 66); Boris Karloff remains the only actor to play both Frankenstein and his monster on screen.

Frankenstein's Monster

Still the most chilling monster of them all, if only because his creation appears to be a distinct medical possibility in this modern age of transplants. Karloff lumbered to stardom in three Universal pictures of the 30s, Christopher Lee did the same at Hammer in 1957; Michael Sarrazin rang the changes in 1974 by appearing as a monster more handsome than his creator.

Boris Karloff	*Frankenstein* (Whale)	USA, 31
Boris Karloff	*Bride Of Frankenstein* (Whale)	USA, 35
Elsa Lanchester	*Bride Of Frankenstein* (Whale)	USA, 35
Boris Karloff	*Son Of Frankenstein* (Lee)	USA, 39
Lon Chaney, Jr.	*The Ghost Of Frankenstein* (Kenton)	USA, 42
Bela Lugosi	*Frankenstein Meets The Wolf Man* (Neill)	USA, 43
Glenn Strange	*House Of Frankenstein* (Kenton)	USA, 44
Glenn Strange	*House Of Dracula* (Kenton)	USA, 45
Glenn Strange	*Abbott & Costello Meet Frankenstein* (Barton)	USA, 48
Christopher Lee	*The Curse Of Frankenstein* (Fisher)	GB, 57
Gary Conway	*I Was A Teenage Frankenstein* (Strock)	USA, 57
Michael Gwynn	*The Revenge Of Frankenstein* (Fisher)	GB, 58
Mike Lane	*Frankenstein — 1970* (Koch)	USA, 58
Sandra Knight	*Frankenstein's Daughter* (Cunha)	USA, 58
Kiwi Kingston	*The Evil Of Frankenstein* (Francis)	GB, 64
Cal Bolder	*Jesse James Meets Frankenstein's Daughter* (Beaudine)	USA, 66
Susan Denberg	*Frankenstein Created Woman* (Fisher)	GB, 67
Freddie Jones	*Frankenstein Must Be Destroyed* (Fisher)	GB, 69
Dave Prowse	*The Horror Of Frankenstein* (Sangster)	GB, 70
John Bloom	*Blood Of Frankenstein* (Adamson)	USA, 70
Dave Prowse	*Frankenstein And The Monster From Hell* (Fisher)	GB, 73
Michael Sarrazin	*Frankenstein: The True Story* (Smight)	USA, 74
Peter Boyle	*Young Frankenstein* (Mel Brooks)	USA, 74
Per Oscarsson	*Victor Frankenstein* (Floyd)	Swe/Ire, 77
Aldo Maccione	*Frankenstein — Italian Style* (Crispino)	It, 77

Note: Charles Ogle appeared as Frankenstein's Monster in Edison's 1910 production of Mary Shelley's story.

Freud, Sigmund

(1856–1939) Famed Austrian pioneer of psychoanalysis; the subject of John Huston's 140-minute biography, *Freud*, a serious, restrained account of the psychiatrist's early struggles for recognition, and also the fictional *The Seven-Per-Cent Solution* in which Freud probes into the broken mind of Sherlock Holmes and then joins him in a thrilling adventure across Europe.

Montgomery Clift	*Freud* (Huston)	USA, 62
Alan Arkin	*The Seven-Per-Cent Solution* (Ross)	GB, 76

Friar Tuck

Plump, jovial friar whose rotund frame invariably provides the humorous incidents in Robin Hood's screen adventures. Despite his bulky appearance, a swordsman of some distinction who joins the outlaws after a memorable duel with Robin Hood in midstream. No definitive screen portrayal, although Eugene Pallette endowed him with an engaging gruffness, shortness of temper and large appetite in Warners' classic of 1938.

Eugene Pallette	*The Adventures Of Robin Hood* (Curtiz/Keighley)	USA, 38
Edgar Buchanan	*The Bandit Of Sherwood Forest* (Sherman/Levin)	USA, 46
Billy House	*Rogues Of Sherwood Forest* (Douglas)	USA, 50
Ben Welden	*Tales Of Robin Hood* (Tinling)	USA, 51
James Hayter	*The Story Of Robin Hood And His Merrie Men* (Annakin)	GB, 52
Reginald Beckwith	*Men Of Sherwood Forest* (Guest)	GB, 54
Niall MacGinnis	*Sword Of Sherwood Forest* (Fisher)	GB, 60
James Hayter	*A Challenge For Robin Hood* (Pennington Richards)	GB, 67
Kenneth Gilbert	*Wolfshead: The Legend Of Robin Hood* (Hough)	GB, 73
Ronnie Barker	*Robin And Marian* (Lester)	USA, 76

Note: Andy Devine voiced Friar Tuck in Walt Disney's 1973 feature cartoon *Robin Hood*; M. Hannafly (USA, 12), H. Holles (USA, 13), Ernest Redding (USA, 14) and Willard Louis (USA, 22) were among the actors who played the role in the silent days.

Friese-Greene, William

(1855–1921) British motion picture pioneer who, in 1889, demonstrated his first celluloid film in public — supposedly to a startled policeman in Hyde Park — and later experimented with both three dimensional and colour photography. Died penniless just a few years after D. W. Griffith had demonstrated in America the enormous potential of film with his classic *Birth of a Nation* (1915).

Robert Donat	*The Magic Box* (John Boulting)	GB, 51

Froman, Jane

(1910–   ) American radio and stage singer, severely crippled in a plane crash in 1943, who struggled to recovery after a leg amputation and sang to US Forces in combat zones in World War II. Her gallantry was admirably conveyed on screen by an Oscar-nominated Susan Hayward who mimed to such Froman soundtracks as 'Blue Moon', 'I'll Walk Alone' and 'Get Happy.'

Susan Hayward   *With A Song In My Heart* (Walter Lang)   USA, 52

Fu Manchu

Chinese master criminal of Sax Rohmer, not unlike Ian Fleming's subsequent Dr. No in that he is cultured, wealthy, intelligent — and deadly! Main aim in life: to destroy the entire white race and become emperor of the world. Sidelines: inventing unpatented tortures and depriving his henchmen of their will-power by cutting into their brains and removing their frontal lobes. First appeared in print in a short story in 1911, then in the novel 'The Mystery Of Fu Manchu' in 1913. Screen career of variable quality, but a notable portrayal by Boris Karloff in Charles Brabin's film of 1932.

Warner Oland	*The Mysterious Dr. Fu Manchu*	(Lee)	USA, 29
Warner Oland	*The Return Of Dr. Fu Manchu*	(Lee)	USA, 30
Warner Oland	*Daughter Of The Dragon*	(Corrigan)	USA, 31
Boris Karloff	*The Mask Of Fu Manchu*	(Brabin)	USA, 32
Henry Brandon	*Drums Of Fu Manchu*	(Witney/English)	USA, 40
Manuel Requena	*The Other Fu Manchu*	(Barreiro)	Spa, 45
Christopher Lee	*The Face Of Fu Manchu*	(Sharp)	GB, 65
Christopher Lee	*The Brides Of Fu Manchu*	(Sharp)	GB, 66
Christopher Lee	*The Vengeance Of Fu Manchu*	(Summers)	GB, 67
Christopher Lee	*The Castle Of Fu Manchu*	(Franco)	
			W.Ger/Spa/It/GB, 68
Christopher Lee	*The Blood Of Fu Manchu*	(Franco)	
			W.Ger/Spa/USA/GB, 68

Note: Harry Agar Lyons appeared as Fu Manchu in two British silent serials: the 15-episode *The Mystery Of Dr. Fu Manchu* (23) and the 8-episode *The Further Mysteries Of Dr. Fu Manchu* (24). Henry Brandon's portrayal in 1940 was another serial performance — in 15 episodes.

G

Gable, Clark

(1901–1960) The 'king' of Hollywood and a man who reigned for nearly thirty years as one of the most personable movie stars on the American screen. Almost impossible to imitate on celluloid, although James Brolin was given the opportunity in Furie's *Gable And Lombard*. The jug handle ears, bootlace moustache and impudent grin were there; the personality, not surprisingly, was missing.

James Brolin   *Gable And Lombard* (Furie)   USA, 76

Galileo, Galilei

(1564–1642) Italian mathematician and astronomer who changed the course of civilization with his revolutionary ideas about the planetary system and mankind's place in the universe. His battles with the hierarchy of the Catholic Church would hardly rank as 'popcorn entertainment', but two recent films have examined his life with some success. Joseph Losey's 1974 film was based on the play by Bertolt Brecht.

Cyril Cusack   *Galileo* (Cavani)   It/Bul, 68
Topol   *Galileo* (Losey)   GB/Can, 74

Galore, Pussy

Another of Ian Fleming's suggestively named bad girls, this time a judo expert and female gangster who runs a fleet of girl pilots for Auric Goldfinger. Hints of latent lesbianism in her character are quickly dispelled after a roll in the hay with 007. Subsequently changes her allegiances to the side of law and order.

Honor Blackman   *Goldfinger* (Hamilton)   GB, 64

Gantry, Elmer

Whoring, whisky-drinking salesman who joins up with a tent pitching revivalist group in the Midwest and, through his talent for rabble rousing, turns the enterprise into big business. A brazen opportunist, he figures in Sinclair Lewis' controversial novel of 1927 and was played on screen in vigorous Oscar-winning style by Burt Lancaster.

Burt Lancaster	*Elmer Gantry* (Brooks)	USA, 60

Garrett, Pat

(1854 ?–1908) A man who earned himself a place in the record books of the American West by shooting down Billy The Kid (in the back and in a darkened room) in New Mexico in July 1881. A former colleague of Bonney, he found that his fame as the killer of the West's most notorious outlaw was short-lived and he eventually went into the ranching and cattle business before meeting a violent death himself at the hands of a fellow rancher. Not always in evidence in films about Billy The Kid, but strikingly played by John Dehner in Arthur Penn's *The Left-Handed Gun* and James Coburn in Peckinpah's *Pat Garrett And Billy The Kid*.

Wallace Beery	*Billy The Kid* (King Vidor)	USA, 30
Wade Boteler	*Billy The Kid Returns* (Kane)	USA, 38
Thomas Mitchell	*The Outlaw* (Hughes)	USA, 43
Charles Bickford	*Four Faces West* (Green)	USA, 48
Robert Lowrey	*I Shot Billy The Kid* (Berke)	USA, 50
Frank Wilcox	*Texas Kid Outlaw* (Neumann)	USA, 50
James Griffith	*The Law vs Billy The Kid* (Castle)	USA, 54
James Craig	*Last Of The Desperadoes* (Newfield)	USA, 55
John Dehner	*The Left-Handed Gun* (Penn)	USA, 58
George Montgomery	*Badman's Country* (Sears)	USA, 58
Fausto Tozzi	*The Man Who Killed Billy The Kid* (Buchs)	
		Spa/It, 67
Glenn Corbett	*Chisum* (McLaglen)	USA, 70
James Coburn	*Pat Garrett And Billy The Kid* (Peckinpah)	
		USA, 73

Gatsby, Jay

Perhaps the most tragic figure in all Scott Fitzgerald's novels of the 20s, a mysterious ex-bootlegger who lives in a luxurious Long Island mansion to be near the woman he once loved and lost. Despite the glamorous performance of Robert Redford in Jack Clayton's 1974 film, it is Alan Ladd who comes closest to Fitzgerald's original conception in Elliott Nugent's flat, but curiously effective adaptation of 1949. Paramount has filmed all three versions of the novel to date.

Alan Ladd	*The Great Gatsby* (Nugent)	USA, 49
Robert Redford	*The Great Gatsby* (Clayton)	USA, 74

Note: Warner Baxter featured as Gatsby in Herbert Brenon's silent version of 1926.

Gauguin, Paul

(1848–1903) French post-impressionist who abandoned his wife and family, and his career as a stockbroker in Paris, to concentrate on his art in the islands of Tahiti. Anthony Quinn's Oscar-winning performance in Minnelli's *Lust For Life* covered Gauguin's period with Van Gogh at Arles; George Sanders' more detailed portrayal in *The Moon And Sixpence* (Somerset Maugham's fictional account of Gauguin's life) incorporated most of his later years.

| George Sanders | *The Moon And Sixpence* (Lewin) | USA, 42 |
| Anthony Quinn | *Lust For Life* (Minnelli) | USA, 56 |

Note: Gauguin was renamed Charles Strickland in the Somerset Maugham novel.

Gehrig, Lou

(1903–1941) One of the legends of American baseball, a renowned hitter who joined the New York Yankees in 1925 and made regular appearances for the next 14 years, playing in a record 2,130 games in succession. The Goldwyn movie of 1942 concentrated on his final years when he was struck down, at the early age of 38, by a rare form of multiple sclerosis.

| Gary Cooper | *Pride Of The Yankees* (Wood) | USA, 42 |

Genghis Khan

(1162–1227) 12th century Mongol Emperor who invaded vast areas of Northern China, Iran and Russia with his barbarous hordes. Film accounts of his ruthless exploits have generally been undistinguished, and, in the case of John Wayne's *The Conqueror* ('You're bewdiful in your wrath') unbelievable!

Marvin Miller	*The Golden Horde* (Sherman)	USA, 51
Manuel Conde	*Genghis Khan* (Salvador)	Philippines, 52
John Wayne	*The Conqueror* (Powell)	USA, 56
Roldano Lupi	*The Mongols* (DeToth/Savona)	Fra/It, 60
Omar Sharif	*Genghis Khan* (Levin)	USA/GB/W.Ger, 65

Geronimo

(1829–1909) The most ferocious of all the Apaches, a renegade who refused to accept the peace treaty of Cochise and operated with a small band of Indians on both sides of the Mexican border. For a man with such a ruthless nature he survived a remarkable 80 years. Two films have centred on his activities, the first with real-life Cherokee Chief Thundercloud, the second with Chuck Connors.

Chief White Horse	*Stagecoach* (Ford)	USA, 39
Chief Thundercloud	*Geronimo!* (Sloane)	USA, 39
Tom Tyler	*Valley Of The Sun* (Marshall)	USA, 42
Chief Thundercloud	*I Killed Geronimo* (Hoffman)	USA, 50
Jay Silverheels	*The Battle At Apache Pass* (Sherman)	USA, 52
Ian MacDonald	*Taza, Son Of Cochise* (Sirk)	USA, 54
Monte Blue	*Apache* (Aldrich)	USA, 54
Jay Silverheels	*Walk The Proud Land* (Hibbs)	USA, 56
Chuck Connors	*Geronimo* (Laven)	USA, 62

Geste, Beau

'Boy's Own Paper' hero of P. C. Wren; one of three brothers who takes the blame for his aunt's theft of a priceless diamond then flees to the Foreign Legion to do battle with the arab hordes and a despotic regimental sergeant. Marty Feldman spoofed the whole thing in his 1977 film with Michael York; Ronald Colman remains the definitive 'let me be the first to die' hero in Herbert Brenon's silent film for Paramount. Wren's novel was first published in 1924.

Ronald Colman	*Beau Geste* (Brenon)	USA, 26
Gary Cooper	*Beau Geste* (Wellman)	USA, 39
Guy Stockwell	*Beau Geste* (Heyes)	USA, 66
Michael York	*The Last Remake of Beau Geste* (Feldman)	USA, 77

Gershwin, George

(1898–1937) American composer who brought his genius to bear on many different aspects of American music in the 20s and 30s — revue, musical comedy, folk opera ('Porgy And Bess'), even concert works ('Rhapsody In Blue'). The Warner Bros biography of 1945, despite the familiar shortcomings, did on occasion capture some of Gershwin's infectious enthusiasm for his work. Among the Gershwin stage shows: 'Lady Be Good', 'Funny Face', 'Strike Up The Band'. Among his songs: 'Fascinating Rhythm', 'S'Wonderful', 'Embraceable You'.

Robert Alda	*Rhapsody In Blue* (Rapper)	USA, 45

Note: Gershwin's brother, Ira, was played by Herbert Rudley in the above film.

Gervaise

The tragic heroine of Emile Zola's 1877 novel 'L'Assommoir', a young girl who struggles against her environment in the slums of mid-19th century Paris then finally succumbs to the sordid life style of her alcoholic husband. The mother of the prostitute Nana whose escapades Zola chronicled in a subsequent novel. Memorably played by Maria Schell in Rene Clement's masterpiece of 1956.

Line Noro	*L'Assommoir* (Roudes)	Fra, 33
Maria Schell	*Gervaise* (Clement)	Fra, 56

Note: Silent portrayals by Alexandre Arguillere in a 1909 French film by Albert Capellani; Irene Browne in the British production *Drink* (17); and Madame Sforza in *L'Assommoir* (Fra, 21).

Gibson, Guy

(1918–1944) British Wing Commander who led the low flying bomber raid that destroyed the Möhne and Eder dams in Germany in 1943. Stoically played by Richard Todd in the 1955 movie which painstakingly recreated the events that led up to the raid, he was awarded the Victoria Cross for bravery and died in 1944 when returning from a mission to the Netherlands.

Richard Todd	*The Dam Busters* (Anderson)	GB, 55

Gigi

15-year-old Parisian schoolgirl who suddenly grows into a beautiful young woman and enslaves the bored rake who has known her since childhood. Created by Colette in her 1945 novel and portrayed twice on film, first in straight drama, then in Vincente Minnelli's Oscar-winning musical.

Daniele Delorme	*Gigi* (Audry)	Fra, 48
Leslie Caron	*Gigi* (Minnelli)	USA, 58

Gilbert, W. S. and Sullivan, Arthur

19th century English composers of a series of comic operas — 'HMS Pinafore', 'The Pirates Of Penzance', 'The Mikado', 'The Gondoliers' — which satirized aspects of Victorian life. The story of their turbulent 18-year partnership which produced 13 operas — and a much publicised quarrel — was related in the Launder/Gilliat biography, *The Story of Gilbert And Sullivan*.

Nigel Bruce (Gilbert)		
Claud Allister (Sullivan)	*Lillian Russell* (Cummings)	USA, 40
Robert Morley (Gilbert)		
Maurice Evans (Sullivan)	*The Story Of Gilbert And Sullivan*	
	(Launder/Gilliat)	GB, 53

Note: In *The Magic Box*, the 1951 Festival of Britain film, conductor-arranger Muir Matheson guested briefly as composer Arthur Sullivan.

Gilda

Only a Christian name, but enough to describe this alluring torch singer who, in 1946, girated her body within a strapless black evening gown 'down South America way'. Marriage to Nazi-styled despot George Macready brought dark tinges to her sensuality; a neat line in wisecracks ('If I'd have been a ranch they would have called me the Bar Nothing') revealed a more appealing side to her nature.

Rita Hayworth	*Gilda* (Charles Vidor)	USA, 46

Note: Hayworth's famous song 'Put The Blame On Mame Boys' was mimed and sung in the movie by Anita Ellis.

Glinka, Mikhail

(1804–1857) Russian composer, a former civil servant, who travelled widely throughout his country in search of the true Russian musical idiom. He introduced a national element into his operas e.g. 'A Life For The Tsar' (1836) and pioneered the style of the Russian national school of composers. Two major screen biographies, both Russian.

Boris Chirkov	*The Great Glinka* (Arnstam)	USSR, 46
B. Smirnov	*Glinka* (Alexandrov)	USSR, 52

Golden Marie (Casque D'Or)

Arguably Simone Signoret's most effective screen role, a Parisian prostitute who embarks on a tragic romance with a young suburban carpenter, drives him twice to murder and then watches him die on the guillotine. Signoret's sensual performance and Jacques Becker's evocation of the Paris underworld of the 1890s helped make the film one of the greatest in the history of the French cinema.

Simone Signoret	*Casque D'Or* (Becker)	Fra, 52

Goldfinger, Auric

Super-villain of the third James Bond movie, a modern Midas obsessed with gold in all its forms. Does well enough in Europe when smuggling millions in his gold-plated Rolls-Royce but comes unstuck when he transfers his attentions to the States and has a crack at Fort Knox. Receives his come-uppance when sucked out of an aircraft at thirty thousand feet!

Gert Frobe	*Goldfinger* (Hamilton)	GB, 64

Goodman, Benny

(1909–   ) The legendary 'King Of Swing' and one of the most important figures in the history of American jazz. Following the box-office success of *The Glenn Miller Story* his life was filmed by Universal in 1955, but despite an electrifying climax at the famous Carnegie Hall concert, the film failed to find the same sympathetic audience. Goodman himself recorded the film's soundtrack and ghosted the clarinet for Steve Allen.

Steve Allen	*The Benny Goodman Story* (Davies)	USA, 55

Note: Goodman and his orchestra appeared as themselves in several Hollywood movies of the 40s e.g. *Syncopation* (42), *Stage Door Canteen* (43), *The Gang's All Here* (43), *Sweet And Lowdown* (44), *A Song Is Born* (48).

Gordon, General Charles

(1833–1885) One of Britain's most popular military figures of the 19th century, an officer of the Royal Engineers who distinguished himself in China and the Sudan before being killed by Arab tribesmen at Khartoum. Basil Dearden's 1966 film explored the motives and character of Gordon in some depth; Charlton Heston's strikingly intelligent performance quelled all doubts about the ability of an American actor to portray an English hero convincingly on screen.

Laidman Browne	*Sixty Glorious Years* (Wilcox)	GB, 38
Charlton Heston	*Khartoum* (Dearden)	GB, 66

Gordon, Flash

Hard-fisted comic strip astronaut, constantly doing his best to save humanity from the evil powers of Ming The Merciless, emperor of the planet Mongo and would-be ruler of the Universe. After three serials and forty episodes he eventually succeeds, but not without a lot of hassle from Shark Men, Death Rays, Zebra-striped Bears, etc, along the way. Created by cartoonist-artist Alex Raymond in 1934 and portrayed on screen by Larry 'Buster' Crabbe.

'Buster' Crabbe	*Flash Gordon* (Stephani)	USA, 36
'Buster' Crabbe	*Flash Gordon's Trip To Mars* (Beebe/Hill)	
'Buster' Crabbe	*Flash Gordon Conquers The Universe*	USA, 38
	(Beebe/Taylor)	USA, 40
Sam Jones	*Flash Gordon* (Hodges)	GB, 80

Note: The three Buster Crabbe serials were all produced by Universal and co-starred Charles Middleton as the despot Ming.

Gorki, Maxim

(1868–1936) The first great writer to emerge from the poverty of the lower classes in Tsarist Russia. A pedlar, dishwasher, gardener and dock hand before turning to writing, he wrote socially realistic novels and dramas ('The Lower Depths') and contributed much of his earnings to the Marxist revolutionary movement. His autobiographical trilogy, written in 1915, was filmed over a period of three years by Mark Donskoi. The films dealt with Gorki's boyhood in provincial Russia and his life as a young man.

Alexei Lyarski	*The Childhood Of Maxim Gorki* (Donskoi)	USSR, 38
Alexei Lyarski	*My Childhood* (Donskoi)	USSR, 39
Y. Valbert	*My Universities* (Donskoi)	USSR, 40

Goya y Lucientes, Francisco de

(1746–1828) Spanish painter, famous for his portraits, religious canvasses and realistic scenes of war, and also the 'Maja Nude' which aroused considerable speculation when it was first unveiled to the public. Henry Koster's 1959 Hollywood film revolved around the romance between Goya and the Duchess of Albany, supposedly the model for the portrait; the 1971 Spanish biography invited more serious study.

| Anthony Franciosa | *The Naked Maja* (Koster) | USA, 59 |
| Francisco Rabal | *Goya* (Vedo) | Spa, 71 |

Graham, Barbara

33-year-old American, known as 'Bloody Babs', who was found guilty of murdering an elderly woman during a house burglary in Burbank in 1953. Not a major figure in the history of American crime, but important in that she may, quite possibly, have been innocent, and had to endure a living hell right up until her death in the gas chamber in San Quentin in 1955. Robert Wise's film of her life and trial cast strong doubts about her guilt; Susan Hayward's acting won her a 1958 Academy Award.

| Susan Hayward | *I Want To Live* (Wise) | USA, 58 |

Gray, Dorian

A man who sells his soul for eternal youth, remaining young while only his portrait reveals the stigma of age and corruption. The central figure in Oscar Wilde's famous morality tale, most ably characterised on screen by Hurd Hatfield in Albert Lewin's definitive film version of 1945. Wilde's novel was first published in 1891.

Hurd Hatfield	*The Picture Of Dorian Gray*	(Lewin)	USA, 45
Helmut Berger	*Dorian Gray* (Dallamano)		It/W.Ger, 70

Note: Lord Henry Wotton, the cynical aristocrat whose evil influence is responsible for Gray embarking on his decadent ways, has been played by George Sanders (45) and Herbert Lom (70); Adam Poulsen (Den, 10), Charles Victor (GB, 16) and Bernd Aldor (Ger, 17) all featured as Dorian Gray in silent screen versions of the story.

Graziano, Rocky

(1922–) New York adolescent who descended into delinquency and crime before boxing his way out of trouble and winning the middleweight championship of the world. Paul Newman's screen portrayal turned him into a major star, in many ways a lucky break, as the role had originally been scheduled for James Dean.

Paul Newman	*Somebody Up There Likes Me*	(Wise)	USA, 56

Greco, El

(1541–1614) Greek-born Spanish painter whose intense, deeply religious portraits inspired a 1964 film biography. Instead of compiling a serious film dedicated to the work of a great artist, the producers opted instead for soap opera, i.e. El Greco's unrequited love for an aristocratic lady and his subsequent inquisition for witchcraft and heresy. Mel Ferrer competed with and lost to the lovely Spanish locations of Toledo.

Mel Ferrer	*El Greco* (Salce)	It/Fra, 64

Grieg, Edvard

(1843–1907) Norwegian composer who reflected the landscapes and history of his homeland in his music. A composer of operas, choral works and concertos, and best-known for his 'Peer Gynt', he was played by Toralv Maurstad in the 140-minute biography directed by Andrew Stone. The film was based on the stage musical first performed on the New York stage in 1944.

Toralv Maurstad	*Song Of Norway* (Stone)	USA, 70

Brothers Grimm

The famed German writers of fairy tales — Wilhelm (1785–1863) and Jacob (1786–1859) — whose lives, fantasies and stories were combined in the early Cinerama production *The Wonderful World Of The Brothers Grimm*. The three stories re-enacted in the film were 'The Cobbler And The Elves', 'The Dancing Princess' and 'The Singing Bone'.

Laurence Harvey (Wilhelm Grimm)
Karl Boehm (Jacob Grimm)   *The Wonderful World Of The Brothers Grimm*
(Levin)   USA, 62

Guevara, Ernesto ('Che')

(1928–1967) Argentine-born revolutionary, popularly known as 'El Che' or 'Che Guevara', who played an important part in the Cuban revolution of 1959 and later served in government posts under Castro. In 1965 he left Cuba to become a guerilla leader in South America and was subsequently captured and killed by government troops in Bolivia. A martyr in popular mythology, he deserves rather better treatment than he has so far received on screen.

Francisco Rabal	*El 'Che' Guevara* (Heusch)	It, 68
Omar Sharif	*Che!* (Fleischer)	USA, 69

Guinevere, Queen

Wife of King Arthur and one of those beautiful heroines forever being abducted and in need of rescue. Her passion for Arthur's favourite knight, Sir Lancelot, is the focal point for most screen characterizations. Ava Gardner played her with controlled twentieth century sensuality in *Knights Of The Round Table*; Vanessa Redgrave with charm and abandon in the Lerner and Loewe musical *Camelot*.

Ava Gardner	*Knights Of The Round Table* (Thorpe)	
		GB, 54
Jean Lodge	*The Black Knight* (Garnett)	GB, 54
Jarma Lewis	*Prince Valiant* (Hathaway)	USA, 54
Jean Wallace	*Lancelot And Guinevere* (Wilde)	GB, 63
Vanessa Redgrave	*Camelot* (Logan)	USA, 67
Laura Duke Condominas	*Lancelot du Lac* (Bresson)	Fra/It, 74
Marie Christine Barrault	*Perceval Le Gallois* (Rohmer)	Fra, 78

Gunga Din

Hindu water carrier who saves a British Indian regiment at the cost of his life; immortalized in Rudyard Kipling's poem ('You're A Better Man Than I, Gunga Din') which appeared in the author's 1892 collection 'Barrack Room Ballads.'

| Sam Jaffe | *Gunga Din* (Stevens) | USA, 39 |

Note: A western version of the story with Gunga Din recast as a freed slave (Sammy Davis Jr.) was filmed as *Sergeants 3* in 1962.

Guthrie, Woody

(1912–1967) American folk singer and composer who became a spokesman for the migrant workers of the Depression years. Wrote over 1000 songs including 'So Long It's Been Good To Know Yuh', 'This Land Is Your Land' and 'Union Maid'. Portrayed as a young man during the 30s by David Carradine in Hal Ashby's *Bound For Glory*, based on Guthrie's own autobiography.

| David Carradine | *Bound For Glory* (Ashby) | USA, 76 |

Gutman, Casper

As personified by Sydney Greenstreet in Huston's *The Maltese Falcon*, the most menacing of all fat screen villains, a mocking, effeminate leader of a small band of international crooks seeking the whereabouts of a priceless statuette. Created by Dashiell Hammett in his private-eye novel of 1930, the character also appeared in an earlier film version of the story, i.e. in 1931 when he was portrayed by Dudley Digges. In the 1936 adaptation, *Satan Met A Lady*, Gutman was renamed Madame Barabbas and resexed by actress Alison Skipworth.

| Dudley Digges | *The Maltese Falcon* (Del Ruth) | USA, 31 |
| Sydney Greenstreet | *The Maltese Falcon* (Huston) | USA, 41 |

Gwyn, Nell

(1650–1687) English comedy actress and mistress of Charles II. Reputedly sold oranges before selling herself and bearing the king two sons between engagements on the London stage. Anna Neagle romped good-naturedly with Cedric Hardwicke in the Herbert Wilcox biography of 1934, Margaret Lockwood explored the realms of slapstick in the Sid Field comedy *Cardboard Cavalier*.

| Anna Neagle | *Nell Gwyn* (Wilcox) | GB, 34 |
| Virginia Field | *Hudson's Bay* (Pichel) | USA, 41 |

| Margaret Lockwood | *Cardboard Cavalier* (Forde) | GB, 49 |
| Anne Neagle | *Lilacs In The Spring* (Wilcox) | GB, 54 |

Note: Dorothy Gish featured as Nell in an earlier, silent Wilcox production of 1926; Lois Sturt featured in a minor role in the 1922 film, *The Glorious Adventure* (GB/USA).

H

Haarmann, Fritz

Possibly the most horrific mass murderer of all time, a meat trader who lured teenage boys to their doom in post-World War I Germany and subsequently sold their bodies for meat. A homosexual who was also an epileptic, he admitted surprise when charged with only 27 murders in 1924; he calculated the number to be nearer 40. He was beheaded the same year, aged 45. Kurt Raab starred as Haarmann in the 1973 German film of Ulli Lommel.

Kurt Raab	*Tenderness Of The Wolves* (Lommel)	W. Ger, 73

Halsey, Vice-Admiral William F.

(1882–1959) Flamboyant, quick-tempered Commander of the Allied Fleets in the South Pacific in World War II. His doggedness in battle earned him the nickname of 'Bull' Halsey and helped bring about several notable victories over the Japanese near Guadalcanal. One detailed screen portrait by James Cagney in *The Gallant Hours*.

James Cagney	*The Gallant Hours* (Montgomery)	USA, 60
James Whitmore	*Tora! Tora! Tora!* (Fleischer)	USA, 70
Robert Mitchum	*Midway* (Smight)	USA, 76
Kenneth Tobey	*MacArthur* (Sargent)	USA, 77

Hamilton, Emma

(c. 1765–1815) Mistress of Lord Nelson, lowly-bred but of great beauty, who attained popularity and influence at the court of Naples (as the wife of Sir William Hamilton) before enslaving England's most popular hero. After Nelson's death she sank swiftly into debt, suffered imprisonment and died in poverty in France. Vivien Leigh's performance in *Lady Hamilton* is overtly romantic, Glenda Jackson's portrayal in *Bequest To The Nation*, too vulgar. The truth lies somewhere in between.

Corinne Griffith	*The Divine Lady* (Lloyd)	USA, 29

Vivien Leigh	*Lady Hamilton*	(Korda)	GB, 41
Michele Mercier	*Lady Hamilton*	(Christian-Jaque)	
			W.Ger/It/Fra/USA, 69
Glenda Jackson	*Bequest To The Nation*	(Jones)	GB, 73

Note: Malvina Longfellow in *Nelson* (GB, 18) and *The Romance Of Lady Hamilton* (GB, 19), Liane Haid in *The Affairs Of Lady Hamilton* (Ger, 21) and Gertrude McCoy in *Nelson* (GB, 26) all featured as Emma Hamilton in silent productions.

Hamlet

Shakespeare's tragic young Danish prince who resolves to avenge the murder of his father when he learns from his father's ghost that his mother has married the assassin. Arguably, the best-known character in the best-known play in the entire Shakespeare canon. Olivier, Burton and Nicol Williamson have all reflected different aspects of the mournful prince; Maximilian Schell starred in a West German adaptation of 1960. The revenge theme has also been adapted into a western, *Johnny Hamlet*, in 1972.

Sohrab Modi	*Hamlet*	(Modi)	Ind, 35
Laurence Olivier	*Hamlet*	(Olivier)	GB, 48
Kishore Sahu	*Hamlet*	(Sahu)	Ind, 54
Maximilian Schell	*Hamlet*	(Wirth)	W.Ger, 60
Innokenti Smoktunovski	*Hamlet*	(Kozintsev)	USSR, 64
Richard Burton	*Hamlet*	(Gielgud)	USA, 64
Nicol Williamson	*Hamlet*	(Richardson)	GB, 69

Note: George Melies produced a version of *Hamlet* in 1907; Charles Raymond (GB, 12) and Sir John Forbes-Robertson (GB, 13) both starred in silent adaptations. The Shakespearean western, *Johnny Hamlet*, was produced in Italy in 1972 and starred Chip Corman.

Hammer, Mike

Private-eye 'hero' of a series of violent and very sexy novels by Mickey Spillane. Devoid of any of the moral virtues of Chandler's Philip Marlowe, he is able to take care of himself in the toughest of situations and is motivated by the theory that the ends justify the means — no matter what! First appeared in print in 'I, The Jury' (1947). Deadliest foes: the commies! Screen career undistinguished except for Aldrich's *Kiss Me Deadly*, a near classic of its kind.

Biff Elliot	*I, The Jury*	(Essex)	USA, 53
Ralph Meeker	*Kiss Me Deadly*	(Aldrich)	USA, 55
Robert Bray	*My Gun Is Quick*	(Victor)	USA, 57
Mickey Spillane	*The Girl Hunters*	(Rowland)	USA, 63

Hammett, Dashiell

(1894–1961) Creator of Sam Spade in *The Maltese Falcon* and Nick Charles in *The Thin Man*, this American writer was responsible for the rise of the hard-boiled private-eye in contemporary fiction and was himself an operator for the famous Pinkerton Detective Agency before turning to writing. His only portrayal on screen has been in *Julia*, set during the 30s when he lived in semi-alcoholic retirement with playwright Lillian Hellman. Jason Robards' performance as Hammett in Zinnemann's film earned him a supporting actor Academy Award.

Jason Robards   *Julia* (Zinnemann)   USA, 77

Handel, George Frederick

(1685–1759) German composer of operas and oratorios; the subject of just one screen biography to date, a 1942 British production which focused on the years when Handel, deprived of Royal patronage and plagued by debtors, wrote his masterpiece, 'The Messiah' (1742).

Wilfrid Lawson   *The Great Mr. Handel* (Walker)   GB, 42

Handy, W. C.

(1873–1958) 'Father of the blues', the man whose compositions expressed the feelings of the Negro and gave America a national music. The son of a former slave turned preacher, he wrote down for the first time many of the Negro spirituals that had been sung over the years. Played on screen by Nat King Cole in the 1958 biography by Allen Reisner.

Nat King Cole   *St. Louis Blues* (Reisner)   USA, 58

Note: Billy Preston featured as the boy Handy in the above film.

Hannay, Richard

Heroic adventurer of novelist John Buchan; a young South African mining engineer who finds himself enmeshed in murder and espionage and being hunted across the Scottish countryside in the days preceeding World War I. A three-time screen hero in *The Thirty Nine Steps* (first published in 1915), he has only once been portrayed in the correct period, i.e. in the most recent version starring Robert Powell. Hannay is also the central character of two other Buchan novels, 'Greenmantle' (1916) and 'The Three Hostages' (1924); neither have been filmed to date.

Robert Donat   *The Thirty Nine Steps* (Hitchcock)   GB, 35

| Kenneth More | *The Thirty Nine Steps* | (Thomas) | GB, 59 |
| Robert Powell | *The Thirty Nine Steps* | (Sharp) | GB, 78 |

Hannibal

(247–183 B.C.) Carthaginian general who spent his life fighting against the Romans and gained fame by invading his enemies after crossing the Alps with a team of elephants. Unfortunately, all the heroic effort proved futile for he lost anyway. Victor Mature provided a one-dimensional Hannibal in 1960; earlier, in the musical *Jupiter's Darling* (based on Robert Sherwood's 'The Road To Rome'), Howard Keel dallied too long with Esther Williams and missed his chance to invade.

| Howard Keel | *Jupiter's Darling* | (Sidney) | USA, 55 |
| Victor Mature | *Hannibal* | (Ulmer/Bragaglia) | It/USA, 60 |

Harlow, Jean

(1911–1937) MGM's most glamorous sex symbol of the 30s, a 'blonde bombshell' who co-starred with many of the studio's leading actors, especially Gable, before meeting a tragically early death at the age of 26. Neither of the screen biographies produced during the 60s was satisfactory, although the opening scenes of studio activity in Gordon Douglas' film remain some of the most realistic ever put on celluloid.

| Carol Lynley | *Harlow* | (Segal) | USA, 65 |
| Carroll Baker | *Harlow* | (Douglas) | USA, 65 |

Note: Carroll Baker's Rina Marlowe in *The Carpetbaggers* (64) was also fashioned after Harlow.

Paul Bern, Harlow's husband who committed suicide shortly after their marriage, was played by Hurd Hatfield in the Alex Segal film and by Peter Lawford in the Douglas movie.

Harper, Lew

In many ways, Philip Marlowe updated to the 60s, better dressed and more tanned in the handsome personage of Paul Newman, but still retaining the snap, crackle and pop dialogue. Two screen cases to date, one involving a millionaire kidnap victim in Los Angeles, the other set in the steaming swamplands and colonial mansions of Louisiana. A hip Newman wins out both times. Harper is the creation of novelist Ross Macdonald who has written over twenty thrillers about the private-eye. In the novels he is known as Lew Archer.

| Paul Newman | *The Moving Target* | (Smight) | USA, 66 |
| Paul Newman | *The Drowning Pool* | (Rosenberg) | USA, 75 |

Harris, Andrew 'Crocker'

Terence Rattigan's supreme creation, a lonely middle-aged schoolmaster whose life both as a teacher and husband has been a failure and whose ill-health causes his premature retirement from the school in which he has taught for twenty years. Michael Redgrave's performance in Anthony Asquith's film touched the heights and was rewarded with a best actor award at the Cannes Film Festival.

Michael Redgrave   *The Browning Version* (Asquith)   GB, 51

Hart, Lorenz

(1895–1943) American lyricist noted for his bittersweet wit and originality of theme. The epitome of the undisciplined genius, he died of alcoholism at the early age of 48, after collaborating with Richard Rodgers on a long series of innovative Broadway musicals. Among their hit songs together: 'Lover', 'Isn't It Romantic', 'Manhattan', 'The Lady Is A Tramp'.

Mickey Rooney   *Words And Music* (Taurog)   USA, 48

Hart, Moss

(1904–1961) Among the most talented of American playwrights, many years in collaboration with George S. Kaufman ('Once In A Lifetime', 'You Can't Take It With You', 'The Man Who Came To Dinner') and later as a screenwriter in Hollywood (*Gentleman's Agreement, A Star Is Born*). His autobiography, 'Act One' (1959), described his early struggles and tentative beginnings on Broadway and was turned into a film by Dore Schary. George Hamilton featured as the young Hart, Jason Robards as the eccentric Kaufman.

George Hamilton   *Act One* (Schary)   USA, 63

Havisham, Miss

Perhaps the most famous recluse in literature, an elderly man-hater who lives alone in a decaying house in Rochester, still dressed in the bridal gown she was wearing when jilted on her wedding eve. A key figure in Dickens' 'Great Expectations' (1860–61), a woman who adopts the young Estella and uses her to wreak vengeance on the male sex. Definitive screen portrait: Martita Hunt in Lean's masterpiece of 1946.

Florence Reed   *Great Expectations* (Walker)   USA, 34
Martita Hunt   *Great Expectations* (Lean)   GB, 46
Margaret Leighton   *Great Expectations* (Hardy)   GB, 75

Note: Grace Barton (USA, 16) and Marie Dinesen (Den, 22) both played Miss Havisham on the silent screen.

Hayes, Billy

A young American student whose attempt to smuggle two kilos of hashish out of Turkey in 1970 resulted in a hideous four-year sentence in Istanbul's Sagamilcar prison. His personal degradation, struggle for survival under torture and spectacular escape were recounted in the award-winning *Midnight Express*.

Brad Davis	*Midnight Express* (Parker)	GB, 78

Heathcliff

Passionate, almost demonic lover of Catherine Earnshaw in Emily Bronte's brooding romance, 'Wuthering Heights'. A tragic figure, drawn on an heroic scale, he has been played three times on the sound screen, although only Olivier has truly captured his wildness, mystery and self-destructive power. The novel, set on the lonely Yorkshire moors, was first published in 1847.

Laurence Olivier	*Wuthering Heights* (Wyler)	USA, 39
Jorge Mistral	*Wuthering Heights* (Bunuel)	Mex, 53
Timothy Dalton	*Wuthering Heights* (Fuest)	GB, 71

Note: Milton Rosmer starred as Heathcliff in a 1920 silent film, directed in England by A. V. Bramble; Cathy has been played by Anne Trevor (20), Merle Oberon (39), Eva Irasema Dilian (53) and Anna Calder-Marshall (71).

Heep, Uriah

The 'ever so 'umble' clerk to solicitor Wickfield in Charles Dickens' 'David Copperfield'. One of the most malignant and hypocritical characters in literature, he blackmails his way into a partnership, defrauds his employer but is eventually unmasked by Mr. Micawber. Roland Young's portrait in George Cukor's 1935 adaptation ranks as the most accomplished screen performance.

Roland Young	*David Copperfield* (Cukor)	USA, 35
Ron Moody	*David Copperfield* (Delbert Mann)	GB, 70

Note: There were two major portrayals of Heep in the silent days — by Jack Hulcup in Thomas Bentley's British production of 1913 and Rasmus Christiansen in A. W. Sandberg's 1923 Danish film.

Heidi

Johanna Spyri's famous child heroine, a Swiss orphan girl who is taken from her grandfather's mountain home to live a more normal but less happy life in the city. A schmaltzy character when Americanised by Shirley Temple, but delightful when played straight, i.e. by Eva Singhammer in the 1965 Austrian film of Werner Jacobs.

Shirley Temple	*Heidi* (Dwan)	USA, 37
Elsbeth Sigmund	*Heidi* (Comencini)	Swi, 52
Elsbeth Sigmund	*Heidi And Peter* (Schnyder)	Swi, 55
Eva Maria Singhammer	*Heidi* (Jacobs)	Aus, 65

Helen Of Troy

According to Greek legend, the most beautiful woman of her time, possessor of a face that launched a thousand ships and caused the Trojan War. Physically well-endowed young actresses have revelled in the role; a more mature but no less attractive Irene Papas featured in Cacoyannis' version of the play by Euripides.

Hedy Lamarr	*The Face That Launched A Thousand Ships* (Allegret)	It, 54
Rossana Podesta	*Helen Of Troy* (Wise)	USA, 55
Dani Crayne	*The Story Of Mankind* (Allen)	USA, 57
Hedy Vessel	*The Trojan Horse* (Ferroni)	Fra/It, 61
Elizabeth Taylor	*Doctor Faustus* (Burton/Coghill)	GB/It, 67
Irene Papas	*The Trojan Women* (Cacoyannis)	USA, 71

Note: Maria Corda appeared in *The Private Life Of Helen Of Troy* (USA, 27) on the silent screen.

Hellman, Lillian

(1905–) American dramatist noted for her plays of psychological conflict, many of which have been filmed, e.g. *The Children's Hour* (twice by Wyler), *The Little Foxes*, *Watch On The Rhine*, *Toys In The Attic*. Jane Fonda portrayed her on screen at the time of her life when she was endeavouring to write her first Broadway play.

Jane Fonda	*Julia* (Zinnemann)	USA, 77

Helm, Matt

America's answer to James Bond, a happy-go-lucky cheesecake photographer who enjoys a double life as a secret service agent for ICE (Organization For Intelligence And Counter Espionage). Curves, rather than patriotism, inevitably motivate his actions. Features in over 15 novels by Donald Hamilton and in four glossy movies.

Dean Martin	*The Silencers* (Karlson)	USA, 66
Dean Martin	*Murderer's Row* (Levin)	USA, 66
Dean Martin	*The Ambushers* (Levin)	USA, 67
Dean Martin	*The Wrecking Crew* (Karlson)	USA, 69

Henry II

(1138–1189) English king, responsible during his reign for many legal reforms, an achievement overlooked in films which have concentrated more on his colourful — and violent — clashes with the Archbishop of Canterbury (*Becket*) and his fiery wife, Eleanor of Aquitaine (*The Lion In Winter*). Peter O'Toole's portrait of Henry as a petulant, frightened neurotic, earned him two Oscar nominations in the 60s, but he lost on both occasions.

Alexander Gauge	*Murder In The Cathedral* (Hoellering)	GB, 51
Peter O'Toole	*Becket* (Glenville)	GB, 64
Peter O'Toole	*The Lion In Winter* (Harvey)	GB, 68

Note: Pamela Brown in *Becket* and Katharine Hepburn in *The Lion In Winter* have both featured as Eleanor Of Aquitaine, the latter winning an Academy Award as best actress of 1968.

Henry V

(1387–1422) Warrior king of England who gained a famous victory at Agincourt in 1415 and became Regent Of France. A stirring, heroic figure in Laurence Olivier's version of Shakespeare's 'Henry V'; mostly a subsidiary character in other movies. Olivier's performance earned him an Oscar nomination and was the first of his four Shakespearean screen roles.

Laurence Olivier	*Henry V* (Olivier)	GB, 45
Dan O'Herlihy	*The Black Shield Of Falworth* (Mate)	USA, 54
Keith Baxter	*Chimes At Midnight* (Welles)	Spa/Swi, 66

Note: Both O'Herlihy and Baxter appeared as Henry before he became king – as the young prince Hal.

Henry VIII

(1491–1547) 16th century British monarch who has coughed, spluttered and died on screen more times than any other British king. Portrayed in Oscar-winning style by Charles Laughton in 1933 and by such distinguished actors as Robert Shaw, Richard Burton and Keith Michell, each of whom elaborated on different aspects of Henry's ebullient personality. The six wives have appeared together in only one film (in

1972); Charles Laughton worked his way through five in *The Private Life Of Henry VIII*.

Charles Laughton	*The Private Life Of Henry VIII* (Korda)	GB, 33
Frank Cellier	*Tudor Rose* (Stevenson)	GB, 36
Montagu Love	*The Prince And The Pauper* (Keighley)	USA, 37
Lyn Harding	*The Pearls Of The Crown* (Guitry-Jaque)	Fra, 37
Iouri Toloubieiev	*The Prince And The Pauper* (Garine/Lokchina) USSR, 43	
James Robertson Justice	*The Sword And The Rose* (Annakin)	GB, 53
Charles Laughton	*Young Bess* (Sidney)	USA, 53
Paul Rogers	*The Prince And The Pauper* (Chaffey)	GB, 62
Robert Shaw	*A Man For All Seasons* (Zinnemann)	GB, 66
Richard Burton	*Anne Of The Thousand Days* (Jarrott)	GB, 69
Sidney James	*Carry On Henry* (Thomas)	GB, 71
Keith Michell	*Henry VIII And His Six Wives* (Hussein)	GB, 72
Charlton Heston	*The Prince And The Pauper* (Fleischer)	GB, 77

Note: Emil Jannings played Henry on the silent screen in Lubitsch's *Anna Boleyn* (Ger, 20). Other actors who appeared as the monarch include Arthur Bourchier in *Henry VIII* (GB, 11), Tefft Johnson in *Cardinal Wolsey* (USA, 12), Robert Broderick in *The Prince And The Pauper* (USA, 15) and Lyn Harding in *When Knighthood Was In Flower* (USA, 22).

Herbert, Victor

(1859–1924) Irish-American composer of some thirty operettas ('Naughty Marietta', 'Sweethearts', etc.) who dominated the Broadway musical stage during the first years of the twentieth century. His romantic and stirring melodies, which included 'March Of The Toys' and 'Ah, Sweet Mystery Of Life', helped maintain the tradition of Viennese operetta, a tradition carried on after his death by Sigmund Romberg. Andrew Stone's 1939 bio-pic centered on Herbert's life in New York at the turn of the century.

Walter Connolly	*The Great Victor Herbert* (Stone)	USA, 39
Paul Maxey	*Till The Clouds Roll By* (Whorf)	USA, 46

Herod Antipas

(Died after A.D. 40) The son of Herod the Great; a man who enjoyed an incestuous marriage to Herodias, leered over Salome, executed the prophet John the Baptist and sent Jesus to Pontius Pilate for trial. Charles Laughton, Jose Ferrer and Christopher Plummer are among the actors who have indulged in his debauchery on screen.

Harry Baur	*Golgotha* (Duvivier)	Fra, 35
Charles Laughton	*Salome* (Dieterle)	USA, 53
Herbert Lom	*The Big Fisherman* (Borzage)	USA, 59
Frank Thring	*King Of Kings* (Ray)	USA, 61
Francesco Leonetti	*The Gospel According To St. Matthew*	
	(Pasolini)	Fra/It, 64
Jose Ferrer	*The Greatest Story Ever Told* (Stevens)	
		USA, 65
Carlos Casaravilla	*The Redeemer* (Breen)	USA/Spa, 65
Christopher Plummer	*Jesus Of Nazareth* (Zeffirelli)	GB, 77

Note: G. Raymond Nye (USA, 18), Mitchell Lewis (USA, 22) and Vincent Coleman (USA, 23) appeared as Antipas in three silent versions of *Salome*.

Herodias has been played by Judith Anderson in *Salome* (53), Martha Hyer in *The Big Fisherman* (59), Rita Gam in *King Of Kings* (61), Franca Cupane in *The Gospel According To St. Matthew* (64), Marian Seldes in *The Greatest Story Ever Told* (65) and Valentina Cortese in *Jesus Of Nazareth* (77).

Herod The Great

(73?–4 B.C.) The King of Judea who ordered the slaughter of the male children of Bethlehem in an attempt to rid himself of the threat of the child Jesus, born in the last year of his reign. Usually only a minor figure in films about Christ, although Claude Rains produced a chilling portrait of near madness in George Stevens' *The Greatest Story Ever Told*.

Edmund Purdom	*Herod The Great* (Genoino)	It/Fra, 59
Gregoire Aslan	*King Of Kings* (Ray)	USA, 61
Amerigo Bevilacqua	*The Gospel According To St. Matthew*	
	(Pasolini)	It/Fra, 64
Claude Rains	*The Greatest Story Ever Told* (Stevens)	USA, 65
Peter Ustinov	*Jesus Of Nazareth* (Zeffirelli)	GB, 77

Note: *Jesus Of Nazareth* was made for television.

Herriot, James

Self-effacing young vet whose amusing, often tender experiences with animals in Yorkshire in the days preceding World War II have been the subject of several best-selling books and a popular TV series starring Christopher Timothy. Two cinema versions of his exploits were filmed prior to the TV series.

Simon Ward	*All Creatures Great And Small*	(Whatham)	GB, 74
John Alderton	*It Shouldn't Happen To A Vet*	(Till)	GB, 76

Note: Siegfried Farnon, Herriot's bluff partner was played by Anthony Hopkins in *All Creatures Great And Small*, and by Colin Blakely in *It Shouldn't Happen To A Vet*.

Heydrich, Reinhard

(1904–1942) The man who created a reign of terror as Nazi 'Protector' of occupied Czechoslovakia in World War II. Second only to Himmler in his total inhumanity, Heydrich was also in charge of the extermination squads who murdered thousands of Jews in the early years of the conflict. His tyrannical career was brought to an abrupt close when he was assassinated by a team of Czech agents in 1942, an event often celebrated on screen, notably in Lang's *Hangmen Also Die*.

Hans V. Twardowski	*Hangmen Also Die*	(Fritz Lang)	USA, 43
John Carradine	*Hitler's Madman*	(Sirk)	USA, 43
Anton Diffring	*Operation Daybreak*	(Gilbert)	GB, 76

Hickok, Wild Bill

(1837–1876) A legendary hero of the American West but, in reality, a gun-happy gambler who served as a scout in the Civil War, helped clean up Abilene as a town marshal and frequented the saloons and whorehouses of Deadwood. Enjoyed a brief acquaintance with Calamity Jane before having his brains blown out by two-bit gambler Jack McCall. The screen has generally followed the legend in portraying him romantically, e.g. Gary Cooper in *The Plainsman*, although two recent performances by Jeff Corey and Charles Bronson have come closer to the truth. Real name: James Butler.

Gary Cooper	*The Plainsman*	(DeMille)	USA, 37
George Houston	*Frontier Scout*	(Newfield)	USA, 38
Roy Rogers	*Young Bill Hickok*	(Kane)	USA, 40
Richard Dix	*Badlands Of Dakota*	(Green)	USA, 41
Bruce Cabot	*Wild Bill Hickok Rides*	(Enright)	USA, 42
Reed Hadley	*Dallas*	(Heisler)	USA, 50
Robert 'Bob' Anderson	*The Lawless Breed*	(Walsh)	USA, 53
Ewing Brown	*Son Of The Renegade*	(Brown)	USA, 53
Douglas Kennedy	*Jack McCall, Desperado*	(Salkow)	USA, 53
Forrest Tucker	*Pony Express*	(Hopper)	USA, 53
Howard Keel	*Calamity Jane*	(Butler)	USA, 53

Tom Brown	*I Killed Wild Bill Hickok* (Talmadge)	
		USA, 56
Robert Culp	*The Raiders* (Daugherty)	USA, 64
Adrian Hoven	*Seven Hours Of Gunfire* (Marchent)	
		Spa/It/W.Ger, 64
Paul Shannon	*The Outlaws Is Coming* (Maurer)	USA, 65
Robert Dix	*Deadwood '76* (Landis)	USA, 65
Don Murray	*The Plainsman* (Rich)	USA, 66
Jeff Corey	*Little Big Man* (Penn)	USA, 70
Charles Bronson	*The White Buffalo* (Lee Thompson)	
		USA, 77

Note: William S. Hart in *Wild Bill Hickok* (23), John Padjan in *The Iron Horse* (24) and J. Farrell MacDonald in *The Last Frontier* (26) all featured as Hickok on the silent screen.

Hitler, Adolf

(1889–1945) Nazi dictator and Führer of the Third Reich who rose to prominence in the 1930s and brought about the Second World War with his invasion of Poland in 1939. Apart from Stuart Heisler's 1962 biography with Richard Basehart, the most detailed screen portrayals of Hitler have been centred on his last few days in the Berlin bunker where he eventually committed suicide with his mistress Eva Braun, i.e. those of Albin Skoda in Pabst's *Ten Days To Die* and Alec Guinness in *Hitler: The Last Ten Days.*

Charles Chaplin	*The Great Dictator* (Chaplin)	USA, 40
Bobby Watson	*The Devil With Hitler* (Douglas)	USA, 42
Bobby Watson	*Hitler — Dead Or Alive* (Grinde)	USA, 43
Bobby Watson	*That Nazty Nuisance* (Tryon)	USA, 43
Ludwig Donath	*The Strange Death Of Adolf Hitler* (Hogan)	
		USA, 43
Bobby Watson	*The Hitler Gang* (Farrow)	USA, 44
V. Savelyov	*The Fall Of Berlin* (Chiaureli)	USSR, 49
M. Astangov	*The Battle Of Stalingrad* (Petrov)	USSR, 50
Luther Adler	*The Desert Fox* (Hathaway)	USA, 51
Luther Adler	*The Magic Face* (Tuttle)	USA, 51
Albin Skoda	*Ten Days To Die* (Pabst)	Aus, 55
Bobby Watson	*The Story Of Mankind* (Allen)	USA, 57
Kenneth Griffith	*The Two-Headed Spy* (de Toth)	GB, 58
Bobby Watson	*On The Double* (Shavelson)	USA, 61
Richard Basehart	*Hitler* (Heisler)	USA, 62
Billy Frick	*Is Paris Burning?* (Clement)	USA/Fra, 66
Rolf Stiefel	*Battle Of Britain* (Hamilton)	GB, 69
Fritz Dits	*The Great Battle* (Ozerov)	
		USSR/Pol/Yug/E.Ger/It, 69
Sidney Miller	*Which Way To The Front?* (Lewis)	USA, 70

Alec Guinness	*Hitler: The Last Ten Days* (De Concini)	
		GB/It, 73
Gunnar Moller	*Day Of Betrayal* (Vavra)	Czech, 74
Peter Sellers	*Soft Beds, Hard Battles* (Roy Boulting)	GB, 74
Helmut Qualtinger	*Ice-Age* (Zadek)	W.Ger/Nor, 75
Kurt Raab	*Adolf And Marlene* (Lommel)	W.Ger, 77

Note: Charles Chaplin gave a satirical portrayal of Hitler in his first sound film, *The Great Dictator*. The Führer was renamed Adenoid Hynkel.

Hogan, Ben

(1912–) Ace American golfer who came back to win the American Open after being seriously injured in a car crash in 1949. The accident and the events that followed were depicted in *Follow The Sun*, the only major feature film to look closely at the career of a top-ranking golf star.

| Glenn Ford | *Follow The Sun* (Lanfield) | USA, 51 |

Holiday, Billie

(1915–1959) A streetwalker at 13 and a victim of drugs and alcohol (a combination that finally killed her), this black singer remains one of the greatest exponents of jazz singing in the history of popular music. Influenced early in her career by Bessie Smith and Louis Armstrong, she once described her singing as 'trying to make my voice behave like an instrument in the hands of a jazz musician'. Her tragic life was portrayed in detail in *Lady Sings The Blues*.

| Diana Ross | *Lady Sings The Blues* (Furie) | USA, 72 |

Hollander, Xaviera

Danish call-girl who took her physical charms and sharp business acumen to the United States where she laid her way to the top and became the madam of one of the most famous bordellos in New York. Several screen portraits in the 70s, although her own performance as a promiscuous movie star in *My Pleasure Is My Business* rated higher than any of the biographical interpretations.

Samantha McClearn	*The Life And Times Of Xaviera Hollander*	
	(Spangler)	USA, 74
Lynn Redgrave	*The Happy Hooker* (Sgarro)	USA, 75
Joey Heatherton	*The Happy Hooker Goes To Washington*	
	(Levey)	USA, 77

Holliday, Doc

(1849–1885) Professional poker player and dentist friend of Wyatt Earp.

A familiar figure in Tombstone in the early 1880s, he joined the Earps in their triumphant gunfight at the O.K. Corral but died of consumption in Colorado four years later. A fair-haired, very small man, usually seen in an overcoat, he was totally unlike any of the actors who have portrayed him on the screen. Jason Robards in John Sturges' historically accurate *Hour Of The Gun* has given the most in-depth performance to date.

Cesar Romero	*Frontier Marshal* (Dwan)	USA, 39
Kent Taylor	*Tombstone, The Town Too Tough To Die* (McGann)	
		USA, 42
Walter Huston	*The Outlaw* (Hughes)	USA, 43
Victor Mature	*My Darling Clementine* (Ford)	USA, 46
James Griffith	*Masterson Of Kansas* (Castle)	USA, 54
Kirk Douglas	*Gunfight At The O.K. Corral* (Sturges)	USA, 57
Arthur Kennedy	*Cheyenne Autumn* (Ford)	USA, 64
Jason Robards	*Hour Of The Gun* (Sturges)	USA, 67
Stacy Keach	*Doc* (Perry)	USA, 71

Note: Harry Carey (as Ed Brant) featured as the Doc Holliday character in Edward L. Cahn's *Law And Order* (32).

Holly, Buddy

(1936–1959) 'Tex-Mex'-style pop singer, enormously popular in the late 50s just prior to his death in a plane crash. His style has been described as a bridge between the harsh rock n' roll of the early innovators and the tean-beat sound of such singers as Frankie Avalon and Ricky Nelson. He enjoyed his first hit, 'Peggy Sue' in 1957 and was the subject of an acclaimed 1978 screen biography starring Gary Busey, who won a best actor Oscar nomination for his performance.

Gary Busey	*The Buddy Holly Story* (Rash)	USA, 78

Holmes, Mycroft

The elder brother of Sherlock, by all accounts no less brilliant, but something of a mysterious figure in that he appears only fleetingly in Conan Doyle's stories. Of more interest in recent years to film-makers, who have begun to dig deeper into his private life at the Diogenes Club and with Her Majesty's government in Whitehall. Christopher Lee, who played Mycroft in Billy Wilder's *The Private Life Of Sherlock Holmes*, is the only actor to have played both Sherlock and Mycroft on the screen.

Robert Morley	*A Study In Terror* (Hill)	GB, 65
Christopher Lee	*The Private Life Of Sherlock Holmes* (Wilder)	GB, 70
Charles Gray	*The Seven-Per-Cent Solution* (Ross)	GB, 76

Holmes, Oliver Wendell

(1841–1935) One of the great judicial figures in American history, a High Court Judge who became known as the 'great dissenter' because of his frequent disagreements with other judges over the rights and problems of the ordinary people. Louis Calhern earned a best actor Oscar nomination for his portrayal in John Sturges' little known screen biography of 1950.

| Louis Calhern | *The Magnificent Yankee* (Sturges) | USA, 50 |

Holmes, Sherlock

The most brilliant detective in English fiction, created in 1887 by Conan Doyle in his novel 'A Study In Scarlet'. Essential requirements when at work on a case: a pipe, a magnifying glass and a deerstalker. Essential requirements for relaxation at 221B Baker Street: tobacco, a violin and a seven-per-cent solution of cocaine. No one actor has yet captured his lonely, introverted personality or the complexities of his brilliant mind. Devotees of pre-war cinema hold Arthur Wontner's performances in high regard, but for most it is Basil Rathbone who most closely fits the bill with his gaunt frame, lack of humour and abrupt manner.

Clive Brook	*The Return Of Sherlock Holmes* (Dean/Brook) USA, 29
Arthur Wontner	*The Sleeping Cardinal* (Hiscott) GB, 31
Raymond Massey	*The Speckled Band* (Raymond) GB, 31
Robert Rendel	*The Hound Of The Baskervilles* (Gundrey) GB, 32
Arthur Wontner	*The Missing Rembrandt* (Hiscott) GB, 32
Arthur Wontner	*The Sign Of Four* (Cutts) GB, 32
Clive Brook	*Sherlock Holmes* (Howard) USA, 32
Martin Fric	*Lelicek In The Service Of Sherlock Holmes* (Lamac) Czech, 32
Reginald Owen	*A Study In Scarlet* (Marin) USA, 33
Arthur Wontner	*The Triumph Of Sherlock Holmes* (Hiscott) GB, 35
Bruno Guttner	*Der Hund Von Baskerville* (Lamac) Ger, 37
Hermann Speelmans	*Sherlock Holmes: The Gray Lady* (Engels) Ger, 37
Arthur Wontner	*Silver Blaze* (Bentley) GB, 37
Hans Albers	*The Man Who Was Sherlock Holmes* (Hartl) Ger, 37
Basil Rathbone	*The Hound Of The Baskervilles* (Lanfield) USA, 39
Basil Rathbone	*The Adventures Of Sherlock Holmes* (Werker) USA, 39
Basil Rathbone	*Sherlock Holmes And The Voice Of Terror* (Rawlins) USA, 42

Basil Rathbone	*Sherlock Holmes And The Secret Weapon* (Neill)	USA, 42
Basil Rathbone	*Sherlock Holmes In Washington* (Neill)	USA, 43
Basil Rathbone	*Sherlock Holmes Faces Death* (Neill)	USA, 43
Basil Rathbone	*Spider Woman* (Neill)	USA, 44
Basil Rathbone	*The Scarlet Claw* (Neill)	USA, 44
Basil Rathbone	*The Pearl Of Death* (Neill)	USA, 44
Basil Rathbone	*The House Of Fear* (Neill)	USA, 45
Basil Rathbone	*The Woman In Green* (Neill)	USA, 45
Basil Rathbone	*Pursuit To Algiers* (Neill)	USA, 45
Basil Rathbone	*Terror By Night* (Neill)	USA, 46
Basil Rathbone	*Dressed To Kill* (Neill)	USA, 46
John Longden	*The Man With The Twisted Lip* (Grey)	GB, 51
Peter Cushing	*The Hound Of The Baskervilles* (Fisher)	GB, 59
Christopher Lee	*Sherlock Holmes And The Deadly Necklace* (Fisher)	W.Ger, 62
John Neville	*A Study In Terror* (Hill)	GB, 65
Robert Stephens	*The Private Life Of Sherlock Holmes* (Billy Wilder)	GB, 70
Radovan Lukavsky	*Sherlock Holmes' Desire* (Skalsky)	Czech, 71
Douglas Wilmer	*The Adventures Of Sherlock Holmes' Smarter Brother* (Gene Wilder)	USA, 75
Nicol Williamson	*The Seven-Per-Cent Solution* (Ross)	USA, 76
Peter Cook	*The Hound Of The Baskervilles* (Morrissey)	GB, 78
Christopher Plummer	*Murder By Decree* (Clark)	GB, 79

Note: Stewart Granger appeared as Holmes in the TV film *The Hound Of The Baskervilles* (72), as did Roger Moore in *Sherlock Holmes In New York* (77); in *They Might Be Giants* (71) George C. Scott appeared as Justin Playfair, a lawyer who believes himself to be the great detective.

More than 60 silent films featured Sherlock Holmes. Among the leading portrayals: Alwin Neuss in *The Hound Of The Baskervilles* (Ger, 15), H. A. Sainsbury in *The Valley Of Fear* (GB, 16), John Barrymore in *Sherlock Holmes* (USA, 22), Eille Norwood in three series of short films for Stoll (GB, 22–24) and Carlyle Blackwell in Richard Oswald's *Der Hund Von Baskerville* (Ger, 29).

Hoover, J. Edgar

(1895–1972) Until recently, a shadowy behind-the-scenes character on screen, just as he was in real life during his 48-year term as Director of the FBI. Larry Cohen's film biography, which covered his life in office from the gang-busting days of the 30s to the behind-closed-doors activities of the 60s, changed all that, and presented Hoover as a repressed figure who remained blind to his own abuse of power.

Erwin Fuller	*Lepke* (Golan)	USA, 75
Broderick Crawford	*The Private Files Of J. Edgar Hoover* (Cohen)	
		USA, 78
Sheldon Leonard	*The Brink's Job* (Friedkin)	USA, 78

Note: James Wainwright played the young Hoover in Cohen's film; the FBI chief appeared briefly as himself in Mervyn LeRoy's *The FBI Story* (59).

Hornblower, Horatio

Heroic British naval captain and adventurer during the wars against Napoleon. Features in a long series of C. S. Forester novels which trace his career from midshipman to admiral, but has appeared on screen only once, a somewhat surprising statistic considering that the solitary film about his exploits was a resounding success. Raoul Walsh's 1951 film was adapted from the novels 'Hornblower And The Atropos', 'The Happy Return' and 'A Ship Of The Line'.

| Gregory Peck | *Captain Horatio Hornblower*   (Walsh) | GB, 51 |

Horrocks, General Sir Brian

(1895–) One of the best-liked British Corps Commanders of World War II. Took part in the Battle of Normandy, the advance to Brussels, the drive through Germany and the tragic Operation Market Garden, code name for the attempt to seize a bridgehead over the Rhine in 1944. Portrayed sympathetically and with style by Edward Fox (*A Bridge Too Far*), during his involvement with the latter mission.

| Edward Fox | *A Bridge Too Far*   (Attenborough) | GB, 77 |

Houdini, Harry

(1874–1926) An escape artist of unsurpassed skill who could free himself from any kind of container. George Marshall's 1953 biography sketched in a number of his remarkable escapes from handcuffs, straitjackets, safes, prison cells, etc. The film also revealed how he died — from the onset of appendicitis while trying to break loose from an upside down position in a glass tank full of water. Houdini appeared in several movies late in his career, among them *Terror Island* (20), *The Soul Of Bronze* (20), *The Man From Beyond* (22). His real name was Erich Weiss.

| Tony Curtis | *Houdini*   (Marshall) | USA, 53 |

Note: Paul Michael Glaser starred as Houdini in Melville Shavelson's *The Great Houdinis*, a TV movie made in 1976.

Hugo, Adele

(1830–1915) The younger daughter of French novelist and poet Victor Hugo, a woman whose relentless pursuit of her former lover to Nova Scotia and Barbados brought about her degradation and insanity. François Truffaut's chronicle of these events resulted in a major French film of the late 70s.

Isabelle Adjani	*The Story Of Adele H*	(Truffaut)	Fra, 76

Note: Hugo himself has not done so well by the screen, the only portrait of any note coming from Victor Varconi in Allan Dwan's *Suez* (38).

Hulot, Monsieur

One of society's most lovable outsiders, a pipe-smoking, accident-prone Frenchman, whose well meaning endeavours invariably make things worse rather than better. During his screen career constantly at odds with all things modern — the mechanics of contemporary living, scientific progress and machinery of all description. First created by Jacques Tati in *Monsieur Hulot's Holiday*.

Jacques Tati	*Monsieur Hulot's Holiday* (Tati)	Fra, 53
Jacques Tati	*Mon Oncle* (Tati)	Fra, 58
Jacques Tati	*Playtime* (Tati)	Fra, 67
Jacques Tati	*Traffic* (Tati)	Fra/It, 71

The Hunchback of Notre Dame

The grotesque bellringer, Quasimodo, of Victor Hugo's masterpiece (1831), a man deafened by the bells he tolls day and night and whose unrequited love for a beautiful gypsy girl leads ultimately to tragedy and death. Generally regarded as a figure of horror, but beneath the hideous surface a character of pathos and sympathy. Chaney's 1923 performance brought out the horror, Laughton's 1939 portrayal ensured the sympathy.

Charles Laughton	*The Hunchback Of Notre Dame* (Dieterle)	
		USA, 39
Ulhas	*Badshah* (Chakrabarty)	Ind, 54
Anthony Quinn	*The Hunchback Of Notre Dame* (Delannoy)	Fra/It, 57

Note: Lon Chaney's famous silent interpretation in Wallace Worsley's film of 1923 was preceded by those of Henry Vorins in Alice Guy's *Esmeralda* (Fra, 06), Henry Krauss in Albert Capellani's *Notre Dame de Paris* (Fra, 11) and Glen White who starred in *The Darling Of Paris*, directed by J. Gordon Edwards in America in 1917.

I

Iago

The epitome of malicious evil; an arch villain whose scheming destroys the Moorish General, Othello, in Shakespeare's tragedy of jealousy and revenge in 15th century Italy. Micheal MacLiammoir's screen Iago suffered more than most, he was hauled up to the castle battlements and left in a cage to be pecked to death by vultures!

Sebastian Cabot	*Othello*	(Mackane)	GB, 46
Micheal MacLiammoir	*Othello*	(Welles)	Mor, 52
Andrei Popov	*Othello*	(Yutkevich)	USSR, 55
Frank Finlay	*Othello*	(Burge)	GB, 65

Note: Patrick McGoohan, as an Iago-type jazz drummer, schemed his way through a modernized version of Othello in *All Night Long* (62), Lance LeGault through the rock musical *Catch My Soul* (73); Werner Krauss appeared as Iago in Dimitri Buchowetzski's German silent film of 1922.

The Invisible Man

H. G. Wells' megalomaniac doctor who succeeds in rendering himself invisible while experimenting with an Indian drug called monocaine. Destroyed on screen when his tell-tale footprints betray him in the snow, he still spawned several descendants at Universal in the 40s, and even had the dubious privilege of meeting up with Abbott and Costello. 44-year-old Claude Rains made his film debut in James Whale's film of 1933, still the only movie to have been adapted from Wells' original novel published in 1897.

Claude Rains	*The Invisible Man* (Whale)	USA, 33
Vincent Price	*The Invisible Man Returns* (May)	USA, 40
Virginia Bruce	*The Invisible Woman* (Sutherland)	USA, 41
Jon Hall	*Invisible Agent* (Marin)	USA, 42
Jon Hall	*The Invisible Man's Revenge* (Beebe)	USA, 44
Arthur Franz	*Abbott And Costello Meet The Invisible Man* (Lamont)	USA, 51

Iscariot, Judas

The most infamous man in history, a disciple of Christ who betrayed his leader to the Jewish priests for thirty pieces of silver. Difficult to play on screen without descending into darkest melodrama, although both David McCallum and Ian McShane gave thoughtful, intelligent performances for directors George Stevens and Franco Zeffirelli. In 1961 John Drew Barrymore achieved a unique double, appearing as both Judas and Christ in *Pontius Pilate*.

James Griffith	*The Day Of Triumph* (Pichel/Coyle)	
		USA, 54
John Drew Barrymore	*Ponzio Pilato* (Callegari)	Fra/It/USA, 61
Rip Torn	*King Of Kings* (Ray)	USA, 61
Otello Sestili	*The Gospel According to St. Matthew* (Pasolini)	
		It/Fra, 64
Manuel Monroy	*The Redeemer* (Breen)	USA/Spa, 65
David McCallum	*The Greatest Story Ever Told* (Stevens)	
		USA, 65
Thomas Leventhal	*The Gospel Road* (Elfstrom)	USA, 73
Scott Wilson	*The Passover Plot* (Campus)	Israel/USA, 76
Ian McShane	*Jesus Of Nazareth* (Zeffirelli)	GB, 77

Note: The Zeffirelli film of 1977 was made for TV; the rock musical *Jesus Christ, Superstar* (73) featured Carl Anderson as a black Judas.

The following actors appeared as Judas in silent productions — Robert Vignola in *From The Manger To The Cross* (USA, 12), Monsieur Jacquinet in *Behold The Man* (USA/Fra, 21), Alexander Granach in *I.N.R.I. A Portrayal Of The Life Of Christ* (Ger. 23) and Joseph Schildkraut in *King Of Kings* (USA, 27).

Ivan The Terrible

(1530–1584) Grand Duke of Moscow and the first to assume the title of Tsar, a mercilessly cruel man who embarked on a reign of terror when he sensed treachery in those serving him. He eventually died, heartbroken after slaying his own son in a fit of rage. The Russian director Sergei Eisenstein planned a screen trilogy on Ivan's life, but completed only two films before his death, both remarkable for their grandiose style and the performances of Nikolai Cherkassov.

Nikolai Cherkassov	*Ivan The Terrible* (Eisenstein)	USSR, 44
Nikolai Cherkassov	*The Boyars Plot* (Eisenstein)	USSR, 46

Note: Conrad Veidt played an insane Ivan in Paul Leni's three-episode German silent film, *Waxworks* (24).

Ivanhoe

Famed Saxon knight of novelist Sir Walter Scott, an adventurer in late

12th century England when Prince John was attempting to usurp the throne of his brother Richard, taken prisoner on his return from the Crusades. Just one sound screen portrayal — by Robert Taylor in MGM's lavish 1952 swashbuckler. Full name, Wilred Of Ivanhoe; novel first published in 1819.

Robert Taylor   *Ivanhoe* (Thorpe)   USA, 52

Note: Two British silent versions of *Ivanhoe* were released in 1913, the first starring Lauderdale Maitland, the second, King Baggot.

J

Jack The Ripper

Perhaps the most notorious murderer of all time, if only for the fact that his identity remains a secret to this day. A favourite character in the movies (he killed and mutilated at least five prostitutes with a knife), he has been variously portrayed as a fanatical woman hater, a surgeon, an escaped lunatic, even a member of the Royal Family. A fictional Sherlock Holmes has tracked him down twice on screen. Not so the real-life detectives of Scotland Yard whose investigations in London's East End during the late autumn of 1888 came to nothing.

Ivor Novello	*The Lodger* (Elvey)	GB, 32
Laird Cregar	*The Lodger* (Brahm)	USA, 44
Valentine Dyall	*Room To Let* (Grayson)	GB, 50
Jack Palance	*Man In The Attic* (Fregonese)	USA, 53
Ewen Solon	*Jack The Ripper* (Baker)	GB, 59
John Fraser	*A Study In Terror* (Hill)	GB, 65
Peter Jonfield	*Murder By Decree* (Clark)	GB, 79
David Warner	*Time After Time* (Meyer)	USA, 79

Note: Novello also played the Ripper in Hitchcock's silent version of *The Lodger* (26); Werner Krauss in *Waxworks* (24) and Gustav Diessl in *Pandora's Box* (29) — both German — were other silent actors who featured as the mass killer.

Jackson, Andrew

(1767–1845) An Indian fighter, a Tennessee backwoods lawyer and an army general, before becoming the 7th President of the United States in 1829. Sometimes known as 'Old Hickory', he was the subject of scandal over his romance with a married woman, a scandal that refused to die and was later used against him by his political enemies. Jackson's stormy private life was recounted in *The President's Lady*; his more vigorous activities at the Battle of New Orleans were highlighted in *The Buccaneer*. Charlton Heston played the President on both occasions.

Lionel Barrymore	*The Gorgeous Hussy* (Brown)	USA, 36
Hugh Sothern	*The Buccaneer* (DeMille)	USA, 38

Edward Ellis	*Man Of Conquest* (Nicholls, Jr.)	USA, 39
Brian Donlevy	*The Remarkable Andrew* (Heisler)	USA, 42
Lionel Barrymore	*Lone Star* (Sherman)	USA, 52
Charlton Heston	*The President's Lady* (Levin)	USA, 53
Basil Ruysdael	*Davy Crockett, King Of The Wild Frontier* (Foster)	USA, 55
Carl Benton Reid	*The First Texan* (Haskin)	USA, 56
Charlton Heston	*The Buccaneer* (Quinn)	USA, 58

Note: George Irving appeared as Jackson in Frank Lloyd's *The Eagle Of The Sea* (USA, 26); Russell Simpson in *The Frontiersman* (USA, 27).

James, Frank

(1843–1915) Older brother of outlaw Jesse James who rode with Quantrill and then his brother's gang before surrendering in 1882, the year of Jesse's death. Early in the twentieth century appeared for a time in a Wild West Show then finished his life peacefully as a starter for a racetrack. Generally portrayed on screen as the more restrained, less flamboyant of the two brothers, notably by Henry Fonda in Fox's two large scale westerns of 39–40.

Michael Worth	*Days Of Jesse James* (Kane)	USA, 39
Henry Fonda	*Jesse James* (Henry King)	USA, 39
Henry Fonda	*The Return Of Frank James* (Fritz Lang)	USA, 40
Tom Tyler	*Badman's Territory* (Whelan)	USA, 46
Tom Tyler	*I Shot Jesse James* (Fuller)	USA, 49
Richard Long	*Kansas Raiders* (Enright)	USA, 50
Don Barry	*Gunfire* (Berke)	USA, 50
Reed Hadley	*The Return Of Jesse James* (Hilton)	USA, 50
Wendell Corey	*The Great Missouri Raid* (Douglas)	USA, 51
Tom Tyler	*Best Of The Badmen* (Russell)	USA, 51
James Brown	*Woman They Almost Lynched* (Dwan)	USA, 53
Jack Buetel	*Jesse James' Women* (Barry)	USA, 54
Jeffrey Hunter	*The True Story of Jesse James* (Ray)	USA, 56
Douglas Kennedy	*Hell's Crossroads* (Andreon)	USA, 57
Jim Davis	*Alias Jesse James* (McLeod)	USA, 59
Robert Dix	*Young Jesse James* (Claxton)	USA, 60
John Pearce	*The Great Northfield Minnesota Raid* (Kaufman)	USA, 72

Note: James Pierce featured in the role in Lloyd Ingraham's 1927 silent production *Jesse James*.

James, Jesse

(1847–1882) Leader of the most notorious outlaw gang of the Wild West, a Missouri-born bank and train robber, who, like Billy The Kid, became a legend in his own lifetime. The beginning of the end occurred in 1876 when his gang was virtually destroyed during the Northfield bank raid; the end of the end came six years later when he was shot in the back by his cousin, Bob Ford. The handsome features of Tyrone Power and Robert Wagner helped Hollywood perpetuate the legend; an unkempt Robert Duvall in *The Great Northfield Minnesota Raid* destroyed all illusions.

Tyrone Power	*Jesse James* (Henry King)	USA, 39
Roy Rogers	*Days Of Jesse James* (Kane)	USA, 39
Roy Rogers	*Jesse James At Bay* (Kane)	USA, 41
Alan Baxter	*Bad Men Of Missouri* (Enright)	USA, 41
Rod Cameron	*The Remarkable Andrew* (Heisler)	USA, 42
Lawrence Tierney	*Badman's Territory* (Whelan)	USA, 46
Dale Robertson	*Fighting Man Of The Plains* (Marin)	USA, 49
Reed Hadley	*I Shot Jesse James* (Fuller)	USA, 49
Audie Murphy	*Kansas Raiders* (Enright)	USA, 50
Macdonald Carey	*The Great Missouri Raid* (Douglas)	USA, 51
Lawrence Tierney	*Best Of The Badmen* (Russell)	USA, 51
Ben Cooper	*Woman They Almost Lynched* (Dwan)	USA, 53
Willard Parker	*The Great Jesse James Raid* (Le Borg)	USA, 53
Don Barry	*Jesse James' Women* (Barry)	USA, 54
Robert Wagner	*The True Story of Jesse James* (Ray)	USA, 56
Henry Brandon	*Hell's Crossroads* (Andreon)	USA, 57
Wendell Corey	*Alias Jesse James* (McLeod)	USA, 58
Ray Stricklyn	*Young Jesse James* (Claxton)	USA, 60
Wayne Mack	*The Outlaws Is Coming* (Maurer)	USA, 65
John Lupton	*Jesse James Meets Frankenstein's Daughter* (Beaudine)	USA, 66
Audie Murphy	*A Time For Dying* (Boetticher)	USA, 69
Robert Duvall	*The Great Northfield Minnesota Raid* (Kaufman)	USA, 72

Note: Jesse James, Jr. in *Jesse James Under The Black Flag* (21) and *Jesse James As The Outlaw* (21), and Fred Thomson in *Jesse James* (27) both appeared in the role on the silent screen.

Clayton Moore featured as James in the serials, *Jesse James Rides Again* (47) and *The Adventures Of Frank And Jesse James* (48), Keith Richards in *The James Brothers Of Missouri* (50).

Jane, Calamity

The most famous woman associated with the Old West and not a bit like Doris Day! A one-time mule skinner who wore men's clothing, she swore, drank and chewed tobacco with the best of them. Once won a 50 dollar bet for shooting a hole in the top of a hat hanging in the rear of a saloon. Supposedly the lover of Wild Bill Hickok, she drifted into drunken obscurity after his murder in Deadwood and died on August

20, 1903, the 27th anniversary of Hickok's death. Real name: Martha Jane Burke or Cannary

Louise Dresser	*Caught* (Sloman)	USA, 31
Jean Arthur	*The Plainsman* (DeMille)	USA, 37
Sally Payne	*Young Bill Hickok* (Kane)	USA, 40
Frances Farmer	*Badlands Of Dakota* (Green)	USA, 41
Jane Russell	*The Paleface* (McLeod)	USA, 48
Yvonne De Carlo	*Calamity Jane And Sam Bass* (Sherman)	USA, 49
Evelyn Ankers	*The Texan Meets Calamity Jane* (Lamb)	USA, 50
Doris Day	*Calamity Jane* (Butler)	USA, 53
Judi Meredith	*The Raiders* (Daugherty)	USA, 64
Gloria Milland	*Seven Hours Of Gunfire* (Marchent)	It/W.Ger/Spa, 64
Abby Dalton	*The Plainsman* (Rich)	USA, 66

Note: Ethel Grey Terry played Calamity Jane in the 1923 silent production *Wild Bill Hickok*.

Javert, Inspector

The police inspector who relentlessly pursues escaped convict Jean Valjean in *Les Miserables*. Unyielding and pitiless, he is basically a tragic figure in that his obsession with the law is due to the fact that he himself was born in prison, the son of a gypsy mother and a criminal father hanged on the gallows. Ultimately commits suicide in the River Seine. A memorable creation of Victor Hugo and one of the 'plum' heavy roles in all cinema. Most famous portrayal: Charles Laughton in Fox's lavish production of 1935.

Charles Vanel	*Les Miserables* (Bernard)	Fra, 34
Charles Laughton	*Les Miserables* (Boleslawski)	USA, 35
Antonio Bravo	*Les Miserables* (Rivero)	Mex, 44
John Hinrich	*Les Miserables* (Freda)	It, 46
Javar Seetharaman	*Ezhai Padum Padu* (Ramanath)	Ind, 50
Robert Newton	*Les Miserables* (Milestone)	USA, 52
Ulhas	*Kundan* (Modi)	Ind, 55
Bernard Blier	*Les Miserables* (Le Chanois)	Fra/It, 58
Anthony Perkins	*Les Miserables* (Glenn Jordan)	GB, 79

Note: There were at least five silent versions of *Les Miserables*. France released a 1909 adaptation; Vitagraph produced a 4-reel adaptation in 1910; J. P. Etievant was Javert in the 1913 French film of Albert Capellani; Hardee Kirkland played the inspector in Frank Lloyd's 1917 production; and Jean Toulout in the 1925 film of Henri Fescourt.

Jesus Christ

(Born between 4 and 6 B.C. and crucified about A.D. 28)

The Messiah predicted by the Old Testament prophets and arguably the most dangerous role for any actor to attempt on screen. Few have been successful not, surprisingly, because of vulgarization but because of an over pious attitude towards the part. Max Von Sydow and Robert Powell both resembled the conventional image of Christ, although the most convincing portrait remains that of Enrique Irazoqui in Pasolini's *The Gospel According to St. Matthew*. In the 1976 film *The Passover Plot*, Christ was portrayed as a political revolutionary who contrives his own crucifixion as a plot against the Roman establishment.

Robert Le Vigan	*Golgotha* (Duvivier)	Fra, 35
Robert Wilson	*The Day Of Triumph* (Pichel/Coyle)	
		USA, 54
Claude Heater	*Ben-Hur* (Wyler)	USA, 59
Jeffrey Hunter	*King Of Kings* (Ray)	USA, 61
John Drew Barrymore	*Ponzio Pilato* (Callegari)	It/Fra, 61
Roy Mangano	*Barabbas* (Fleischer)	It, 62
Enrique Irazoqui	*The Gospel According to St. Matthew* (Pasolini)	
		It/Fra, 64
Luis Alvarez	*The Redeemer* (Breen)	USA/Spa, 65
Max Von Sydow	*The Greatest Story Ever Told* (Stevens)	
		USA, 65
Bernard Verley	*The Milky Way* (Bunuel)	Fra/It, 69
Radomir Reljic	*The Master And Margarita* (Petrovic)	
		Yug/It, 72
Robert Elfstrom	*The Gospel Road* (Elfstrom)	USA, 73
Zalman King	*The Passover Plot* (Campus) Israel/USA, 76	
Robert Powell	*Jesus Of Nazareth* (Zeffirelli)	GB, 77

Note: Macdonald Carey dubbed the voice of Christ for the American version of *The Redeemer*; Ted Neeley appeared in the rock musical, *Jesus Christ, Superstar* (73).

There were many silent portrayals of Christ, among them Howard Gaye in *Intolerance* (USA, 16), George Fisher in *Civilization* (USA, 16), Giovanni Pasquali in *Christus* (It, 17) and H. B. Warner in DeMille's *King of Kings* (27).

Joan Of Arc

(1412–1431) French peasant girl who was inspired by saintly voices to lead the French armies against the British and then, later, tried and burned as a heretic. Falconetti's silent performance apart, a role that has generally proved beyond even the most accomplished of actresses. Best to opt for the ridiculous rather than the sublime, e.g. Hedy Lamarr's Maid in Irwin Allen's historical pageant, *The Story Of Mankind*.

Simone Genevois	*Saint Joan — The Maid* (Gastyne)	Fra, 29
Angela Salloker	*Das Madchen Johanna* (Ucicky)	Ger, 35
Ingrid Bergman	*Joan Of Arc* (Fleming)	USA, 48
Michele Morgan	*Destinees* (Delannoy)	Fra, 53

Diana Ross, Oscar-nominated for her performance as singer Billie Holiday in *Lady Sings The Blues* (Paramount, 1972).

Jane Fonda (as playwright Lillian Hellman) and Jason Robards, Jr. (as crime writer Dashiell Hammett) in *Julia* (Twentieth Century-Fox, 1977).

Ralph Meeker (centre) as Mickey Spillane's rough tough private eye Mike Hammer in Robert Aldrich's *Kiss Me Deadly* (United Artists, 1955).

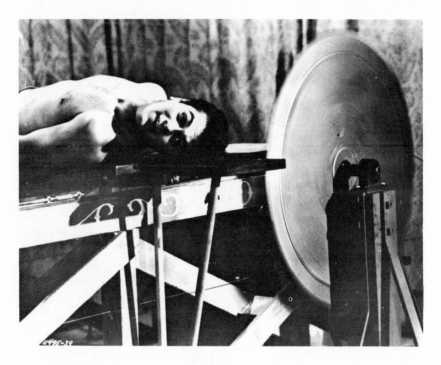

Tony Curtis as the death defying escape artist *Houdini* in Paramount's 1953 biography directed by George Marshall.

Christopher Plummer (left) and James Mason (centre) as Sherlock Holmes and Doctor Watson in the 1979 thriller *Murder By Decree* (Avco Embassy).

Richard Roundtree as black private eye John Shaft with plenty to investigate in MGM's 1971 thriller, *Shaft*.

Emma Hamilton — vulgar, earthy and humorous — as portrayed by
Glenda Jackson in *Bequest To The Nation* (Universal, 1973).

Gary Busey as Buddy Holly, the pioneer innovator of rock 'n' roll in *The Buddy Holly Story* (Innovasions/ECA, 1978). Busey was Oscar-nominated for his performance.

Doc Holliday (Jason Robards, Jr.) and Wyatt Earp (James Garner), far right, in action during the Gunfight at the O.K. Corral in the 1967 western *Hour Of The Gun* (United Artists).

Robert Powell, the most recent of the screen Richard Hannays, in the 1978 version of John Buchan's *The 39 Steps* (Rank).

Jack The Ripper — or at least his lethal knife arm — in the appropriately titled *A Study In Terror* (Columbia, 1965). On the receiving end? Barbara Windsor.

Larry Parks in the second of his two portrayals of Al Jolson in *Jolson Sings Again* (Columbia, 1949).

Fred Astaire and Red Skelton as songwriters Bert Kalmar and Harry Ruby in the 1950 MGM musical *Three Little Words*.

Julie Andrews as Gertrude Lawrence in the lavish 'Jenny' number in the Fox musical *Star!* (1968).

Seduction nymphet style! Sue Lyon issues an irresistible invitation to James Mason in Stanley Kubrick's *Lolita* (MGM, 1962).

In two minds. Fred Clark is not quite sure about Dickie Owen in *The Curse Of The Mummy's Tomb* (Columbia, 1964).

Misty Rowe re-enacts Marilyn Monroe's famous skirt billowing scene in *Goodbye, Norma Jean* (GTO, 1975), a biography of the actress's early years in movies.

Gregory Peck as two widely differing characters of World War II. Above, getting his come-uppance as Nazi doctor Josef Mengele in *The Boys From Brazil* (ITC, 1978) and below, starring as American general, *MacArthur* (Universal, 1977). Also in the picture — Dan O'Herlihy as Franklin Roosevelt.

Humphrey Bogart, the most famous of the screen Philip Marlowes, in
Howard Hawks' classic thriller, *The Big Sleep* (Warners, 1946).

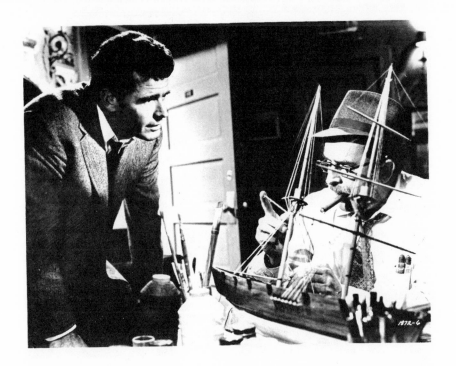

Another portrayal of Raymond Chandler's private eye. James Garner in *Marlowe* (MGM, 1969), a version of 'The Little Sister'.

Killer! An almost unrecognisable Alain Delon as Ramon Mercader, the murderer of Russian exile Trotsky in Joseph Losey's 1972 film, *The Assassination Of Trotsky* (MGM/EMI).

Oriental sleuth. Peter Lorre (seated) as John P. Marquand's wily little detective Mr. Moto, a role he played on several occasions.

Ageing master criminal Professor Moriarty (Laurence Olivier) in the 1976 Sherlock Holmes adventure *The Seven-Per-Cent Solution* (Universal).

Jean Seberg	*Saint Joan* (Preminger)	GB, 57
Hedy Lamarr	*The Story Of Mankind* (Allen)	USA, 57
Florence Carrez	*The Trial Of Joan Of Arc* (Bresson)	Fra, 62

Note: Michele Morgan's performance in the three-part film *Destinees* (*Love, Soldiers And Women*) was in the episode *Jeanne*; Geraldine Farrar in DeMille's *Joan The Woman* (17) and Falconetti in Dreyer's *The Passion Of Joan Of Arc* (28) were among the silent actresses to appear as Joan.

John The Baptist

The forerunner of Christ who preached in the wilderness about the coming of the Messiah and eventually lost his head when he denounced Herod's incestuous marriage to Herodias. Robert Ryan roared his defiant warnings for director Nicholas Ray, Charlton Heston for George Stevens and Michael York for Franco Zeffirelli.

Alan Badel	*Salome* (Dieterle)	USA, 53
Jay Barney	*The Big Fisherman* (Borzage)	USA, 59
Robert Ryan	*King Of Kings* (Ray)	USA, 61
Mario Socrate	*The Gospel According to St. Matthew* (Pasolini)	It/Fra, 64
Charlton Heston	*The Greatest Story Ever Told* (Stevens)	USA, 65
Larry Lee	*The Gospel Road* (Elfstrom)	USA, 73
Harry Andrews	*The Passover Plot* (Campus)	Israel/USA, 76
Michael York	*Jesus Of Nazareth* (Zeffirelli)	GB, 77

Note: Albert Roscoe appeared as John The Baptist in the 1918 silent version of *Salome* (USA).

John, Prince

(1167–1216) The youngest son of Henry II and Eleanor of Aquitaine who succeeded his brother Richard to the throne and was forced to sign the Magna Carta (1215) by English barons, which decreed that the king's power should be limited by law. In movies, usually the sly, cunning heavy in the Robin Hood adventures. Claude Rains retains the crown as the softest spoken but most menacing of all the screen Prince Johns.

Ramsay Hill	*The Crusades* (DeMille)	USA, 35
Claude Rains	*The Adventures Of Robin Hood* (Curtiz/Keighley)	USA, 38
George Macready	*Rogues Of Sherwood Forest* (Douglas)	USA, 50
Guy Rolfe	*Ivanhoe* (Thorpe)	GB, 52
Hubert Gregg	*The Story Of Robin Hood And His Merrie Men* (Annakin)	GB, 52
Nigel Terry	*The Lion In Winter* (Harvey)	GB, 68
Peter Ustinov	*Robin Hood* (Disney)	USA, 73

Note: Peter Ustinov voiced the role in Disney's 1973 cartoon; George Courtenay in *Ivanhoe* (USA, 13) and Sam de Grasse in *Robin Hood* (USA, 22) were among those who played Prince John in the silent days.

Johnson, Amy

(1903–1941) English woman aviator who made the first solo flight from England to Australia in 1930. Herbert Wilcox's 1942 biography with Anna Neagle was released just a year after Johnson's death. She was a pilot in the Air Transport Auxiliary, and drowned after baling out over the Thames estuary.

Anna Neagle	*They Flew Alone* (Wilcox)	GB, 42

Johnson, Andrew

(1808–1875) Vice-president of America at the time of Lincoln's assassination and the man who tried to carry through Lincoln's policy of reconciliation with the South at the end of the Civil War. His subsequent conflicts with Congress resulted in his near-impeachment. His turbulent Presidential career was recounted in William Dieterle's *Tennessee Johnson* in 1942.

Van Heflin	*Tennessee Johnson* (Dieterle)	USA, 42

Jolson, Al

(1886–1950) Star of the first talkie, *The Jazz Singer* (27), a brash vaudeville performer who sang and knelt his way to the top with a large repertoire of hit songs — 'Mammy', 'Swannee', 'April Showers'. Known as the Minstrel of Broadway and the star of several movies, he declined in popularity during the 30s but enjoyed a rebirth when Columbia filmed his life story in 1946.

Larry Parks	*The Jolson Story* (Green)		USA, 46
Larry Parks	*Jolson Sings Again* (Levin)		USA, 49
Norman Brooks	*The Best Things In Life Are Free* (Curtiz)		USA, 56
Buddy Lewis	*Harlow* (Segal)		USA, 65

Note: Jolson sang all the songs on the soundtracks of both film biographies. In the second film he actually meets on screen his film impersonator, Larry Parks.

Jones, John Paul

(1747–1792) Scottish-born American naval officer, famed for his exploits in the Revolutionary War and founder of the US Navy. Afforded a lavish Warner biography in 1959 by director John Farrow who, along with Raoul Walsh, was never happier than when his cameras were focused on ships at sea.

Robert Stack   *John Paul Jones* (Farrow)   USA, 59

Jones, Tom

Rumbustious hero of one of the masterpieces of English literature, a wild, lusty country boy who wenches his way across the West Country to London in 18th century England and nearly pays for his philandering on the gallows. The novel was written by Henry Fielding in 1749; the definitive screen portrayal given by Albert Finney in the Oscar-winning film of Tony Richardson.

Albert Finney   *Tom Jones* (Richardson)   GB, 63
Nicky Henson   *The Bawdy Adventures Of Tom Jones* (Owen)   GB, 76

Note: Langhorne Burton played the role in Edwin Collins' British silent film of 1917.

Joplin, Scott

(1868–1917) Black ragtime pianist-composer, famous for his celebrated 'Maple Leaf Rag' and also 'The Entertainer' which was used so effectively on the soundtrack of the Oscar-winning *The Sting*. His life, a tragic one ruined by syphilis, was the subject of a realistic, often harrowing film made in 1977.

Billy Dee Williams *Scott Joplin* (Kagan)   USA, 77

Juarez, Benito Pablo

(1806–1872) Zapotec Indian who became President of Mexico in 1857 and fought and defeated the French-supported regime of Maximilian. In 1939 William Dieterle told his story in 132 absorbing minutes and drew from Paul Muni one of the most authoritative performances of his distinguished career.

Paul Muni   *Juarez* (Dieterle)   USA, 39
Jason Robards, Sr. *The Mad Empress* (Torres)   Mex, 40

K

K, Joseph

Helpless victim of Franz Kafka's nightmarish novel 'The Trial' (1925), a nameless young bank clerk who is awakened at night by the police and placed under arrest for a crime of which he knows nothing. The country is nameless, the crime never explained; the whole piece reflects the desperate confrontation of the individual against a mindless bureaucracy. The story was filmed in a suitably bizarre fashion by Orson Welles in 1962.

Anthony Perkins   *The Trial*   (Welles)   Fra/Ger/It, 62

Kahn, Gus

(1886–1941) German-born lyricist of pop songs: 'Makin' Whoopee', 'Liza', 'You Stepped Out Of A Dream'. Numerous musicals at MGM during the 30s. The subject of a detailed biography by Michael Curtiz in 1952.

Danny Thomas   *I'll See You In My Dreams*   (Curtiz)   USA, 52

Kalmar and Ruby

American songwriting team responsible for numerous Broadway shows and Marx Brothers movie scripts during the 20s and 30s. The story of their often turbulent relationship was related in MGM's musical biography of 1950. Among their movies: *Animal Crackers* (30), *Horse Feathers* (32), *Duck Soup* (33). Among their song hits: 'Three Little Words', 'I Loved You So Much', 'Nevertheless', 'Who's Sorry Now?'

Fred Astaire & Red Skelton   *Three Little Words*   (Thorpe)   USA, 50

Note: Bert Kalmar was born in 1884 and died in 1947; Harry Ruby (1895–1974) survived him by 27 years.

Karenina, Anna

The most tragic of Tolstoy's heroines. A tortured, passionate woman who flaunts the conventions of 19th century Russian society by abandoning her husband and son and embarking on an ill-fated romance with a young army officer. A titanic part for any actress, yet one that has never quite been satisfactorily interpreted on screen, despite the fact that Garbo (twice) and Vivien Leigh both made ambitious attempts.

Greta Garbo	*Anna Karenina*	(Brown)	USA, 35
Vivien Leigh	*Anna Karenina*	(Duvivier)	GB, 48
Tatiana Samoilova	*Anna Karenina*	(Zarkhi)	USSR, 67

Note: Garbo also played the role in MGM's 1927 silent production, *Love*. M. Sorokhtina (11) and M. Guermanova (14) both featured as Anna in early Russian adaptations and film versions of the novel were produced in the USA (15), Italy (17), and Germany (20).

Keaton, Buster

(1895–1966) Silent screen comedian (referred to by one critic as 'the supreme clown poet') who rivalled Chaplin as the king of slapstick comedy during the 20s, with a series of classic features: *Sherlock Junior* (24), *The Navigator* (24), *The General* (27). Known as the great stoneface because of his doleful expression, he declined rapidly in the 30s due to alcoholism and his inability to transfer his style of humour to the sound medium. Featured in only minor roles in some 30 movies until his death in 1966.

Donald O'Connor	*The Buster Keaton Story*	(Sheldon)	USA, 57

Keller, Helen

(1880–1968) Struck deaf and blind when she was just nineteen months old, this remarkable American lecturer/writer was taught to speak at the age of seven by her equally remarkable teacher, Annie Sullivan. The arduous months of Keller's agonizing education — she was taught to read with her fingers, and hear by feeling the vibrations of the throat — were related in Arthur Penn's *The Miracle Worker*, based on the 1959 stage play by William Gibson. Both Patty Duke and Anne Bancroft (as Annie Sullivan) received Academy Awards for their performances.

Patty Duke	*The Miracle Worker*	(Penn)	USA, 62

Kellermann, Annette

(1888–1975) Australian swimming star who achieved prominence and notoriety in the early part of the century by swimming into the record books and wearing a brief, revolutionary one piece bathing suit.

Hollywood beckoned and she subsequently appeared in several movies for Universal and Fox: *Neptune's Daughter* (14), *A Daughter Of The Gods* (16), *Queen Of The Sea* (18), etc. The 1952 screen biography proved to be the most substantial role of Esther Williams' aquatic career.

| Esther Williams | *Million Dollar Mermaid* (LeRoy) | USA, 52 |

Kelly, Ned

(1855–1880) Legendary Irish-born outlaw and horse thief who plagued the Australian authorities with his bushranging activities in Victoria and New South Wales during the 1870s. Eventually hanged for murder at the ripe old age of 25. Played by British pop star Mick Jagger in Tony Richardson's bio-pic of 1970.

| Mick Jagger | *Ned Kelly* (Richardson) | GB, 70 |

Kennedy, President John F.

(1917–1963) The youngest man ever to be elected to the American Presidency, assassinated by Lee Harvey Oswald in Dallas, Texas, in November 1963. To date, only his war experiences (as the commander of a PT Boat in the South Pacific) have been recounted on screen, although a documentary, *John F. Kennedy: Years Of Lightning, Days Of Drums*, covering his 2 year 10 month term of office was released in 1964.

Cliff Robertson	*PT 109* (Martinson)	USA, 63
William Jordan	*The Private Files of J. Edgar Hoover* (Cohen)	
		USA, 78

Note: An assassination plot by right-wing Americans to guard their interests against Kennedy's liberal policies was the subject of the 1973 thriller, *Executive Action*.

Kenny, Sister Elizabeth

(1886–1954) Australian bush nurse who gained international prominence for her methods of treating the crippling disease of polio. The one film about her career traces her life from her early days in the Australian bush to her constant battles with the world's medical boards over her controversial treatment. Rosalind Russell's portrayal was honoured with a best actress Oscar nomination.

| Rosalind Russell | *Sister Kenny* (Nichols) | USA, 46 |

Kern, Jerome

(1885–1945) The father of the modern musical theatre, a composer whose music greatly influenced the later work of Gershwin, Youmans and Richard Rodgers. Nearly 40 Broadway shows including 'Sally', 'Show Boat' and 'Roberta'; several movies, *Swing Time*, *High Wide And Handsome*, *Cover Girl*, etc. and innumerable hit songs of exceptional tenderness — 'All The Things You Are', 'They Didn't Believe Me', 'The Last Time I Saw Paris'. The subject of a lavish MGM biography in 1946.

Robert Walker   *Till The Clouds Roll By*   (Whorf)   USA, 46

Kidd, Captain William

(*c.* 1645–1701) Scottish-born sea captain and officer who turned pirate in 1699 and for two years plundered the Caribbean, earning a reputation for cruelty and torture. He surrendered on the promise of a pardon but nevertheless was promptly arrested in Boston and hanged at Execution Dock, London. Now something of a legendary figure, he was played by Charles Laughton in a minor biography of 1945.

Charles Laughton	*Captain Kidd* (Lee)	USA, 45
Alan Napier	*Double Crossbones* (Barton)	USA, 50
Charles Laughton	*Abbott And Costello Meet Captain Kidd* (Lamont)	
		USA, 52
Robert Warwick	*Against All Flags* (Sherman)	USA, 52
Anthony Dexter	*Captain Kidd And The Slave Girl* (Landers)	
		USA, 54

The Killers

Not just any old bunch of thugs, but the two sharp-talking American assassins of Hemingway's classic short story. Portrayed twice on screen, first in 1946 in a faithful recreation of the story with the two gunmen waiting in a roadside diner to kill an ex-boxer, then again in a modernized version in 1964.

Charles McGraw & William Conrad	*The Killers* (Siodmak)	
		USA, 46
Lee Marvin & Clu Gulager	*The Killers* (Siegel)	
		USA, 64

Kim

Young Irish-born orphan boy (real name Kimball O'Hara) who adventures through India for the British Secret Service in the days of Victorian colonialism. Created by Rudyard Kipling in his 1901 novel 'Kim.'

Dean Stockwell   *Kim* (Saville)   USA, 51

Kimmel, Admiral Husband

(1882–1968) Commander-in-chief of the US Pacific Fleet during the Japanese attack on Pearl Harbour on December 7, 1941. He was removed from command just ten days after the attack and took no further part in the war. Martin Balsam's portrayal in *Tora! Tora! Tora!* covers the few days prior to and during Pearl Harbour.

Martin Balsam	*Tora! Tora! Tora!* (Fleischer)	USA/Japan, 70

Kipling, Rudyard

(1865–1936) British author of numerous stories of 19th century imperialist India ('Kim', 'Gunga Din'); portrayed on screen as part of his own story 'The Man Who Would Be King', a wry, witty and sobering tale of two British army sergeants adventuring in Kafiristan in the 1880s.

Christopher Plummer	*The Man Who Would Be King* (Huston)	USA, 75

Kipps, Arthur

H. G. Wells' 'simple soul', an Edwardian draper's assistant who comes into a fortune, tastes the fruits of high society then retreats back into his own less ambitious world and happiness. Michael Redgrave's portrait in Carol Reed's 1941 film remains the definitive portrayal; Tommy Steele's exuberant performance in the musical version includes the songs 'Half A Sixpence' and 'What A Picture'.

Michael Redgrave	*Kipps* (Reed)	GB, 41
Tommy Steele	*Half A Sixpence* (Sidney)	GB, 68

Note: George K. Arthur played the role in Harold Shaw's British silent version of 1921.

Knievel, Evel

Spectacular motor cycle stuntman who has successfully flirted with death for many years and become something of a legend in his own lifetime. He has featured in two movies, the first a biography starring George Hamilton, the second a crime thriller in which he appeared as himself. Most famous stunt: bike jumping from a ramp over a line of twenty adjacent cars.

George Hamilton	*Evel Knievel* (Chomsky)	USA, 72
As himself	*Viva Knievel!* (Douglas)	USA, 77

Krupa, Gene

(1909–1973) Arguably the most accomplished white jazz drummer of all time, at his best when improvising in small groups, but also inventive when contributing to the big bands of Red Nichols, Benny Goodman, Tommy Dorsey. Sal Mineo's performance in *Drum Crazy* covered fifteen years of Krupa's life, following his rise to the top, his downfall when arrested for carrying marijuana, and his subsequent comeback.

Sal Mineo	*Drum Crazy* (Weis)	USA, 59

Kurten, Peter

The frightening model for Peter Lorre's haunted child murderer in Fritz Lang's *M*. A mild-looking, middle-aged German factory worker, he created a reign of terror in Düsseldorf when he committed nine sexual murders between 1929 and 1930. He was eventually guillotined in 1931, after a plea of insanity had been rejected. The locale of Joseph Losey's remake was changed to Los Angeles.

Peter Lorre	*M* (Fritz Lang)	Ger, 31
David Wayne	*M* (Losey)	USA, 51
Robert Hossein	*The Vampire Of Dusseldorf* (Hossein)	Fra, 64

L

Lafitte, Jean

(c. 1780–1854) French-born pirate whose band of smugglers and buccaneers came to the aid of Andrew Jackson against the British in the War of 1812. This bizarre association, culminating in the Battle of New Orleans, has been depicted twice on celluloid — in 1938 by Cecil B. DeMille and twenty years later in Anthony Quinn's remake. After the war, Lafitte returned to smuggling and piracy but eventually settled for respectability and a quiet life as a wealthy married merchant.

Fredric March	*The Buccaneer* (DeMille)	USA, 38
Paul Henreid	*Last Of The Buccaneers* (Landers)	USA, 50
Yul Brynner	*The Buccaneer* (Quinn)	USA, 58

Note: Ricardo Cortez featured as Lafitte in Frank Lloyd's 1926 silent film *The Eagle Of The Sea.*

Lampton, Joe

The 'determined to make it in one bounce' working class hero of novelist John Braine. The antithesis of Osborne's Jimmy Porter, he sets his sights on the top and succeeds in his aim by seducing the daughter of a wealthy industrialist. Lives unhappily — but in comfort — ever after. First created in the novel 'Room At The Top', later a popular character on TV.

Laurence Harvey	*Room At The Top* (Clayton)	GB, 59
Laurence Harvey	*Life At The Top* (Kotcheff)	GB, 66
Kenneth Haigh	*Man At The Top* (Vardy)	GB, 73

Lancelot

The most valiant of the knights of King Arthur's Round Table. More often than not, a simple cut and thrust swashbuckler on screen, although Franco Nero's performance in *Camelot* conveyed much of his tragic passion for Queen Guinevere, a passion which destroyed his friendship with Arthur and led to the break-up of the Order of the Round Table.

Robert Taylor	*Knights Of The Round Table* (Thorpe)		GB, 54
Don Megowan	*Prince Valiant* (Hathaway)		USA, 54
Cornel Wilde	*Lancelot And Guinevere* (Wilde)		GB, 63
Franco Nero	*Camelot* (Logan)		USA, 67
Luc Simon	*Lancelot du lac* (Bresson)		Fra/It, 74
John Cleese	*Monty Python And The Holy Grail* (Gillam/Jones)		
			GB, 75

Note: Wilfred McDonald played Lancelot in the silent version of *A Connecticut Yankee At King Arthur's Court* (21).

Landru, Henri-Desire

France's infamous 'Bluebeard', a bald, unprepossessing little family man who delighted in growing roses and dealing in antiques. Unfortunately, he also dabbled in murder, disposing of ten rich widows between 1915 and 1919, the motive on each occasion being money. When brought to trial he denied all charges but was eventually guillotined in February, 1922. Claude Chabrol's 1962 film is the definitive screen biography, its only fault being that the lovely Danielle Darrieux, Hildegarde Neff and Michele Morgan rank among the victims.

George Sanders	*Bluebeard's Ten Honeymoons* (Lee Wilder)	GB, 60
Charles Denner	*Landru* (Chabrol)	Fra, 62

Note: Chaplin's *Monsieur Verdoux* (USA, 47), about an elegant French murderer of rich widows, was closely modelled on the career of Landru.

Langsdorff, Captain Hans

(1890–1939) One of the honourable figures of 'the phoney war', the German commander of the pocket battleship 'Graf Spee' which sank several ships before being trapped by three British cruisers — 'Ajax', 'Exeter' and 'Achilles' — near Montevideo harbour. Realising escape was impossible, Langsdorff landed his crew and prisoners of war before scuttling his ship and committing suicide.

Peter Finch	*The Battle Of The River Plate* (Powell/Pressburger)	
		GB, 56

Largo, Emilio

The man with one eye and two atom bombs in the fourth James Bond movie, *Thunderball*. A Sicilian millionaire who works for SPECTRE, he hijacks a NATO aircraft carrying two nuclear bombs and demands a £100 million ransom in diamonds from the western powers. Bond, despite being trapped in a sealed shark pool at one point, eventually foils his evil ambitions.

Adolfo Celi	*Thunderball* (Young)	GB, 65

Larsen, Wolf

Nietzschean figure, created by Jack London in his powerful novel 'The Sea Wolf' (1904). A ruthless yet educated captain of the schooner 'Ghost', he is finally destroyed by his mutinous crew and his own manic depression which finally gives way to blindness and madness. The 1950 version of the story, *Barricade*, was adapted into a western with Larsen recast as the owner of a gold mine utilizing slave labour.

Milton Sills	*The Sea Wolf* (Santell)	USA, 30
Edward G. Robinson	*The Sea Wolf* (Curtiz)	USA, 41
Raymond Massey	*Barricade* (Godfrey)	USA, 50
Barry Sullivan	*Wolf Larsen* (Jones)	USA, 58

Note: Hobart Bosworth (13), Noah Beery (20) and Ralph Ince (26) all appeared in silent versions of the role.

Lawrence, Gertrude

(1898 or 1902–1952) Vivacious British revue star of the 20s, associated for many years with Noel Coward and famous for her singing and dancing stage roles — 'Lady In The Dark', 'The King And I', etc. Never achieved anywhere near the same success on screen, appearing in only a handful of films, but played with vigour and authority by Julie Andrews in Robert Wise's underrated biography, *Star!*

Julie Andrews	*Star!* (Wise)	USA, 68

Lawrence, Marjorie

(1907–1979) Australian-born operatic soprano whose brilliant career as a Wagnerian singer was cruelly curtailed by an attack of polio in 1941. Succeeded in making a courageous comeback but subsequently concentrated on teaching in American universities and running summer opera workshops. Eleanor Parker won an Oscar nomination for her portrayal of Miss Lawrence in 1955.

Eleanor Parker	*Interrupted Melody* (Bernhardt)	USA, 55

Lawrence, T. E.

(1888–1935) Enigmatic British soldier and scholar who during his two years in Arabia in the First World War succeeded in uniting the Arab tribes against the Turks and became known as the legendary 'El Aurens.' Once described by Winston Churchill as 'the greatest living Englishman,' he died in obscurity in a motor cycle accident in Dorset after serving in the RAF under the name of Shaw. Peter O'Toole's performance as Lawrence in David Lean's film turned him into a major star; Albert Finney, first choice for the role, turned the part down.

Peter O'Toole	*Lawrence Of Arabia* (Lean)	GB, 62

King Lear

Legendary British king who seeks nothing but peace in his old age but declines into madness after enduring long and bitter conflicts with his three daughters. The central figure in what is generally considered to be Shakespeare's greatest work, he has been portrayed only twice on the sound screen, both versions being released in 1971. Peter Brook's film, in particular, reflected the sadness of a man growing old before his time.

Paul Scofield	*King Lear* (Brook)	GB/Den, 71
Yuri Jarvet	*King Lear* (Kozintsev)	USSR, 71

Note: Edward Dmytryk's *Broken Lance* with Spencer Tracy as a cattle baron at odds with his three sons, was a reworking of the Lear theme in a western setting; Frederick Warde appeared as Lear in a 1916 silent production and there were several Italian versions filmed between 1909 and 1912.

Ledbetter, Huddie

(1885–1949) Black blues singer/songwriter who learned the blues the hard way — breaking rocks in a chain gang in the Deep South. One of America's most widely acknowledged folksingers, his influence remains a significant force in music even thirty years after his death. Among his compositions: 'Good Night, Irene', 'Midnight Special', 'Rock Island Line', 'Cotton Fields', 'Bring Me L'il Water Silvy.' The songs in the 1976 biography *Leadbelly* were sung by HiTide Harris.

Roger E. Mosley	*Leadbelly* (Parks)	USA, 76

Lee, Gypsy Rose

(1913–1970) The best known stripper in show business, she appeared on stage with her sister (June Havoc) from the age of six. An undistinguished career in films but a sensation on stage. The Broadway musical 'Gypsy' (59) celebrated her early career and baptism into burlesque, notably with the song 'Let Me Entertain You'. Real name: Louise Hovick.

Natalie Wood	*Gypsy* (LeRoy)	USA, 62

The Lemon Drop Kid

Celebrated Damon Runyon character, a race track tipster who has to raise 10,000 dollars by Christmas Day in order to pay off his debt to a gang of mobsters. The 1951 production, partly rewritten and directed (uncredited) by Frank Tashlin, provided Bob Hope with one of his most amusing roles.

Lee Tracy	*The Lemon Drop Kid* (Neilman)	USA, 34
Bob Hope	*The Lemon Drop Kid* (Lanfield)	USA, 51

Lenin, Nikolai

(1870–1924) Russian revolutionary and profound student of Marxism who first took part in revolutionary activity in the 1890s and then led the Bolsheviks to supreme power in October 1917. Many notable portrayals on the Soviet screen, e.g. Boris Shchukin in *Lenin In October* and *Lenin In 1918*, and Maxim Shtraukh in *Lenin In Poland*.

Boris Shchukin	*Lenin In October* (Romm)	USSR, 37
Maxim Shtraukh	*The Man With A Gun* (Yutkevich)	USSR, 38
K. Miuffko	*Great Dawn* (Chiaureli)	USSR, 38
Boris Shchukin	*Lenin In 1918* (Romm)	USSR, 39
Maxim Shtraukh	*The Vyborg Side* (Kozintsev/Trauberg)	USSR, 39
Maxim Shtraukh	*His Name Is Sukhe-Bator* (Zarkhi/Heifits)	USSR, 42
Nikolai Kolesnikov	*Light Over Russia* (Yutkevich)	USSR, 47
I. Molchanov	*The Unforgettable Year, 1919* (Chiaureli)	USSR, 52
Nikolai Plotnikov	*Prologue* (Dzigan)	USSR, 56
Maxim Shtraukh	*Stories About Lenin* (Yutkevich)	USSR, 58
V. Chestnokov	*In The October Days* (Vasiliev)	USSR, 58
Maxim Shtraukh	*Lenin In Poland* (Yutkevich)	USSR, 66
Yuri Kayurov	*The Sixth Of July* (Karasik)	USSR, 68
John Gabriel	*Oh! What A Lovely War* (Attenborough)	GB, 69
Michael Bryant	*Nicholas And Alexandra* (Schaffner)	USA, 71

Note: In Eisenstein's 1928 film about the Revolution, *October*, the role of Lenin was played by Nikandrov.

Leopold, Nathan
Loeb, Richard

Two rich Chicago youths who, in 1924, murdered a 14-year-old schoolboy in order to prove their Nietzschean theory that their intellectual superiority exempted them from moral law. Leopold, who engaged in perverse sexuality, and Loeb, an overt homosexual, were defended by Clarence Darrow, a lifelong campaigner against capital punishment. Each received 99 years for murder and kidnapping. Neither of the two films based on their gruesome activities have identified Leopold and Loeb by name.

Farley Granger & John Dall	*Rope* (Hitchcock)	USA, 48
Dean Stockwell & Bradford Dillman	*Compulsion* (Fleischer)	USA, 59

Note: In 1936 Loeb was stabbed to death for sexually molesting another inmate. Leopold died, aged 71, while on parole in Puerto Rico.

Lepke, Louis

(–1943) A killer and top executive in Murder Inc, an organization set up by Al Capone and the Mafia in the late 20s to handle contracts on Syndicate opponents. A powerful colleague of Lucky Luciano and Albert Anastasia, he died in the electric chair in 1943 after surrendering himself to J. Edgar Hoover. Until Tony Curtis' detailed performance in Menahem Golan's film, an unknown character in the *genre* of true life American gangster films. Real name: Louis 'Lepke' Buchalter.

David J. Stewart	*Murder Inc* (Balaban/Rosenberg)	USA, 60
Tony Curtis	*Lepke* (Golan)	USA, 75
Gordon Zimmerman	*The Private Files Of J. Edgar Hoover* (Cohen)	USA, 78

Lestrade, Inspector

Inept Scotland Yard inspector whose incompetence is forever throwing the deductory powers of Sherlock Holmes into even sharper light in Conan Doyle's famous series of detective stories. Described by Dr. Watson as 'little, sallow, rat-faced, and dark-eyed', he is generally a subsidiary figure on screen, although Frank Finlay has made something of him in two recent Holmes adventures, *A Study In Terror* and *Murder By Decree*.

Philip Hewland	*The Sleeping Cardinal* (Hiscott)	GB, 31
Philip Hewland	*The Missing Rembrandt* (Hiscott)	GB, 32
Alan Mowbray	*A Study In Scarlet* (Marin)	USA, 33
Charles Mortimer	*The Triumph Of Sherlock Holmes* (Hiscott)	GB, 35

John Turnbull	*Silver Blaze* (Bentley)	GB, 37
Dennis Hoey	*Sherlock Holmes And The Secret Weapon* (Neill)	USA, 42
Dennis Hoey	*Sherlock Holmes Faces Death* (Neill)	USA, 43
Dennis Hoey	*Spider Woman* (Neill)	USA, 44
Dennis Hoey	*The Pearl Of Death* (Neill)	USA, 44
Dennis Hoey	*The House Of Fear* (Neill)	USA, 45
Dennis Hoey	*Terror By Night* (Neill)	USA, 46
Frank Finlay	*A Study In Terror* (Hill)	GB, 65
Frank Finlay	*Murder By Decree* (Clark)	GB, 79

Note: Arthur Bell appeared as Lestrade in the first few films in the Stoll series made by Maurice Elvey in Britain in the early 20s.

Levi, Dolly

Thornton Wilder's formidable matchmaking heroine of turn-of-the century New York. A scheming, affable widow, she is the central figure in both Wilder's New York play 'The Matchmaker' and the subsequent Broadway musical 'Hello, Dolly!' (1964). Louis Armstrong's hit title number is a valentine to her matchmaking abilities; the song 'Put On Your Sunday Clothes' celebrates her own vigorous intentions.

| Shirley Booth | *The Matchmaker*   (Anthony) | USA, 58 |
| Barbra Streisand | *Hello, Dolly!*   (Kelly) | USA, 69 |

Liar, Billy

Young undertaker's clerk (real name, Billy Fisher) who escapes from his humdrum life in a Northern industrial town through a series of elaborate fantasies in which he imagines himself the ruler of the mythical kingdom of Ambrosia. A likeable, yet finally tragic character; when he does at last get the chance to start a new life in London he loses his nerve and returns to the world of his dreams. Created by Keith Waterhouse and Willis Hall in the stage play of 1960.

| Tom Courtenay | *Billy Liar*   (Schlesinger) | GB, 63 |

Lime, Harry

A trafficker in diluted penicillin in the ruins of post-war Vienna. One of the screen's most famous villains, remembered with affection despite the fact that his smuggling activities bring agonizing deaths to scores of young children. Ends up, appropriately enough, as a corpse among the sewer rats of the city.

| Orson Welles | *The Third Man*   (Reed) | GB, 49 |

Note: Although created by Graham Greene in 1949, Lime was conceived some twenty years earlier when Greene scribbled a note on the back of an envelope, 'I had paid my last farewell to Harry a week ago, when his coffin was lowered into the frozen February ground so that it was with incredulity that I saw him pass by, without a sign of recognition among the host of strangers in the Strand!'

Lincoln, Abraham

(1809–1865) The most distinguished of all American Presidents; a former storekeeper, postmaster, surveyor and lawyer who was twice elected to the Presidency (in 1861 and 1865) and served during the dark and turbulent years of his country's Civil War. His days as a lawyer in Springfield were conveyed with affection by John Ford in *Young Mr. Lincoln*, his political career recounted in *Abraham Lincoln* and *Abe Lincoln in Illinois*, and the events leading to his assassination examined in *The Lincoln Conspiracy*. During the 30s, Frank McGlynn starred regularly as Lincoln in minor screen portrayals.

Walter Huston	*Abraham Lincoln* (Griffith)	USA, 30
Frank McGlynn	*The Littlest Rebel* (Butler)	USA, 35
Frank McGlynn	*Hearts In Bondage* (Ayres)	USA, 36
Frank McGlynn	*The Prisoner Of Shark Island* (Ford)	USA, 36
Frank McGlynn	*The Plainsman* (DeMille)	USA, 37
Frank McGlynn	*Wells Fargo* (Lloyd)	USA, 37
John Carradine	*Of Human Hearts* (Brown)	USA, 38
Henry Fonda	*Young Mr. Lincoln* (Ford)	USA, 39
Frank McGlynn	*The Mad Empress* (Torres)	Mex, 39
Raymond Massey	*Abe Lincoln In Illinois* (Cromwell)	USA, 40
Victor Kilian	*Virginia City* (Curtiz)	USA, 40
Jeff Corey	*Transcontinent Express* (Kane)	USA, 50
Leslie Kimmell	*The Tall Target* (Anthony Mann)	USA, 51
Stanley Hall	*Prince Of Players* (Dunne)	USA, 55
Austin Green	*The Story Of Mankind* (Allen)	USA, 57
Raymond Massey	*How The West Was Won* (Hathaway/Marshall/Ford)	USA, 62
John Anderson	*The Lincoln Conspiracy* (Conway)	USA, 77

Note: Lincoln was also a popular figure on the silent screen. D. W. Griffith selected Joseph Henabery for the role in his *Birth Of A Nation* (15); Judge Charles Edward Bull appeared for John Ford in *The Iron Horse* (24) and George Billings featured in the 1924 biography, *Abraham Lincoln*. Like McGlynn, Billings made a small career out of playing Lincoln, appearing several times as the President in the 20s, e.g. *Barbara Frietchie* (24), *The Man Without A Country* (25) and *Hands Up* (26).

Lindbergh, Charles A.

(1902–1974) American aviator who made the first solo non-stop transatlantic flight (from New York to Paris) in 1927. The name of the plane, 'The Spirit Of St. Louis', was also that of Lindbergh's Pulitzer Prize-winning book of 1954. James Stewart's *tour-de-force* portrayal in Wilder's 1957 film took in both the background to the flight and the flight itself.

James Stewart	*The Spirit Of St. Louis* (Wilder)	USA, 57

Liszt, Franz

(1811–1886) Hungarian composer and virtuoso pianist, a child prodigy who first performed in public at the age of nine. A favourite subject for film-makers, especially as he found time to appreciate the physical attractions of Lola Montez between composing his twenty Hungarian rhapsodies. Ken Russell's fantasy biography with Roger Daltrey was a rock conception of Liszt's life and innovatory music and looked at the composer as an early superstar.

Daniel Lecourtis	*Un Amour de Frederic Chopin* (Bolvary)	Fra, 35
Brandon Hurst	*Suez* (Dwan)	USA, 38
Fritz Leiber	*The Phanton Of The Opera* (Lubin)	USA, 43
Stephen Bekassy	*A Song To Remember* (Charles Vidor)	USA, 45
Henry Daniell	*Song Of Love* (Brown)	USA, 47
Svyatoslav Richter	*Glinka* (Alexandrov)	USSR, 52
Jacques Francois	*At The Order Of The Tsar* (Haguet)	Fra, 54
Will Quadflieg	*Lola Montes* (Ophuls)	Fra/Ger, 55
Carlos Thompson	*Magic Fire* (Dieterle)	USA, 56
Dirk Bogarde	*Song Without End* (Charles Vidor)	USA, 60
Henry Gilbert	*Song Of Norway* (Stone)	USA, 70
Imre Sinkovits	*The Loves Of Liszt* (Keleti)	Hung/USSR, 70
Roger Daltrey	*Lisztomania* (Russell)	GB, 75

Little John

Along with Friar Tuck, the most easily identifiable member of Robin Hood's outlaw band and a character who appears not only in several ballads, but in Walter Scott's 1825 novel 'The Talisman'. His battle with Robin with quarter-staves on a log spanning a stream was first depicted on film in the famous Warner swashbuckler of 1938. Burley Hollywood character actor Alan Hale played him three times; Nicol Williamson portrayed him as an old man in Richard Lester's *Robin And Marian*.

Alan Hale	*The Adventures Of Robin Hood* (Curtiz/Keighley)	USA, 38
Ray Teal	*The Bandit Of Sherwood Forest* (Sherman/Levin)	USA, 46
Walter Sande	*Prince Of Thieves* (Bretherton)	USA, 48

Alan Hale	*Rogues Of Sherwood Forest* (Douglas)	
		USA, 50
Wade Crosby	*Tales Of Robin Hood* (Tinling)	USA, 51
James Robertson Justice	*The Story Of Robin Hood And His Merrie*	
	Men (Annakin)	GB, 52
Leslie Linder	*Men Of Sherwood Forest* (Guest)	GB, 54
George Woodbridge	*Son Of Robin Hood* (Sherman)	GB, 58
Nigel Green	*Sword Of Sherwood Forest* (Fisher)	GB, 60
Leon Greene	*A Challenge For Robin Hood*	
	(Pennington Richards)	GB, 67
John Baldry	*Up The Chastity Belt* (Kellett)	GB, 71
Dan Meaden	*Wolfshead: The Legend Of Robin Hood*	
	(Hough)	GB, 73
Nicol Williamson	*Robin And Marian* (Lester)	USA, 76

Note: Little John was voiced by Phil Harris in Disney's 1973 cartoon, *Robin Hood*; Dean Martin played the equivalent role to that of Little John in *Robin And The Seven Hoods* (64), a modern gangster version of the story.

Little Women

Four teenage sisters who find maturity and romance as they grow up in a Massachussetts household during the turbulent days of the Civil War. Louisa May Alcott's novel, a timeless, gentle tale of lavender and lace, was published in 1868–9; the definitive screen portrayal of the tomboyish Jo, the headstrong, literary member of the family, belongs safely in the hands of Katharine Hepburn.

The sisters have been played as follows in the four silent and sound versions of the story:

Jo March

Ruby Miller	*Little Women*	(Samuelson/Butler)	GB, 17
Dorothy Bernard	*Little Women*	(Knowles)	USA, 19
Katharine Hepburn	*Little Women*	(Cukor)	USA, 33
June Allyson	*Little Women*	(LeRoy)	USA, 49

Amy March

Daisy Burrell	*Little Women*	(Samuelson/Butler)	GB, 17
Florence Finn	*Little Women*	(Knowles)	USA, 19
Joan Bennett	*Little Women*	(Cukor)	USA, 33
Elizabeth Taylor	*Little Women*	(LeRoy)	USA, 49

Beth March

Muriel Myers	*Little Women*	(Samuelson/Butler)	GB, 17
Lilian Hall	*Little Women*	(Knowles)	USA, 19
Jean Parker	*Little Women*	(Cukor)	USA, 33
Margaret O'Brien	*Little Women*	(LeRoy)	USA, 49

Meg March

Mary Lincoln	*Little Women*	(Samuelson/Butler)	GB, 17
Isabel Lamon	*Little Women*	(Knowles)	USA, 19
Frances Dee	*Little Women*	(Cukor)	USA, 33
Janet Leigh	*Little Women*	(LeRoy)	USA, 49

Livingstone, David

(1813–1873) Scottish explorer and medical missionary who was 'found' in Africa in 1871 by Henry Stanley, but who holds somewhat higher claims to fame in the world's history books, i.e. exposing the slave trade and discovering the Victoria Falls and Lake Nyasa. There have been two biographies of his life, one silent, one sound, and also a version of the Stanley incident. Nothing since.

Percy Marmont	*David Livingstone*	(Fitzpatrick)	GB, 36
Cedric Hardwicke	*Stanley And Livingstone*	(Henry King)	USA, 39
Neal Arden	*The Best House In London*	(Saville)	GB, 69

Note: M. A. Wetherell starred as *Livingstone* in a British production of 1925.

Lolita

The most famous nymphet in literature, an unconsciously seductive twelve-year-old who enslaves a middle-aged American lecturer — with hilarious, pathetic, and ultimately tragic results. The central figure in Vladimir Nabokov's 1955 novel of murder and lust; turned into a teenager in Kubrick's film version in order to appease the censor.

| Sue Lyon | *Lolita* | (Kubrick) | USA/GB, 62 |

Loman, Willy

Arthur Miller's ageing travelling salesman who, after a lifetime of failure and self delusion, comes home to die with his family. One of the most important figures in post-war literature in that his final disenchantment symbolises the fact that American get-rich-quick philosophy and worship of success is little more than a phoney dream. Memorably played on stage by Lee J. Cobb, equally so on screen by Fredric March.

| Fredric March | *Death Of A Salesman* | (Benedek) | USA, 51 |

Lombard, Carole

(1908–1942) High-spirited, inimitable Hollywood comedienne who featured in several of America's brightest film comedies of the 30s (*Twentieth Century, My Man Godfrey, Nothing Sacred*) before meeting an untimely death in a plane crash in 1942. Her tempestuous ten year love affair with Hollywood 'king' Clark Gable (they were married in 1939), was related in Sidney Furie's 1976 bio-pic *Gable And Lombard*.

| Jill Clayburgh | *Gable And Lombard*   (Furie) | USA, 76 |

London, Jack

(1876–1916) San Francisco-born author who served as a hobo, sailor and Klondike goldminer before becoming the highest-paid American writer of the early 1900s. His violent, socialistic stories — 'Martin Eden', 'Call Of The Wild', 'The Sea Wolf' — all reflect his experiences during his poverty-stricken youth; Alfred Santell's unpretentious film biography effectively transferred London's adventurous life to the screen.

| Michael O'Shea | *Jack London*   (Santell) | USA, 43 |
| Jeff East | *Klondike Fever*   (Carter) | USA, 79 |

Lone Wolf, The

Louis Joseph Vance's society detective, an ex-jewel thief turned gentleman benefactor who re-embraces his old profession in order to bring down the American crime rate. Bert Lytell set to work as The Lone Wolf (Michael Lanyard) in the silent days; Warren William played the reformed cracksman during the 40s. The Lone Wolf first appeared in print in 1914.

Bert Lytell	*The Lone Wolf's Daughter* (Rogell)	USA, 29
Bert Lytell	*Last Of The Lone Wolf* (Boleslavsky)	USA, 30
Thomas Meighan	*Cheaters At Play* (MacFadden)	USA, 32
Melvyn Douglas	*The Lone Wolf Returns* (Neill)	USA, 36
Francis Lederer	*The Lone Wolf In Paris* (Rogell)	USA, 38
Warren William	*The Lone Wolf Spy Hunt* (Godfrey)	USA, 39
Warren William	*The Lone Wolf Strikes* (Salkow)	USA, 40
Warren William	*The Lone Wolf Meets A Lady* (Salkow)	USA, 40
Warren William	*The Lone Wolf Takes A Chance* (Salkow)	USA, 41
Warren William	*The Lone Wolf Keeps A Date* (Salkow)	USA, 41
Warren William	*Secrets Of The Lone Wolf* (Dmytryk)	USA, 41
Warren William	*Counter-Espionage* (Dmytryk)	USA, 42
Warren William	*One Dangerous Night* (Gordon)	USA, 43
Warren William	*Passport To Suez* (DeToth)	USA, 43
Gerald Mohr	*The Notorious Lone Wolf* (Lederman)	USA, 46
Gerald Mohr	*The Lone Wolf In Mexico* (Lederman)	USA, 47
Gerald Mohr	*The Lone Wolf In London* (Goodwins)	USA, 47
Ron Randell	*The Lone Wolf And His Lady* (Hoffman)	USA, 49

Note: Bert Lytell featured as the Lone Wolf in the silent films *The Lone Wolf* (17), *The Lone Wolf Returns* (26), *Alias The Lone Wolf* (27). Henry B. Walthall in *The False Faces* (19) and Jack Holt in *The Lone Wolf* (24) also appeared in the role.

Lonsdale, Gordon

The major figure in the true life Portland Spy case of 1961, a Russian agent who posed as a Canadian and blackmailed an ex-Navy man into stealing secret documents from the Underwater Weapon Establishment at Portland. He was eventually apprehended, along with a London bookseller and his wife, who transmitted the information by radio to Moscow.

William Sylvester   *Ring Of Spies* (Tronson)   GB, 64

Note: The naval 'leak', Henry Houghton, was played by Bernard Lee; the bookseller and his wife, the Krogers, by David Kossoff and Nancy Nevinson.

Lord Jim

In many ways, the most representative of Joseph Conrad's characters, a young British naval officer who makes lifelong efforts to atone for an act of instinctive cowardice (abandoning his ship when it appears to be sinking) and succeeds only when he achieves an honourable death among a tribe of Far East natives. The complex theme of honour and its redemption have so far eluded both sound and silent film-makers. The Conrad novel was published in 1900.

Peter O'Toole   *Lord Jim* (Brooks)   USA/GB, 65

Note: The only other version of the novel was produced in 1925. Percy Marmont starred as Lord Jim under Victor Fleming's direction.

Louis, Joe

(1914–) Real name, Joseph Louis Barrow. Prior to the rise of Muhammad Ali, the most famous of the modern American heavyweights. Known as 'The Brown Bomber', he reigned as world champion from 1936 to 1948 and defended his title 25 times. He won 68 of his 71 fights. A minor screen biography was produced in 1953, two years after Louis had retired from the ring.

Coley Wallace   *The Joe Louis Story* (Gordon)   USA, 53

Luciano, Charles 'Lucky'

Together with Al Capone, one of the most powerful criminals America has ever known, a gangster who began in the 20s selling protection to madams and their girls and then quickly rose to become a millionaire and Mafia overlord. Although involved in numerous gangland killings, he did not, for a change, finish up with a bullet in his brain, but died of a heart attack in 1962 after serving a jail sentence and being deported to Italy. Franco Rosi told his story in the 1973 film *Lucky Luciano*.

Cesar Romero	*A House Is Not A Home* (Rouse)	USA, 64
Angelo Infanti	*The Valachi Papers* (Young)	Fra/It, 73
Gian Maria Volonte	*Lucky Luciano* (Rosi)	It/Fra, 73
Vic Tayback	*Lepke* (Golan)	USA, 75
Lee Montague	*The Brass Target* (Hough)	USA, 78

Ludwig II

(1845–1886) Mad king of Bavaria, the subject of two recent film biographies and also a German film of the 50s which traced his bizarre life from his youth as patron of Richard Wagner, through his struggles with Bismarck and ultimate death in an asylum. Helmut Kautner's film was shot in many of the extravagant castles built by Ludwig during his lifetime.

O. W. Fischer	*Ludwig II* (Kautner)	Ger, 55
Gerhard Riedmann	*Magic Fire* (Dieterle)	USA, 56
Harry Baer	*Ludwig — Requiem For A Virgin King* (Syberberg)	W.Ger, 72
Helmut Berger	*Ludwig* (Visconti)	It/Fra/W.Ger, 73

Luther, Martin

(1483–1546) German religious cleric who changed the course of history when he led the Protestant Reformation in Europe in the 16th century. The subject of a 1961 stage play by John Osborne, transferred to the screen in 1973 by Guy Green.

Niall McGinnis	*Martin Luther* (Pichel)	USA/Ger, 53
Stacy Keach	*Luther* (Green)	USA/GB/Can, 73

M

MacArthur, General Douglas

(1880–1964) 'I shall return' was the rallying cry of this flamboyant American general when early Japanese victories forced him to leave the Philippines in 1942. He was as good as his word and in 1945 received the surrender of the Japanese on the battleship 'Missouri'. One of America's controversial heroes of World War II, he was later relieved of command in Korea after refusing to obey orders from President Truman. Usually a subsidiary figure in movies, he has also been the subject of a full-length screen biography, Joseph Sargent's *MacArthur*.

Robert Barrat	*They Were Expendable* (Ford)	USA, 45
Robert Barrat	*American Guerilla In The Philippines* (Fritz Lang)	
		USA, 50
Dayton Lummis	*The Court Martial Of Billy Mitchell* (Preminger)	
		USA, 55
Gregory Peck	*MacArthur* (Sargent)	USA, 77
Laurence Olivier	*Inchon* (Young)	USA, 80

Macbeth

Shakespeare's Scots nobleman, driven to commit murder for the throne by the supernatural prophecies of three witches and the ambitions of his power-crazed wife. Orson Welles' cheaply budgeted *Macbeth* resembled, at times, 'Dante's Inferno'; Roman Polanski's 1971 adaptation came closest to the description of the play as being 'a nightmare study in fear'. 'Macbeth' was first performed on stage in 1606.

Ratnaprabha	*Macbeth*	(Vinayak)	Ind, 38
David Bradley	*Macbeth*	(Blair)	USA, 46
Orson Welles	*Macbeth*	(Welles)	USA, 48
Maurice Evans	*Macbeth*	(Schaefer)	GB, 61
Jon Finch	*Macbeth*	(Polanski)	GB, 71

Note: Toshiro Mifune starred as a Japanese Macbeth in Kurosawa's *Throne Of Blood* (57), Paul Douglas as the modern gangster equivalent, *Joe Macbeth* in 1955 (GB); Frank Benson (GB, 11) and Sir Herbert Beerbohm Tree (USA, 16) appeared in the role in silent versions.

The following actresses have starred as Lady Macbeth: Constance Benson (11), Constance Collier (16), Jain Wilimovsky (46), Jeanette Nolan (48), Judith Anderson (61) and Francesca Annis (71).

Ruth Roman appeared in *Joe Macbeth*; Isuzu Yamada in *Throne Of Blood*.

Macheath

Highwayman-adventurer of John Gay's 'The Beggar's Opera' (1728) and subsequently Bertolt Brecht's updated 'Die Dreigroschenoper'. Renamed in the latter as Mackie Messer (Mac The Knife), he operates in a seamy Victorian London where he marries the daughter of Soho's underworld boss and is eventually betrayed by his former mistress. The satirical Brecht musical (with lyrics by Kurt Weill) was premiered exactly 200 years after the first performance of Gay's ballad opera. One screen version of the original, two of 'Die Dreigroschenoper' ('The Threepenny Opera').

Rudolf Forster	*Die Dreigroschenoper*	(Pabst)	Ger, 31
Laurence Olivier	*The Beggar's Opera*	(Brook)	GB, 53
Curt Jurgens	*Die Dreigroschenoper*	(Staudte)	Fra/W.Ger, 63

Note: Polly Peachum, Macheath's wife, was played by Caroline Neher in 1931, Dorothy Tutin in 1953 and June Ritchie in 1963; Pirate Jenny, his former mistress, by Lotte Lenya (31) and Hildegard Neff (63).

Madame X

Long-suffering martyr of Alexandre Brisson's 1910 play, a tragic woman, forced to abandon her husband and child, who sinks to the depths and then years later finishes up accused of murder, defended by a son who doesn't recognise her. One of the most artificial of all tearjerking roles, yet one that is still brought out and dusted with surprising regularity. Lana Turner's fall from gloss to gloom is the best-known of the talkie interpretations.

Ruth Chatterton	*Madame X*	(Barrymore)	USA, 29
Gladys George	*Madame X*	(Wood)	USA, 37
Mme Kyveli	*Madame X*	(Laskos)	Gre, 60
Lana Turner	*Madame X*	(Rich)	USA, 66

Note: Dorothy Donnelly (15) and Pauline Frederick (20) both appeared in silent screen versions of the story.

The Mahdi

(1843–1885) Fanatical Sudanese religious leader who believed himself to be 'the expected one of Mohammed' and led a successful revolt against Egyptian rule in Eastern Sudan in the 1880s. He died just five months after witnessing General Gordon's head on a pole at Khartoum. Laurence Olivier, in an impressive piece of off-beat casting, played The Mahdi (full name, Mohammed Ahmed) in Basil Dearden's 1966 film *Khartoum*.

John Laurie	*The Four Feathers* (Zoltan Korda)	GB, 39
Laurence Olivier	*Khartoum* (Dearden)	GB, 66

Mahler, Gustave

(1860–1911) Austrian composer whose symphonies have become increasingly popular in recent decades. The only screen biography to date, starring Robert Powell, was directed by Ken Russell who recalled, in flashback, the events and people who influenced the composer's life. Some inspired visual passages were offset by scenes of Powell composing three symphonies at once and uttering the line, 'I don't care a shit for military band music'.

Robert Powell	*Mahler* (Russell)	GB, 74

Note: The character of Gustave von Aschenbach, the dying composer in Luchino Visconti's *Death In Venice* (71) was based on Mahler. Dirk Bogarde starred as Aschenbach.

Maid Marian

'Welcome to Sherwood, my lady!' Few screen heroines can have received such an engaging welcome as Olivia de Havilland in *The Adventures Of Robin Hood*. The handsome Errol Flynn made the greeting and a suitably wet-eyed Miss de Havilland made the most of it. Unfortunately, subsequent Maid Marians have been decidedly wishy-washy, all, that is, except the lovely ageing Marian of Audrey Hepburn in Richard Lester's *Robin And Marian*.

Olivia de Havilland	*The Adventures Of Robin Hood* (Curtiz/Keighley)	USA, 38
Patricia Morison	*Prince Of Thieves* (Bretherton)	USA, 48
Diana Lynn	*Rogues Of Sherwood Forest* (Douglas)	USA, 50
Mary Hatcher	*Tales Of Robin Hood* (Tinling)	USA, 51
Joan Rice	*The Story Of Robin Hood And His Merrie Men* (Annakin)	GB, 52
Sarah Branch	*Sword Of Sherwood Forest* (Fisher)	GB, 60
Gay Hamilton	*A Challenge For Robin Hood* (Pennington Richards)	GB, 67
Rita Webb	*Up The Chastity Belt* (Kellett)	GB, 71
Ciaran Madden	*Wolfshead: The Legend Of Robin Hood* (Hough)	GB, 73
Audrey Hepburn	*Robin And Marian* (Lester)	USA, 76

Note: Monica Evans voiced Maid Marian in Disney's cartoon feature of 1973; Barbara Rush played the modern equivalent in the 1964 gangster film *Robin And The Seven Hoods*; Barbara Tennant (USA, 12), Gerda Holmes (USA, 13), Enid Bennett (USA, 22) all played the role on the silent screen.

Maigret, Jules

Pipe-smoking police inspector of Georges Simenon, in many ways the French equivalent of Sherlock Holmes, but relying less on intellectual deduction and more on an uncanny intuition to solve his cases. Played only once on the English-speaking screen — by Charles Laughton in *The Man On The Eiffel Tower* — although Rupert Davies, who scored such a triumph as Maigret on British TV, also featured in a German production of 1966. Jean Gabin and Albert Prejean both appeared three times as the Inspector; author Simenon first created Maigret in 'Death Of Monsieur Gallet' in 1931.

Pierre Renoir	*La Nuit du Carrefour* (Renoir)	Fra, 32
Abel Tarride	*La Chien Jaune* (Tarride)	Fra, 32
Harry Baur	*La Tête d'un Homme* (Duvivier)	Fra, 33
Albert Prejean	*Picpus* (Pottier)	Fra, 43
Albert Prejean	*Cecile est Morte* (Tourneur)	Fra, 44
Albert Prejean	*Les Caves du Majestic* (Pottier)	Fra, 45
Charles Laughton	*The Man On The Eiffel Tower* (Meredith)	USA, 50
Michel Simon	*Brelan D'As* (Verneuil)	Fra, 52
Maurice Manson	*Maigret Mene L'Enquete* (Cordier)	Fra, 56
Jean Gabin	*Maigret Sets A Trap* (Delannoy)	Fra, 58
Jean Gabin	*Maigret et L'Affaire St. Fiacre* (Delannoy)	Fra, 59
Jean Gabin	*Maigret Voit Rouge* (Grangier)	Fra, 63
Gino Cervi	*Maigret a 'Pigalle* (Landi)	Fra/It, 66
Rupert Davies	*Maigret Spielt Falsch* (Weidenmann)	W. Ger, 66
Heinz Ruhmann	*Maigret und Sein Grosster Fall* (Weidenmann)	Aus/Fra/It, 66

Auntie Mame

Patrick Dennis' one and only eccentric aunt, a volatile, high-living but warm-hearted extrovert whose sophisticated way of life is suddenly disrupted when she finds herself responsible for her young nephew's upbringing. Vividly described by Dennis in his best-selling book which was later adapted for the stage by Jerome Lawrence and Robert E. Lee and then into a hit musical.

Rosalind Russell	*Auntie Mame* (DaCosta)	USA, 58
Lucille Ball	*Mame* (Saks)	USA, 75

Manon Lescaut

Luxury-craving whore who enslaves her weak-willed student lover and drives him to petty crime and murder before meeting her own violent end in the desert. A sordid, unregenerate character, first created by Abbe Prevost in 1731, many times interpreted on the screen, notably by Cecile Aubry in Clouzot's 1949 updating which set her story in the brothels of post-war Paris and the deserts of Palestine.

Alida Valli	*Manon Lescaut* (Gallone)	It, 39
Cecile Aubry	*Manon* (Clouzot)	Fra, 49
Myriam Bru	*The Loves Of Manon Lescaut* (Costa)	It/Fra, 54
Catherine Deneuve	*Manon 70* (Aurel)	Fra/W.Ger/It, 68

Note: Silent portrayals included those by Lina Cavalieri (USA, 14), Lya Mara (Ger, 19), Lya de Putti (Ger, 26) and Dolores Costello in Alan Crosland's 1927 film *When A Man Loves*.

Manson, Charles

Described by the prosecution as 'one of the most evil, satanic men who ever walked the face of the earth', this demented psychopath and his followers were responsible for the murder of Roman Polanski's wife, Sharon Tate, and five other victims in Hollywood in August, 1969. Manson, regarded by his followers as a 'Christ-like figure', was sentenced to life imprisonment in 1970 and was the subject of a 1976 film *Helter Skelter*. A 1972 documentary was also made of his life and trial.

Steve Railsback	*Helter Skelter* (Gries)	USA, 76

Marlowe, Philip

The one American private-eye who continues to hold the fascination of movie audiences the world over. Tough, honest and laconic, he has operated in a nightmare world of drugs, murder and double-cross since the 1940s. The creation of Raymond Chandler and always worth listening to ('It was a nice little front yard. O.K. for the average family only you'd need a compass to go to the mail box'), he first appeared in print in 1939 in 'The Big Sleep'. Bogart's performance in Hawks' 1946 film remains the most famous screen interpretation. Chandler himself wanted Cary Grant to play the part.

Dick Powell	*Farewell My Lovely* (Dmytryk)	USA, 44
Humphrey Bogart	*The Big Sleep* (Hawks)	USA, 46
Robert Montgomery	*Lady In The Lake* (Montgomery)	USA, 46
George Montgomery	*The Brasher Doubloon* (Brahm)	USA, 47
James Garner	*Marlowe* (Bogart)	USA, 69

Elliott Gould	*The Long Goodbye* (Altman)	USA, 73
Robert Mitchum	*Farewell My Lovely* (Richards)	USA, 75
Robert Mitchum	*The Big Sleep* (Winner)	GB, 78

Note: *The Brasher Doubloon* was a version of Chandler's 'The High Window'; *Marlowe*, an adaptation of 'The Little Sister'.

Mary, Queen Of Scots

(1542–1587) 16th century Queen of Scotland, from the Catholic viewpoint the rightful claimant to the throne of England, but eventually brought to trial and executed for conspiring against Elizabeth. Two compelling, if historically inaccurate screen performances — by Katharine Hepburn in John Ford's *Mary Of Scotland* and Vanessa Redgrave, an Oscar nominee for *Mary, Queen Of Scots*.

Katharine Hepburn	*Mary Of Scotland* (Ford)	USA, 36
Jacqueline Delubac	*The Pearls Of The Crown* (Guitry/Jaque)	
		Fra, 37
Zarah Leander	*Heart Of A Queen* (Froelich)	Ger, 40
Esmeralda Ruspoli	*Seven Seas To Calais* (Mate)	It, 62
Vanessa Redgrave	*Mary, Queen Of Scots* (Jarrott)	GB, 71

Note: On the silent screen Mary was played by Mary Fuller in *Mary Stuart* (USA, 13), Fay Compton in *Loves Of Mary, Queen Of Scots* (GB, 23) and Maisie Fisher in *The Virgin Queen* (GB, 23).

Mata Hari

(1876–1917) The stage name of the most notorious female spy in history. Under her real name of Margarete Gertrude Zelle, she might not have fared so well, but as dancer Mata Hari she was as alluring an espionage agent as the Germans could have wished for, achieving notable success before finishing up in front of a French firing squad in 1917. The highspot of George Fitzmaurice's 1932 film was Greta Garbo's exotic temple dance.

| Greta Garbo | *Mata Hari* (Fitzmaurice) | USA, 32 |
| Jeanne Moreau | *Mata Hari, Agent H-21* (Richard) | Fra/It, 65 |

Note: Magda Sonja was a silent Mata Hari in *Mata Hari: The Red Dancer* (28); Ludmilla Tcherina *The Daughter Of Mata Hari* in the 1954 French/Italian co-production directed by Carmine Gallone and Renzo Merusi.

Maugham, W. Somerset

(1874–1965) Distinguished English novelist and short story writer, twice played on screen by Herbert Marshall in the 40s, i.e. in *The Moon And Sixpence* (as Geoffrey Wolfe) and *The Razor's Edge*. In the post-war years he appeared as himself when he introduced three omnibus films of his short stories — *Quartet* (48), *Trio* (50), *Encore* (51).

| Herbert Marshall | *The Moon And Sixpence* (Lewin) | USA, 42 |
| Herbert Marshall | *The Razor's Edge* (Goulding) | USA, 46 |

Note: Maugham's days as a medical student before he turned to a writing career were reflected in his 1915 novel 'Of Human Bondage'. The character of the young Philip Carey who becomes infatuated with a worthless tart was a semi-autobiographical portrait. Carey has been played three times on film — by Leslie Howard in 1934, Paul Henreid in 1946 and Laurence Harvey in 1964. Bette Davis, Eleanor Parker and Kim Novak bitched their way through the respective adaptations.

Melba, Dame Nellie

(1861–1931) Australian soprano who became the prima donna of the Royal Opera at Covent Garden. The wonderful purity of her voice won her world fame, as did her stage surname which inspired not only two operas but the delicacies peach melba and melba toast. One of the few opera stars to be given a screen biography, she was played by Patrice Munsel in Lewis Milestone's bio-pic of 1953. Real name: Helen Porter Armstrong.

| Patrice Munsel | *Melba* (Milestone) | GB, 53 |

Mengele, Dr. Josef

The world's most wanted criminal, a sadistic ex-Nazi doctor, known as 'The Angel of Death', who was directly responsible for the destruction of 300,000 Jews in Auschwitz. Now living under presidential protection in Paraguay, he is still the number one target of famed Nazi hunter Simon Wiesenthal. Portrayed on screen by Gregory Peck in Ira Levin's bizarre thriller *The Boys From Brazil*.

| Gregory Peck | *The Boys From Brazil* (Schaffner) | USA, 78 |

Note: Wiesenthal has been played by Shmuel Rodensky in Ronald Neame's *The Odessa File* (74) and by Laurence Olivier (as Ezra Lieberman) in *The Boys From Brazil*.

Mercader, Ramon

(1914–1978) A man of many aliases but whose real name is firmly etched in the history books as the assassin of the exiled Leon Trotsky. As Frank

Jacson he infiltrated the Trotsky household in Mexico and on August 21, 1940, drove an ice pick into the skull of the Communist ideologist who died the following day. Jacson served twenty years in prison but never once revealed the names of his paymasters. The weeks leading up to the assassination were reconstructed in Joseph Losey's 1972 film, with Alain Delon as Jacson and Richard Burton as Trotsky.

| Alain Delon | *The Assassination Of Trotsky* (Losey) | Fra/It/GB, 72 |

Merlin

Legendary magician, generally hovering in the background in movies about the Round Table, but whose magical powers helped Arthur remain invincible during his reign on the throne. Legend has it that he was destroyed by the Lady In The Lake, a sorceress who tired of him and imprisoned him forever in an enchanted tower, an event not yet conveyed on film, but which offers intriguing possibilities, nonetheless!

Brandon Hurst	*A Connecticut Yankee* (Butler)	USA, 31
Murvyn Vye	*A Connecticut Yankee In King Arthur's Court* (Garnett)	USA, 49
Felix Aylmer	*Knights Of The Round Table* (Thorpe)	GB, 54
John Laurie	*Siege Of The Saxons* (Juran)	GB, 63
Mark Dignam	*Lancelot And Guinevere* (Wilde)	GB, 63
Laurence Naismith	*Camelot* (Logan)	USA, 67
Ron Moody	*The Spaceman And King Arthur* (Mayberry)	GB, 79

Note: Karl Swenson voiced Merlin in Disney's cartoon *The Sword And The Stone* (63), Chinese showman Tony Randall donned the disguise of Merlin in *The Seven Faces Of Dr. Lao* (64); on the silent screen William V. Mong featured as the character in the 1921 version of *A Connecticut Yankee At King Arthur's Court*.

Micawber, Wilkins

The eternal optimist of 'David Copperfield' (1850), always on the bread line but forever confident that something will 'turn up'. For most of his life it usually does, in the form of his creditors. In the end, though, his joviality and kindness to Dickens' boy hero serve him well and he emigrates to Australia to become a magistrate. Ralph Richardson's screen Micawber comes closest to Dickens' original conception; W. C. Fields' unique vaudeville turn defies criticism.

| W. C. Fields | *David Copperfield* (Cukor) | USA, 35 |
| Ralph Richardson | *David Copperfield* (Delbert Mann) | GB, 70 |

Note: Micawber was played by H. Collins in Thomas Bentley's British silent version of 1913 and by Frederik Jensen in A. W. Sandburg's Danish film of 1923.

Michelangelo

(1475–1564) Renaissance painter, sculptor and poet whose conflict with Pope Julius II during his four-year painting of the ceilings of the Sistine Chapel provided the basis for Irving Stone's novel, and later Carol Reed's film, *The Agony And The Ecstasy*. Charlton Heston suffered producing a masterpiece of decorative design, Rex Harrison fretted as the impatient Julius.

Wilfred Fletcher	*The Cardinal* (Hill)	GB, 36
Andrea Bosic	*The Magnificent Adventurer* (Freda)	
		It/Fra/Spa, 63
Charlton Heston	*The Agony And The Ecstasy* (Reed)	USA, 65

Milady de Winter

Beautiful *femme fatale* in many of the screen versions of Dumas' 'The Three Musketeers', a spy for Cardinal Richelieu and former wife of Athos, she murders without compunction and is eventually executed by the musketeers. A bejewelled Faye Dunaway sparkled with venom in Richard Lester's two films of the 70s; Lana Turner was even more effective in George Sidney's 1948 version for MGM.

Dorothy Revier	*The Iron Mask* (Dwan)	USA, 29
Margot Grahame	*The Three Musketeers* (Lee)	USA, 35
Binnie Barnes	*The Three Musketeers* (Dwan)	USA, 39
Lana Turner	*The Three Musketeers* (Sidney)	USA, 48
Yvette Lebon	*Milady And The Musketeers* (Cottafavi)	It, 51
Yvonne Sanson	*The Three Musketeers* (Hunebelle)	Fra, 53
Dawn Addams	*Le Vicomte de Bragelonne* (Cerchio)	Fra/It, 55
Mylene Demengeot	*The Three Musketeers* (Borderie)	Fra, 61
Faye Dunaway	*The Three Musketeers* (Lester)	Panama/Spa, 74
Faye Dunaway	*The Four Musketeers* (Lester)	Panama/Spa, 75

Note: Barbara La Marr starred as Milady in Fred Niblo's 1921 silent *The Three Musketeers*, Mademoiselle Claude Merelle in Berger's 18-part serial of 1922.

Miller, Glenn

(1904–1944) American bandleader who brought a new sound to popular dance music in the 30s and 40s and whose music enjoyed a rebirth a decade after his death with the release of Universal's *The Glenn Miller Story*. Lost in a World War II plane crash, Miller earned his enormous popularity with such hit numbers as 'Moonlight Serenade', 'In The Mood' and 'String Of Pearls'. He featured with his band in the Fox musicals, *Orchestra Wives* and *Sun Valley Serenade*.

| James Stewart | *The Glenn Miller Story* (Anthony Mann) | USA, 54 |
| Ray Daley | *The Five Pennies* (Shavelson) | USA, 59 |

Miller, Marilyn

(1898–1938) Tiny blonde musical comedy star of the 20s who appeared in several revues for Ziegfeld, as well as the hit Broadway shows 'Sally', 'Sunny' and 'As Thousands Cheer'. Helped make popular such songs as 'Who?', 'Wild Rose' and 'Easter Parade'. Her career, including her early vaudeville days with her mother and stepfather, was recounted in the Warner biography *Look For The Silver Lining*. Judy Garland featured as Miller in *Till The Clouds Roll By*.

Rosina Lawrence	*The Great Ziegfeld* (Leonard)	USA, 36
Judy Garland	*Till The Clouds Roll By* (Whorf)	USA, 46
June Haver	*Look For The Silver Lining* (Butler)	USA, 49

Miniver, Mrs.

Middle-class British housewife who takes all the Nazis can throw at her home and country in World War II. In William Wyler's famous film of 1942 she reads to her children in an air raid shelter, waits for her husband to return from Dunkirk and even captures a German airman in her back garden. Whether or not many Mrs. Minivers actually existed in Britain during the war is difficult now to ascertain. If they didn't, they should have! Played to perfection in two movies by Greer Garson.

| Greer Garson | *Mrs. Miniver* (Wyler) | USA, 42 |
| Greer Garson | *The Miniver Story* (Potter) | GB, 50 |

Miss Julie

The repressed daughter of a Swedish nobleman who tempts her father's valet into seducing her then commits suicide rather than face the consequences of her act. The central figure of Strindberg's 1888 play in which the author explores the social conflict between the working classes and decadent aristocracy of 19th century Sweden. Faultlessly played by Anita Bjork in Sjoberg's 1950 screen version.

Amelia Bence	*Miss Julie* (Soffici)	Arg, 47
Anita Bjork	*Miss Julie* (Sjoberg)	Swe, 50
Helen Mirren	*Miss Julie* (Phillips)	GB, 72

Note: Three silent film versions were made of Strindberg's play — a 1912 Swedish film with Manda Bjorling, a 1915 Russian adaptation with Olga Preobrajenskaia, and a 1921 German version with Asta Nielsen.

Miss Marple

Spinster sleuth of crime writer Agatha Christie, the very antithesis of her other detective Hercule Poirot. Tall and thin in the 16 novels but short and chubby in the four films of Margaret Rutherford. Fussy and gossipy in both! First case: 'Murder At The Vicarage' (30). Vaguely based on the character of Christie's own grandmother.

Margaret Rutherford	*Murder She Said* (Pollock)	GB, 61
Margaret Rutherford	*Murder At The Gallop* (Pollock)	GB, 63
Margaret Rutherford	*Murder Most Foul* (Pollock)	GB, 64
Margaret Rutherford	*Murder Ahoy* (Pollock)	GB, 64

Note: Miss Marple (again played by Margaret Rutherford) also makes a fleeting guest appearance in Tashlin's 1966 Poirot melodrama *The Alphabet Murders*.

Mitchell, Reginald

(1895–1937) English aircraft designer of the famous Spitfire fighter plane used with such devastating effect by the RAF in World War II. The development and testing of the plane are covered in detail in Leslie Howard's bio-pic *The First Of The Few*.

Leslie Howard	*The First Of The Few* (Howard)	GB, 42

Molière

(1622–1673) Satirical French playwright, a master of prose and comic verse, and sometimes referred to as the father of modern French comedy. In 1978 afforded the luxury of a four and a quarter hour screen biography by director Ariane Mnouchkine.

Fernand Gravey	*Versailles* (Guitry)	Fra, 54
Philippe Caubere	*Molière* (Mnouchkine)	Fra, 78

Note: Frederic Ladonne played Molière as a child in the Mnouchkine biography.

Monroe, Marilyn

(1926–1962) Real name, Norma Jean Baker. In many ways the last of the great Hollywood sex symbols, blonde, wide-eyed and innocently appealing. Regarded with more affection than any other star of her period (the 50s), she desired only one thing in life, i.e. to become a movie star, but was subsequently destroyed by the very system in which she functioned so effectively. Her sordid, early life, up until the time she broke into films by signing a contract with a major studio was recounted in *Goodbye, Norma Jean*.

Misty Rowe	*Goodbye, Norma Jean* (Buchanan)	USA/Austral, 75

Montes, Lola

(1818–1861) 19th century adventuress and dancer who crammed into her 43 years more 'living' than perhaps any other woman of her century. On screen, she emerges frequently in films about Liszt and King Ludwig of Bavaria, just two of her many illustrious lovers. She was given star treatment in the last film of Max Ophuls, who traced her career in flashback from the time of her love affairs with Liszt and Ludwig, to her final degradation as a circus sideshow attraction.

Rebecca Wassem	*Wells Fargo* (Lloyd)	USA, 37
Yvonne De Carlo	*Black Bart* (Sherman)	USA, 48
Martine Carol	*Lola Montes* (Ophuls)	Fra/Ger, 55
Larissa Trembovelskaya	*The Loves Of Liszt* (Keleti)	
		Hung/USSR, 70
Ingrid Caven	*Ludwig — Requiem For A Virgin King*	
	(Syberberg)	W.Ger, 72
Anulka Dziubinska	*Lisztomania* (Russell)	GB, 75
Florinda Bolkan	*Royal Flash* (Lester)	GB, 75

Montgomery, Field Marshal Bernard

(1887–1976) Britain's most celebrated commander of World War II (a hero of El Alamein and Commander-in-Chief of the British armies in France and Germany) but not yet awarded a major screen biography to go alongside those of Patton and MacArthur. Michael Bates, in Schaffner's *Patton*, showed Monty to be a somewhat petulant figure, in constant rivalry with his American colleagues.

Trevor Reid	*The Longest Day* (Wicki/Marton/Annakin)	
		USA, 62
Michael Rennie	*Desert Tanks* (Padget)	It/Fra, 68
Michael Bates	*Patton* (Schaffner)	USA, 70

Note: Ironically, Montgomery's 'stand-in', Clifton James, has been given wider exposure on screen. The film, *I Was Monty's Double*, showed how the British fooled the Germans on the eve of D-Day by sending his look-alike to review the troops in the Middle East while the real Monty was putting the final touches to the plans for the invasion of Europe. Clifton James played himself in the film which was released in 1958.

Moore, Grace

(1901–1947) Operatic singer who enjoyed a brief movie career at Columbia during the 30s. An Oscar nominee for *One Night Of Love* (34), she retired from the screen in 1939 and met a premature death in a Copenhagen aircrash just eight years later. Warners' screen biography focused on her life up until her debut at the Metropolitan Opera in 1928.

Kathryn Grayson	*So This Is Love* (Douglas)	USA, 53

Moran, Bugs

American gangster who took over Chicago's North Side Mob after the murder of Dion O'Bannion in the bootlegging wars of the 20s. By a lucky chance escaped death in the St. Valentine's Day Massacre of 1929 when six of his gang were shot down in a garage by Al Capone's men. Never again a force to be reckoned with, he turned to petty crime and died in prison in 1957. A substantial performance was given by Ralph Meeker in Roger Corman's film of 1967.

Ben Hendricks, Jr.	*The Public Enemy* (Wellman)	USA, 31
Murvyn Vye	*Al Capone* (Wilson)	USA, 58
Ralph Meeker	*The St. Valentine's Day Massacre* (Corman)	
		USA, 67
Robert Phillips	*Capone* (Carver)	USA, 75

More, Sir Thomas

(1478–1535) 16th century statesman who refused as a matter of conscience to sign the Act of Succession which condoned Henry VIII's divorce from Catherine of Aragon and marriage to Anne Boleyn. After resigning the post of Lord Chancellor, he was imprisoned, tried for high treason and executed. Fred Zinnemann's film of Robert Bolt's stage play, 'A Man For All Seasons' (1961) examined the man and his principles; Paul Scofield's performance won him a best actor Academy Award.

Paul Scofield	*A Man For All Seasons* (Zinnemann)	GB, 66
William Squire	*Anne Of The Thousand Days* (Jarrott)	GB, 70
Michael Goodliffe	*Henry VIII And His Six Wives* (Hussein)	GB, 72

Morgan, Harry

Tough, disillusioned Hemingway hero of 'To Have And Have Not'

(1937), a man who wearies of hiring out his motor boat for unprofitable fishing trips and becomes involved with smugglers and racketeers. Portrayed by Bogart in the famous 1944 film of Howard Hawks, but more effectively by John Garfield in Michael Curtiz's adaptation, *The Breaking Point*.

Humphrey Bogart	*To Have And Have Not* (Hawks)	USA, 44
John Garfield	*The Breaking Point* (Curtiz)	USA, 50
Audie Murphy	*The Gun Runners* (Siegel)	USA, 58

Morgan, Helen

(1900–1941) Famed torch singer, at her peak during the 20s and early 30s. Success and acclaim in vaudeville and on Broadway, but failure and alcoholism in her private life. Introduced 'Bill' and 'Can't Help Lovin' Dat Man' in 'Show Boat', appeared in the movies *Applause* (29), *Show Boat* (30), *Marie Galante* (34), etc. Gogi Grant dubbed the musical numbers for Ann Blyth in Michael Curtiz' 1957 bio-pic.

Ann Blyth	*The Helen Morgan Story* (Curtiz)	USA, 57

Morgan, Sir Henry

(*c.* 1635–1688) Notorious Welsh buccaneer who reformed to become the Lieutenant Governor of Jamaica and who died, not as the result of a rope around the neck or a sword through the chest, but of simple dissipation. Portrayed as a swashbuckler by Steve Reeves in *Morgan The Pirate*, and as the overlarge, ageing governor by Laird Cregar in *The Black Swan*.

Laird Cregar	*The Black Swan* (Henry King)	USA, 42
Robert Barrat	*Double Crossbones* (Barton)	USA, 50
Torin Thatcher	*Blackbeard The Pirate* (Walsh)	USA, 52
Steve Reeves	*Morgan The Pirate* (De Toth/Zeglio)	It, 60
Timothy Carey	*The Boy And The Pirates* (Gordon)	USA, 60
Robert Stephens	*Pirates Of Tortuga* (Webb)	USA, 61

Moriarty

In the words of Sherlock Holmes, 'the Napoleon of crime,' a master criminal with a far-flung organization, who is forever lurking in the background in the Holmes stories and finally meets his death amid the roaring waters of the Reichenbach Falls. More in the thick of things in the movies, especially in *The Adventures of Sherlock Holmes* in which he attempts to steal the Crown Jewels. No definitive screen portrait as yet but several enjoyable ones from Zucco, Atwill, Daniell and co.

Harry T. Morey	*The Return Of Sherlock Holmes* (Dean/Brook)	
		USA, 29
Ernest Torrence	*Sherlock Holmes* (Howard)	USA, 32
Lyn Harding	*The Triumph Of Sherlock Holmes* (Hiscott)	GB, 35
Lyn Harding	*Silver Blaze* (Bentley)	GB, 37
George Zucco	*The Adventures Of Sherlock Holmes* (Werker)	
		USA, 39
Lionel Atwill	*Sherlock Holmes And The Voice Of Terror*	
	(Rawlins)	USA, 42
Henry Daniell	*The Woman In Green* (Neill)	USA, 45
Hans Sohnker	*Sherlock Holmes And The Secret Necklace* (Fisher)	
		W.Ger, 62
Leo McKern	*The Adventures Of Sherlock Holmes' Smarter Brother*	
	(Gene Wilder)	USA, 75
Laurence Olivier	*The Seven-Per-Cent Solution* (Ross)	GB, 76

Note: Booth Conway in *The Valley Of Fear* (GB, 16) and Gustav von Seyffertitz in *Sherlock Holmes* (USA, 22) both featured as Moriarty on the silent screen; John Huston played the notorious Professor in the 1976 TV movie *Sherlock Holmes In New York*.

Moses

The Hebrew lawgiver who led the Israelites out of Egypt, through the wilderness and to the promised land. According to the Bible, the meekest of men; according to Hollywood, somewhat more dominant in the form of Charlton Heston, who parted the Red Sea without any difficulty and took the tablets on top of Mount Sinai.

Charlton Heston	*The Ten Commandments* (DeMille)	USA, 56
Francis X. Bushman	*The Story Of Mankind* (Allen)	USA, 57
Burt Lancaster	*Moses* (De Bosio)	It/GB, 75

Note: William Lancaster played the young Moses in the 1975 film; Theodore Roberts appeared for DeMille as the lawgiver in the silent version of *The Ten Commandments* (USA, 23), Hans Marr for Michael Curtiz in the Austrian production, *Moon Of Israel* (24).

Rameses II, the Pharaoh who oppressed the Jews at the time of the Exodus from Israel, has been played by Charles de Roche (23), Yul Brynner (56) and Mario Ferrari (75).

Mr. Moto

Oriental super sleuth of Pulitzer Prize-winning novelist John P. Marquand. Shrewd, courteous and more active than his elderly competitors, Charlie Chan and Mr. Wong, he frequently worked under cover and employed many disguises during his cases. First appeared in print in 'Saturday Evening Post' serials then graduated to the screen in the person of Peter Lorre, whose well-known features were partly obscured by steel-rimmed glasses, plastered down hair and false buck teeth.

Peter Lorre	*Think Fast, Mr. Moto* (Foster)	USA, 37
Peter Lorre	*Thank You, Mr. Moto* (Foster)	USA, 37
Peter Lorre	*Mr. Moto's Gamble* (Tinling)	USA, 38
Peter Lorre	*Mr. Moto Takes A Chance* (Foster)	USA, 38
Peter Lorre	*Mysterious Mr. Moto* (Foster)	USA, 38
Peter Lorre	*Mr. Moto's Last Warning* (Foster)	USA, 39
Peter Lorre	*Mr. Moto In Danger Island* (Leeds)	USA, 39
Peter Lorre	*Mr. Moto Takes A Vacation* (Foster)	USA, 39
Henry Silva	*The Return Of Mr. Moto* (Morris)	USA, 65

Mowgli

The 'Boy Cub' of Rudyard Kipling's two-volume fable 'The Jungle Book' (1894–5), a foundling who is raised by a family of wolves and instructed in the lore of the jungle. On screen, best known as the animated character in Walt Disney's full-length cartoon, but portrayed earlier by Sabu in a 1942 Korda film in which he ventures out against wild animals, wicked natives and discovers the treasures of a lost city.

| Sabu | *The Jungle Book* (Zoltan Korda) | USA, 42 |
| Bruce Reitherman (voice only) | *The Jungle Book* (Disney) | USA, 67 |

Mozart, Wolfgang

(1756–91) Austrian composer and child prodigy, a supreme musical genius who produced more than 600 works in his 35 years, including concertos, symphonies and the operas 'The Marriage of Figaro', 'Don Giovanni' and 'The Magic Flute'. Unlike Liszt, Wagner and Chopin, he has received distinguished treatment from film-makers, possibly because Hollywood has yet to explore his extraordinary career. The two films of Karl Hartl rank as the definitive screen life stories. Kirschner's 1976 film concentrated on Mozart's boyhood and youth.

Stephen Haggard	*Whom The Gods Love* (Dean)	
		GB, 36
Gino Cervi	*Eternal Melodies* (Gallone)	It, 39
Hannes Stelzer	*Die Kleine Nachtmusik* (Hainisch)	
		Ger, 39
Hans Holt	*Whom The Gods Love* (Hartl)	
		Aus, 42
Oscar Werner	*Mozart — Put Your Hand In Mine Dear* (Hartl)	Aus, 55
Diego Crovetti and Santiago Ziesmer	*Mozart: A Childhood Chronicle* (Kirschner)	W.Ger, 76

Note: In Kirschner's film Diego Crovetti played Mozart when he was 12, Santiago Ziesmer when he was 20.

Muhammad Ali

(1942–   ) The only man ever to win the heavyweight championship of the world three times and, without doubt, the supreme boxer of the post-war generation. His life, from his early years when he won the light heavyweight gold medal at the Rome Olympics, to his regaining the title from George Foreman in Zaire, was recounted in Tom Gries' *The Greatest*. To no-one's surprise, Ali played himself.

| Muhammad Ali | *The Greatest* (Gries) | USA, 77 |

Note: The 18-year-old Cassius Clay was played in the film by Phillip 'Chip' McAllister; Ernest Borgnine appeared as Angelo Dundee, Roger E. Mosley as Sonny Liston.

The Mummy

Since 1932, one of the great figures of screen horror, a 3700-year-old mummified Egyptian priest who guards the tomb of a princess and is accidentally brought back to life by an English archaeologist. Known as Imhotep in Karl Freund's film and, more usually, Kharis in the sequels. Changed sex in the 1971 movie, *Blood From The Mummy's Tomb*. There have been just two versions of the original story, the first with Karloff, the second with Christopher Lee.

Boris Karloff	*The Mummy* (Freund)	USA, 32
Tom Tyler	*The Mummy's Hand* (Cabanne)	USA, 40
Lon Chaney, Jr.	*The Mummy's Tomb* (Young)	USA, 42
Lon Chaney, Jr.	*The Mummy's Ghost* (Le Borg)	USA, 44
Lon Chaney, Jr.	*The Mummy's Curse* (Goodwins)	USA, 45
Eddie Parker	*Abbott And Costello Meet The Mummy* (Lamont)	USA, 55
Christopher Lee	*The Mummy* (Fisher)	GB, 59
Dickie Owen	*The Curse Of The Mummy's Tomb* (Carreras)	GB, 64
Toolsie Persaud	*The Mummy's Shroud* (Gilling)	GB, 67
Valerie Leon	*Blood From The Mummy's Tomb* (Holt)	GB, 71

Munch, Edvard

(1863–1944) Melancholic Norwegian artist of portraits and landscapes, a pioneer of modern art who became one of the most influential figures in European Expressionism. Peter Watkins' 215-minute film chronicled his turbulent years in Norway and photographed all Munch's major canvases.

Geir Westby   *Edvard Munch*   (Watkins)   Swe/Nor, 76

Note: Erik Allum appeared as Munch, aged five, and Amund Berge as the artist, aged fourteen.

Murphy, Audie

(1924–1971) America's most decorated hero of World War II; later a movie star in over thirty double-feature westerns. Appeared as himself in Universal's version of his war experiences, *To Hell And Back*. Died in a plane crash in 1971.

Audie Murphy   *To Hell And Back*   (Hibbs)   USA, 56

Mussolini, Benito

(1883–1945) 'Il Duce', the Italian dictator who marched on Rome with his black shirts in October, 1922 and ruled Italy with force — and efficiency — until the Second World War brought about his collapse. Chaplin satirized him through Jack Oakie's Benzini Napaloni in *The Great Dictator*; Rod Steiger portrayed him in the last days of his life when he was hounded across Italy by partisans and finally executed by firing squad.

Jack Oakie	*The Great Dictator* (Chaplin)	USA, 40
Joe Devlin	*The Devil With Hitler* (Douglas)	USA, 42
Joe Devlin	*That Nazty Nuisance* (Tryon)	USA, 43
Ivo Garrani	*The Great Battle* (Ozerov)	
	USSR/Pol/Yug/E.Ger/It, 69	
Mario Adorf	*The Assassination Of Matteotti* (Vancini)	It, 73
Vladimir Stach	*Day Of Betrayal* (Vavra)	Czech, 74
Rod Steiger	*The Last Days Of Mussolini* (Lizzani)	It, 74

N

Nana

The prostitute daughter of Gervaise in Zola's 'Nana' (1880). Yet another victim of her slum environment, she goes from man to man in the Paris of the 1880s, ruining both her lovers and herself until she dies a lingering death from smallpox. Her hard, unrepentant nature has appealed to many actresses, although none has yet managed to capture her true character on screen. For the Sam Goldwyn version starring Anna Sten, Rodgers and Hart were commissioned to write a torch song called 'That's Love'.

Anna Sten	*Nana* (Arzner)	USA, 34
Lupe Velez	*Nana* (Gorostiza)	Mex, 44
Martine Carol	*Nana* (Christian-Jaque)	Fra/It, 55
Anna Gael	*Take Me, Love Me* (Ahlberg)	Swe/Fra, 70

Note: Silent portrayals include those of Ellen Lumbye (Den, 12), Lilla Pescatori (It, 14) and Catherine Hessling, who featured in Jean Renoir's French version of 1926.

Napoleon Bonaparte

(1769–1821) Emperor of France and possibly the only historical figure to have been viewed from every standpoint on screen. Boyer and Brando concentrated on his romantic excesses, Herbert Lom and Vladislav Strzhelchik on his retreat from Moscow, Rod Steiger his defeat at Waterloo and Kenneth Haig his imprisonment on St. Helena. The following list is the most comprehensive yet published about Napoleon on film. When two names appear against the pictures of Sacha Guitry, the first refers to the actor who played the young Bonaparte, the second to the performer who appeared as the older Napoleon.

Paul Gunther	*Luise, Königin von Preussen* (Froelich)	Ger, 31
Paul Irving	*The Count Of Monte Cristo* (Lee)	USA, 34
Esme Percy	*Invitation To The Waltz* (Merzbach)	GB, 35
Rollo Lloyd	*Anthony Adverse* (LeRoy)	USA, 36
Charles Boyer	*Maria Walewska* (Brown)	USA, 37

Jean-Louis Barrault		
Emile Drain	*The Pearls Of The Crown* (Guitry-Jaque)	
		Fra, 37
Claude Martin		
Emile Drain	*Champs-Elysees* (Guitry)	Fra, 38
Pierre Blanchar	*A Royal Divorce* (Raymond)	GB, 38
Jean-Louis Barrault		
Sacha Guitry	*Le Destin Fabuleux de Desiree Clary* (Guitry)	
		Fra, 42
Herbert Lom	*The Young Mr. Pitt* (Reed)	GB, 42
Sergei Mezhinsky	*Kutuzov/1812* (Petrov)	USSR, 44
Emile Drain	*La Diable Boiteux* (Guitry)	Fra, 48
Arnold Moss	*The Reign Of Terror* (Anthony Mann)	
		USA, 49
Gerard Oury	*Sea Devils* (Walsh)	GB, 53
Daniel Gelin		
Raymond Pellegrin	*Napoleon* (Guitry)	Fra, 54
Marlon Brando	*Desiree* (Koster)	USA, 54
Emile Drain	*Versailles M'Etait Conte* (Guitry)	Fra, 54
Robert Cornthwaite	*The Purple Mask* (Humberstone)	USA, 55
Herbert Lom	*War and Peace* (King Vidor)	USA/It, 56
Dennis Hopper	*The Story Of Mankind* (Allen)	USA, 57
Rene Deltgen	*Queen Luise* (Liebeneiner)	Ger, 57
Pierre Mondy	*Austerlitz* (Gance)	Fra/It/Yug, 60
Julien Bertheau	*Madame Sans-Gene* (Christian-Jaque)	
		It/Fra/Spa, 61
Janusz Zakrzenski	*Ashes* (Wajda)	Pol, 65
Gyula Bodrogi	*Hary Janos* (Szinetar)	Hung, 65
Vladislav Strzhelchik	*War And Peace* (Bondarchuk)	USSR, 66–67
Giani Esposito	*The Sea Pirate* (Rowland)	Fra/Spa/It, 67
Rod Steiger	*Waterloo* (Bondarchuk)	It/USSR, 70
Eli Wallach	*The Adventures Of Gerard* (Skolimowski)	
		GB/It/Swi, 70
Kenneth Haig	*Eagle In A Cage* (Cook)	GB, 71
James Tolkan	*Love And Death* (Woody Allen)	USA, 75
Aldo Maccione	*The Loves And Times Of Scaramouche*	
		(Castellari) It/Yug, 76

Note: The most famous silent screen Napoleon was Albert Dieudonne who appeared in Abel Gance's 1927 French epic *Napoleon*, filmed in a revolutionary triple-screen process. The picture was reassembled with a synchronised stereophonic soundtrack in 1936 and again in a revamped $4^{1}/_{2}$ hour version in 1971.

Nelson, George 'Baby Face'

(–1935) Real name: Lester Gillis. One of the nastiest hoodlums to flourish in Depression America. Just 5 ft 5 in tall and with the face of a choir boy, he was a cold-blooded killer of the most ruthless kind and, after the death of Dillinger, with whom he teamed for a while, featured prominently on the FBI's wanted list. He was eventually killed in Illinois in a shootout with two FBI agents. Nelson's ruthlessness was most accurately conveyed in Don Siegel's 1957 biography with Mickey Rooney.

Mickey Rooney	*Baby Face Nelson* (Siegel)	USA, 57
William Phipps	*The FBI Story* (LeRoy)	USA, 59
John Ashley	*Young Dillinger* (Morse)	USA, 64
Richard Dreyfuss	*Dillinger* (Milius)	USA, 73

Nelson, Horatio

(1758–1805) British naval hero of the battles of the Nile and Trafalgar, but of more interest to film-makers for his victories below decks, i.e. with Lady Hamilton, than those against Napoleon. Nonetheless, a major figure in several screen biographies, both silent and sound. The romanticised *Lady Hamilton* was said to be one of the favourite films of Winston Churchill who reputedly saw it many times.

Victor Varconi	*The Divine Lady* (Lloyd)	USA, 29
John Burton	*Lloyds Of London* (Henry King)	USA, 36
Laurence Olivier	*Lady Hamilton* (Korda)	GB, 41
Stephen Haggard	*The Young Mr. Pitt* (Reed)	GB, 42
Roland Bartrop	*Austerlitz* (Gance)	Fra/It/Yug, 60
Richard Johnson	*Lady Hamilton* (Christian-Jaque)	
		W.Ger/It/Fra/USA, 69
Peter Finch	*Bequest To The Nation* (Jones)	GB, 73

Note: Jimmy Thompson spoofed Nelson in *Carry On Jack* (64); Donald Calthrop in *Nelson* (GB, 18), Humberstone Wright in *The Romance Of Lady Hamilton* (GB, 19), Conrad Veidt in Richard Oswald's *The Affairs Of Lady Hamilton* (Ger, 21) and Cedric Hardwicke in *Nelson* (GB, 26) all played him on the silent screen.

Nemo, Captain

The megalomaniac genius of Jules Verne's novels, '20,000 Leagues Under The Sea' and 'The Mysterious Island' (both 1870); an embittered inventor who finds a new world for himself beneath the ocean as he patrols the lower depths in his revolutionary 19th century submarine *Nautilus.* Numerous portrayals in spin-offs from the original story but played with most conviction by James Mason in Disney's relatively straight adaptation of 1954.

Lionel Barrymore	*The Mysterious Island* (Hubbard)	USA, 29
James Mason	*20,000 Leagues Under The Sea* (Fleischer)	
		USA, 54

Herbert Lom	*Mysterious Island* (Endfield)	GB, 62
Robert Ryan	*Captain Nemo And The Underwater City* (Hill)	
		GB, 69
Omar Sharif	*The Mysterious Island* (Bardem) Fra/It/Spa, 73	
Jose Ferrer	*The Amazing Captain Nemo* (March) USA, 78	

Note: Nemo was renamed Dakkar in the 1929 version with Lionel Barrymore; Allan Holubar played the role in a 1916 production released by Universal.

Nero

(A.D. 37–68) Mad Roman emperor who supposedly fiddled while Rome burned, kicked his mistress Poppaea and her unborn child to death and fed hundreds of Christians to the lions. A natural for any actor with a tendency towards ham, as was proved by Charles Laughton's Nero which was laced with effeminacy, and that of Peter Ustinov who combined humour with the sadism and insanity and won himself an Academy Award nomination.

Charles Laughton	*The Sign Of The Cross* (DeMille)	USA, 32
Francis L. Sullivan	*Fiddlers Three* (Watt)	GB, 44
Peter Ustinov	*Quo Vadis* (LeRoy)	USA, 51
Gino Cervi	*O.K. Nero!* (Soldati)	It, 51
Jacques Aubuchon	*The Silver Chalice* (Saville)	USA, 54
Alberto Sordi	*Nero's Big Weekend* (Steno)	It/Fra, 56
Peter Lorre	*The Story Of Mankind* (Allen)	USA, 57
Gianni Rizzo	*The Ten Desperate Men* (Parolini)	It, 63
Vladimir Medar	*Revenge Of The Gladiators* (Malatesta)	It, 63

Note: Emil Jannings featured as Nero in a silent Italian version of *Quo Vadis* (24).

Poppaea has not appeared in all the films about the emperor but has been played by the following actresses: Claudette Colbert in *The Sign Of The Cross*, Patricia Laffan in *Quo Vadis*, Silvana Pampanini in *O.K. Nero!*, Brigitte Bardot in *Nero's Big Weekend*, Margaret Taylor in *The Ten Desperate Men* and Moira Orfei in *Revenge Of The Gladiators*.

Nevsky, Alexander

(1218–1263) Legendary Russian prince who led his country's peasants to great victories against the invading Teutonic Knights during the war between Russia and Germany in the 13th century. Presented as a hero of epic proportions by Sergei Eisenstein in his 1938 film, which included the famous battle on the ice of Lake Peipus.

| Nikolai Cherkasov | *Alexander Nevsky* (Eisenstein) | USSR, 38 |

Nicholas II

(1868–1918) The last emperor of Russia, a Tsar whose ill-fated reign was filled with political blunders, social upheaval, and ended violently in the Bolshevik revolution of 1917. Often a shadowy figure in films made about his turbulent times, he was put into historical perspective in *Nicholas And Alexandra* which focused on the final decay of the Romanovs during the years 1904 to 1918.

Paul Otto	*Rasputin* (Trotz)	Ger, 32
Ralph Morgan	*Rasputin And The Empress* (Boleslawsky)	
		USA, 32
Reinhold Schuenzrel	*1914 : The Last Days Before The War* (Oswald)	
		Ger, 32
Jean Worme	*Rasputin* (L'Herbier)	Fra, 39
Ugo Sasso	*The Nights Of Rasputin* (Chenal)	Fra/It, 60
Paul Daneman	*Oh! What A Lovely War* (Attenborough)	
		GB, 69
Michael Jayston	*Nicholas And Alexandra* (Schaffner)	USA, 71

Note: H. C. Simmons in *Into Her Kingdom* (USA, 26) and Erwin Kalser in *Rasputin And The Holy Devil* (Ger, 28) were among the actors who appeared as Nicholas on the silent screen.

Nichols, Red

(1905–1965) Jazz trumpeter of the 20s and 30s who led several large and small bands, notably 'The Five Pennies', on his rise to the top. Mel Shavelson's sentimental biography included a guest appearance by Louis Armstrong and several soundtrack solos by Nichols. Top numbers: 'Indiana', 'Runnin' Wild' and 'My Blue Heaven'.

Danny Kaye	*The Five Pennies* (Shavelson)	USA, 59

Note: Nichols appeared as himself in the movies *Wabash Avenue* (50), *Disc Jockey* (51) and *The Gene Krupa Story* (59).

Nightingale, Florence

(1820–1910) English nurse and hospital reformer, known as 'The Lady With The Lamp', who founded the modern nursing profession when she set up a hospital with other nurses to tend the wounded in the Crimean War. A natural role for Anna Neagle in the refined, patriotic 50s and the last in her long line of portraying real life British heroines.

Joyce Bland	*Sixty Glorious Years* (Wilcox)	GB, 38
Anna Neagle	*The Lady With The Lamp* (Wilcox)	GB, 51

Note: Elizabeth Risdon starred in Maurice Elvey's silent biography, *Florence Nightingale* (GB, 15).

Nijinsky, Vaslav

(1890–1950) Legendary Russian dancer, an outstanding member of the Diaghilev company and the first man to appear as Petrouchka in Stravinsky's ballet of 1911. Herbert Ross' film hinged on Nijinsky's sexual relationships with impresario Diaghilev and the young Russian girl Romola de Pulsky, a relationship that culminated in Nijinsky's decline and ultimate descent into madness.

George de la Pena	*Nijinsky* (Ross)	USA, 79

Note: The role of Diaghilev was played by Alan Bates in *Nijinsky*.

Nimitz, Admiral Chester W.

(1885–1966) Commander-in-Chief of all US naval forces in the Pacific from December 17, 1941 (when Kimmel was relieved of command) to the end of World War II. An outstanding strategist, he was responsible for re-establishing the power of the American Fleet after the disaster of Pearl Harbour, i.e. at the famous Battle of Midway in 1942.

Selmer Jackson	*Hellcats Of The Navy* (Juran)	USA, 57
Selmer Jackson	*The Gallant Hours* (Montgomery)	USA, 60
Henry Fonda	*Midway* (Smight)	USA, 76
Addison Powell	*MacArthur* (Sargent)	USA, 77

Ninotchka

Garbo's favourite role, a cold Soviet envoy who learns the meaning of laughter and love from a debonair American in Paris (Melvyn Douglas). Twenty years later the same character was again warmed up, this time by impresario Fred Astaire, in the Cole Porter musical *Silk Stockings*.

Greta Garbo	*Ninotchka* (Lubitsch)	USA, 39
Cyd Charisse	*Silk Stockings* (Mamoulian)	USA, 57

Nitribitt, Rosemarie

Frankfurt call girl, no more important than countless others in her sordid trade, but whose murder caused sensational headlines when it was discovered that she included among her clients several leading West German industrialists. Her murder was never solved and started a political scandal that was reflected in two films of the late 50s.

| Nadja Tiller | *The Girl Rosemarie* (Thiele) | Ger, 58 |
| Belinda Lee | *Love Now, Pay Later* (Jugert) | Ger, 59 |

No, Dr.

The first 007 master villain to reach the screen, a handless Chinese scientist who causes havoc among the Western powers when he diverts American rocket missiles through the use of atomic power. His black gloved steel claws allow him the luxury of cigarette smoking, but ultimately let him down when he slides slowly into a bubbling pool of radioactive acid. A key member of the SPECTRE organization, based in the Caribbean. First appeared in print in 1958.

| Joseph Wiseman | *Dr. No* (Young) | GB, 62 |

Nobile, General Umberto

(1885–1978) Italian airship designer whose attempt to reach the North Pole by dirigible in 1928 ended in disaster when the airship crashed in a blizzard and many lives were lost. Amundsen, flying to the rescue, perished in the attempt; Nobile and a handful of survivors were rescued.

| Peter Finch | *The Red Tent* (Kalatozov) | It/USSR, 71 |

Nolan, Gypo

Liam O'Flaherty's tragic, doom-laden police informer who sells his best friend for a £20 reward during the Sinn Fein rebellion of the 20s. The central figure in O'Flaherty's 1925 novel 'The Informer'. Victor McLaglen won an Oscar for his portrait of Nolan in 1935; the third version of the story, *Uptight*, was updated to an all-black Cleveland setting.

Lars Hansen	*The Informer* (Robinson)	GB, 29
Victor McLaglen	*The Informer* (Ford)	USA, 35
Julian Mayfield	*Uptight* (Dassin)	USA, 68

O

Oakley, Annie

(1859–1926) Famed western sharpshooter — a crackshot from the age of 9 — who reigned as a top attraction in Buffalo Bill's Wild West Show for some 17 years. Her feud with vaudeville performer Frank Butler, whom she later married, has been the subject of several movies, i.e. George Stevens' *Annie Oakley* and the MGM musical *Annie Get Your Gun*. Her full name was Phoebe Anne Oakley Mozee. She was partially paralysed by injury in a train wreck in 1902, but continued her sharpshooting after the accident.

Barbara Stanwyck	*Annie Oakley* (Stevens)	USA, 35
Betty Hutton	*Annie Get Your Gun* (Sidney)	USA, 50
Gail Davis	*Alias Jesse James* (McLeod)	USA, 59
Nancy Kovack	*The Outlaws Is Coming* (Maurer)	USA, 65
Angela Douglas	*Carry On Cowboy* (Thomas)	GB, 66
Geraldine Chaplin	*Buffalo Bill And The Indians, or Sitting Bull's History Lesson* (Altman)	USA, 76

Oddjob

Korean bodyguard and chauffeur of Auric Goldfinger — mute, powerful and deadly! A karate expert, he kills by hurling his steel-brimmed bowler hat at the necks of his victims and, on more subtle occasions, by covering the bodies of beautiful girls with gold paint. The physical master of 007, but not the electricity system, as he finds out to his cost when electrocuted in Fort Knox.

Harold Sakata	*Goldfinger* (Hamilton)	GB, 64

Orlac, Stephen

Celebrated concert pianist who has the hands of a murderous psychopath grafted onto his wrists when he is badly mutilated in an accident. A favourite horror character who has grown steadily in popularity since he was first adapted for the screen in 1925. First appeared in Maurice Renard's 1920 novel 'Les Mains d'Orlac'.

Colin Clive	*Mad Love* (Freund)	USA, 35
Mel Ferrer	*The Hands of Orlac* (Greville)	GB/Fra, 60
James Stapleton	*Hands Of A Stranger* (Newt Arnold)	USA, 62

Note: Conrad Veidt was the first actor to appear in the role in Robert Wiene's German silent of 1925.

Othello

The man who 'loved not wisely but too well', a noble Moor who murders his wife Desdemona in a jealous rage after the scheming Iago has cast doubts in his mind about her infidelity. The central figure in Shakespeare's tragedy of 1604. Three distinguished screen performances to date: by Orson Welles (52) who filmed the story among the old Arab citadels of North Africa, Sergei Bondarchuk (55) and Laurence Olivier (65) who repeated for the cameras, his performance at Britain's National Theatre.

John Slater	*Othello* (Mackane)	GB, 46
Orson Welles	*Othello* (Welles)	Mor, 52
Sergei Bondarchuk	*Othello* (Yutkevich)	USSR, 55
Laurence Olivier	*Othello* (Burge)	GB, 65

Note: Paul Harris (as a black jazz pianist) featured as the Othello character in a modern updating of the story, *All Night Long* (62), Richie Havens starred in a loose rock musical adaptation, *Catch My Soul* (73); Emil Jannings played the Moor in a German silent version of 1922.

The innocent Desdemona has been played by Luanna Shaw (46), Suzanne Cloutier (52), Irina Skobtseva (55) and Maggie Smith (65); Marti Stevens featured in *All Night Long*, Season Hubley in *Catch My Soul*.

P

Palmer, Harry

A poor man's 007 but far, far removed from Fleming's super-hero in that he is working-class, unenthusiastic and basically a loser. A liking for good food is just about the only thing he has in common with Bond. Featured in three movies during the 60s, but, like most of 007's competitors, quickly faded from the scene. The first of Len Deighton's novels, 'The Ipcress File' was published in 1962. Palmer remains unnamed in all of Deighton's books.

Michael Caine	*The Ipcress File* (Furie)	GB, 65
Michael Caine	*Funeral In Berlin* (Hamilton)	GB, 66
Michael Caine	*Billion Dollar Brain* (Russell)	GB, 67

Papillon

The nickname (meaning 'Butterfly') of Frenchman Henri Charriere, falsely accused of murder in the 1930s and who survived the horrors of the infamous penal colony on Devil's Island. An indestructible hero-victim, he survived all the system could throw at him and escaped to tell his tale in a novel that became a best-seller the world over.

Steve McQueen	*Papillon* (Schaffner)	USA, 73

Pasteur, Louis

(1822–1895) Dedicated French chemist who succeeded in pasteurizing milk in order to free it from harmful bacteria and also discovered vaccines for anthrax and rabies. A man constantly at odds with his own profession and the subject of the first of Warners' famous screen biographies of the 30s. For his performance as Pasteur, Paul Muni won the best actor Academy Award of 1936.

Sacha Guitry	*Pasteur* (Guitry)	Fra, 35
Paul Muni	*The Story Of Louis Pasteur* (Dieterle)	USA, 36

Patton, General George S.

(1885–1945) Old 'Blood And Guts' to his men, this controversial American general was one of the leaders of the Allied march across France and Germany during the latter stages of World War II. At one time relieved of his command for slapping the face of a soldier suffering from combat fatigue, he later made a decisive intervention in the Battle of the Bulge. Franklin Schaffner's three-hour account of his final years remains one of the most distinguished biographies of a military leader ever to reach the screen.

John Larch	*Miracle Of The Wild Stallions* (Hiller)	USA, 63
Kirk Douglas	*Is Paris Burning?* (Clement)	Fra/USA, 66
George C. Scott	*Patton* (Schaffner)	USA, 70
George Kennedy	*Brass Target* (Hough)	USA, 78

Peace, Charles Frederick

(1832–1879) A man frequently referred to as Britain's most notorious criminal, yet one who has been portrayed only once in sound cinema — by Michael Martin Harvey in 1949. His criminal career lasted for nearly twenty years and included countless burglaries and two murders. In between times he became an accomplished violinist, reciter of monologues, woodweaver, picture framer and pacifist. He ate his pre-execution breakfast with great calm but quickly complained, 'This is bloody rotten bacon!'

Michael Martin Harvey	*The Case Of Charles Peace* (Lee)	GB, 49

Note: Walter Haggar in the 1905 British film *Charles Peace*, and Jeff Barlow in *Charles Peace, King Of Criminals* (1914) both played the role in the silent days.

Pepe-Le-Moko

Parisian jewel thief who finds temporary safety from the police in the Algerian Casbah only to be tempted into the outside world and certain death because of his love for a beautiful woman. As portrayed in the original French film by Duvivier, a doomed tragic figure fighting against authority; as played by Charles Boyer and Tony Martin in the remakes little more than a crook on the run.

Jean Gabin	*Pepe-Le-Moko* (Duvivier)	Fra, 37
Charles Boyer	*Algiers* (Cromwell)	USA, 38
Tony Martin	*Casbah* (Berry)	USA, 48

Peter, St.

Disciple who, after Christ's death on the cross, travelled as a missionary preaching God's word. History has it that in 66 A.D. he was crucified upside down because he believed himself unworthy to suffer the same fate as Jesus. Screen portraits have covered most periods of his life, Finlay Currie featuring as the aged Peter in MGM's *Quo Vadis*.

Finlay Currie	*Quo Vadis* (LeRoy)	USA, 51
Michael Rennie	*The Robe* (Koster)	USA, 53
Michael Rennie	*Demetrius And The Gladiators* (Daves)	USA, 54
Lorne Greene	*The Silver Chalice* (Saville)	USA, 54
Tyler McVey	*The Day Of Triumph* (Pichel / Coyle)	USA, 54
Howard Keel	*The Big Fisherman* (Borzage)	USA, 59
Harry Andrews	*Barabbas* (Fleischer)	It, 62
Settimio Di Porto	*The Gospel According to St. Matthew* (Pasolini) It/ Fra, 64
Gary Raymond	*The Greatest Story Ever Told* (Stevens)	USA, 65
Antonio Vilar	*The Redeemer* (Breen)	Spa/USA, 65
Jean Clarieux	*The Milky Way* (Bunuel)	Fra/It, 69
Paul Smith	*The Gospel Road* (Elfstrom)	USA, 73
James Farentino	*Jesus Of Nazareth* (Zeffirelli)	GB, 77

Note: Philip Toubus featured as Peter in *Jesus Christ, Superstar* (USA, 73); Ernest Torrence played the disciple in DeMille's silent *King Of Kings* (USA, 27).

Petrovich, Porfiri

Wily Russian police inspector who patiently breaks down the will of the haunted murderer Raskolnikov in 'Crime And Punishment'. A master of psychological observation, he is the cat figure in Dostoievsky's famous cat and mouse crime story and simply awaits the confession he knows will come. The performance of Frank Silvera in the 1959 updating, *Crime And Punishment, USA*, is one of the most accomplished interpretations of the role. Dostoievsky's novel was published in 1866.

Harry Baur	*Crime And Punishment* (Chenal)	Fra, 35
Edward Arnold	*Crime And Punishment* (von Sternberg)	USA, 35
Sigurd Wallen	*Crime And Punishment* (Faustman)	Swe, 45
Jean Gabin	*Crime And Punishment* (Lampin)	Fra, 56
Pelegri	*Pickpocket* (Bresson)	Fra, 59
Frank Silvera	*Crime And Punishment, USA* (Sanders)	USA, 59
Innokenti Smoktounovski	*Crime And Punishment* (Kulidjanov)	USSR, 70

Note: Andrei Gromov in the Russian 1910 adaptation and Pavel Pavlov in Robert Wiene's 1923 German film both appeared in silent versions of Dostoievsky's novel.

Petruchio

The wily opportunist who tames and weds the fiery man-eater Katharina in Shakespeare's 'The Taming Of The Shrew' (1594). Douglas Fairbanks portrayed him (opposite real-life wife Mary Pickford) in the first talking screen version of a Shakespearean play; Richard Burton roared his way through the part in Zeffirelli's opulent production of 1967. Elizabeth Taylor, then Mrs. Burton, fought tooth and nail to get on even terms.

Douglas Fairbanks	*The Taming Of The Shrew*	(Taylor)	USA, 29
Miklos Hajmassy	*The Taming Of The Shrew*	(Banky)	Hung, 43
Alberto Closas	*The Taming Of The Shrew*	(Roman)	Fra/Spa, 55
Richard Burton	*The Taming Of The Shrew*	(Zeffirelli)	USA/It, 67

Note: Katharina has been played by Mary Pickford (29), Enni Buttykay (43), Carmen Sevilla (55) and Elizabeth Taylor (67).

In Cole Porter's musical *Kiss Me Kate* (53), Howard Keel and Kathryn Grayson featured as a married couple whose offstage lives intertwine with their performances in 'The Taming Of The Shrew'. Snatches of Shakespearean dialogue combined with such classic Porter songs as 'So In Love', 'Too Darn Hot' and 'Wunderbar'.

The Phantom Of The Opera

Gaston Leroux's classical figure of horror, a demented musician with a disfigured face who haunts the underground caves of the Paris Opera House and secretly aids a young prima donna in her career. Known as Erik in the classic silent version of 1925, Enrique in 1943, The Phantom in 1962 and Winslow in Brian DePalma's rock updating of 1974. Gaston Leroux's novel was first published in 1911.

Lon Chaney	*The Phantom Of The Opera*	(Julian)	USA, 25
Claude Rains	*The Phantom Of The Opera*	(Lubin)	USA, 43
Herbert Lom	*The Phantom Of The Opera*	(Fisher)	GB, 62
William Finley	*Phantom Of The Paradise*	(DePalma)	USA, 74

Piaf, Edith

(1915–1963) The French singer (real name, Edith Gassion) whose life was described by Sacha Guitry as being so sad it was almost too beautiful to be true. Raised in a brothel and blind until she was seven, she was noisy, demanding, egotistical and possessor of that magical talent which only the greatest artistes enjoy. Primarily a stage performer, she appeared in just a handful of films (including Renoir's *French Can Can*) and made famous such songs as 'La Vie en Rose' and 'Je ne Regrette Rien'. Guy Casaril's film covered her early years; Betty Mars mimed the songs to Brigitte Ariel's performance.

Brigitte Ariel	*The Sparrow Of Pigalle* (Casaril)	Fra, 74

Picasso, Pablo

(1881–1973) Prolific Spanish-born painter, creator of Cubism and generally considered to be the greatest of the twentieth century masters. The Swedish film, *The Adventures Of Picasso*, paid affectionate homage in a crazy, comic vein; Clouzot's 75-minute documentary, *The Mystery Of Picasso*, observed the artist at work on some 15 original pictures, especially painted for the cameras.

Himself	*The Mystery Of Picasso* (Clouzot)	Fra, 56
Goesta Ekman	*The Adventures Of Picasso* (Danielsson)	Swe, 78

Pickwick, Samuel

Benign founder of the adventurous Pickwick Club in Charles Dickens' novel 'The Pickwick Papers', published in 1836–37. The first of the author's optimistic heroes, jovial, benevolent, cast in the Micawber mould and only once portrayed on the sound screen, although the novel was filmed twice in the silent days.

James Hayter	*The Pickwick Papers* (Langley)	GB, 53

Note: John Bunny in the three-part *The Pickwick Papers* (GB, 13) and Fred Volpe in *The Adventures Of Mr. Pickwick* (GB, 21) were the actors who played Pickwick on the silent screen.

Pilate, Pontius

The Roman governor of Judaea who presided over the trial of Jesus and eventually ordered his crucifixion, despite being unable to find him guilty of any crime. A challenging, if brief role in which many actors have excelled, notably Rod Steiger in Zeffirelli's *Jesus Of Nazareth*. Telly Savalas earned himself world fame by shaving his head for the part in George Stevens' *The Greatest Story Ever Told*.

Basil Gill	*The Wandering Jew* (Elvey)	GB, 33
Basil Rathbone	*The Last Days Of Pompeii* (Schoedsack)	USA, 35
Jean Gabin	*Golgotha* (Duvivier)	Fra, 35
Richard Boone	*The Robe* (Koster)	USA, 53
Basil Sydney	*Salome* (Dieterle)	USA, 53
Lowell Gilmore	*The Day Of Triumph* (Pichel/Coyle)	USA, 54
Frank Thring	*Ben-Hur* (Wyler)	USA, 59
Hurd Hatfield	*King Of Kings* (Ray)	USA, 61
Jean Marais	*Ponzio Pilato* (Callegari)	It/Fra, 61
Arthur Kennedy	*Barabbas* (Fleischer)	It, 62
Alessandro Tasca	*The Gospel According To St. Matthew* (Pasolini)	It/Fra, 64
Telly Savalas	*The Greatest Story Ever Told* (Stevens)	USA, 65

Antonio Vilar	*The Redeemer* (Breen)	USA/Spa, 65
Ljuba Tadic	*The Master And Margarita* (Petrovic)	Yug/It, 72
Donald Pleasence	*The Passover Plot* (Campus)	Israel/USA, 76
Rod Steiger	*Jesus Of Nazareth* (Zeffirelli)	GB, 77

Note: Barry Dennen featured as the Pilate character in *Jesus Christ, Superstar* (73); Werner Krauss (Ger, 23), Victor Varconi (USA, 27) and Charles McCaffrey (USA, 28) all appeared in the role in silent productions.

Pip

The simple name for one of Charles Dickens' most famous characters, a young country blacksmith who becomes a gentleman in London society through the generosity of an unknown benefactor. Despite the drama of his adult life, he is best remembered for his frightening childhood encounter with the convict Magwitch on the lonely marshes of Kent. The central figure in Dickens' 1861 novel 'Great Expectations'; impeccably played by Anthony Wager (as the boy Pip) and John Mills (as the adult Pip) in David Lean's classic film of 1946.

As a boy:

George Breakston	*Great Expectations* (Walker)	USA, 34
Anthony Wager	*Great Expectations* (Lean)	GB, 46
Simon Gipps-Kent	*Great Expectations* (Hardy)	GB, 75

As a man:

Phillips Holmes	*Great Expectations* (Walker)	USA, 34
John Mills	*Great Expectations* (Lean)	GB, 46
Michael York	*Great Expectations* (Hardy)	GB, 75

Note: Jack Pickford in Robert Vignola's 1916 American version and Martin Herzberg in the 1922 Danish film of A. W. Sandberg both featured as the boy Pip on the silent screen.

Pitt, William

(1759–1806) For many historians, the greatest of English Prime Ministers, a major reformer who enjoyed one of the longest ministries in English history — from 1783 to 1801 and again between 1804–5. Carol Reed's biography followed his career in the days preceding and during the first phase of the Napoleonic wars and drew strong parallels with Britain's fight against the Nazis.

Robert Donat	*The Young Mr. Pitt* (Reed)	GB, 42
Anthony Nicholls	*The Laughing Lady* (Stein)	GB, 46
Paul Rogers	*Beau Brummel* (Bernhardt)	GB, 54
Anthony Stuart	*Austerlitz* (Gance)	Fra/It/Yug, 60

Note: Ernest Thesiger featured as Pitt in Maurice Elvey's 1918 British production, *Nelson*.

Poe, Edgar Allan

(1809–1849) American poet and short story writer whose tortured private life was reflected in many of his macabre stories of the supernatural — 'The Black Cat', 'The Fall Of The House Of Usher', 'The Tell-Tale Heart', etc. Credited with establishing the form of the modern short story, Poe has been featured many times on screen, i.e. as a struggling writer in *The Loves Of Edgar Allan Poe*, an alcoholic poet in *The Man With A Cloak*, and an explorer of the occult in *The Spectre Of Edgar Allan Poe*. He died of exhaustion and alcoholism in 1849.

John Shepperd	*The Loves Of Edgar Allan Poe* (Lachman)	USA, 42
Joseph Cotten	*The Man With A Cloak* (Markle)	USA, 51
Laurence Payne	*The Tell-Tale Heart* (Morris)	GB, 60
Robert Walker	*The Spectre Of Edgar Allan Poe* (Quandour)	
		USA, 74

Note: John Shepperd who appeared in the 1942 film later became known as Shepperd Strudwick.

Poirot, Hercule

Dapper Belgian detective who features in more than 40 Agatha Christie novels. Almost a comic figure — fastidious, short and sporting a waxed moustache — he solves his cases through a fine intellect and massive ego. Until Finney's portrayal in *Murder On The Orient Express*, an unappealing character on screen, although Charles Laughton and Francis L. Sullivan were both admirable stage Poirots during the 30s.

Austin Trevor	*Alibi* (Hiscott)	GB, 31
Austin Trevor	*Black Coffee* (Hiscott)	GB, 31
Austin Trevor	*Lord Edgware Dies* (Edwards)	GB, 34
Tony Randall	*The Alphabet Murders* (Tashlin)	GB, 66
Albert Finney	*Murder On The Orient Express* (Lumet)	GB, 74
Peter Ustinov	*Death On The Nile* (Guillermin)	GB, 78

Pollyanna

Heroine of Eleanor Porter's 1913 novel; a young orphan girl who goes to live with her wealthy aunt in a small New England town and changes the lives of everyone she comes in contact with, primarily because of her uncanny knack of always looking on the bright side of things. The most delightful optimist in modern literature.

Hayley Mills   *Pollyanna* (Swift)   USA, 60

Note: Mary Pickford played Pollyanna on the silent screen in a version
directed by Paul Powell in 1920.

Poppins, Mary

The most famous fictional nanny of them all, P. L. Travers' magical
child-minder who floats from the skies, complete with umbrella and
carpetbag, spreading delight and wisdom all over early twentieth
century London. In her own words, 'practically perfect'. Just one screen
portrayal — by Julie Andrews in the classic film of Walt Disney; he was
kept waiting for 16 years (1944–1960) before securing the screen rights!

Julie Andrews   *Mary Poppins* (Stevenson)   USA, 64

Porter, Cole

(1892–1964) Elegant, witty American lyricist/composer whose stage
shows — 'Anything Goes', 'Kiss Me Kate', 'Silk Stockings' — rank with
some of the best ever produced on Broadway. Seriously disabled as a
result of a riding accident, he continued to write into the 50s and was
played and sung ('You're The Top') by Cary Grant in Warners' 1946
biography *Night And Day*. Among his film scores: *You'll Never Get Rich*,
High Society, *Les Girls*. Among his hit songs: 'You Do Something To Me',
'I Get A Kick Out Of You', 'Begin The Beguine'.

Cary Grant   *Night And Day* (Curtiz)   USA, 46
Ron Randell   *Kiss Me Kate* (Sidney)   USA, 53

Porter, Jimmy

The original 'angry young man' of John Osborne's 1957 stage play
'Look Back In Anger', a working-class hero whose rebellion against the
establishment emerged as a powerful comment on the mood of Britain
in the mid-50s. A star part if ever there was one, although Richard
Burton's screen Porter was too mature and less convincing than those
of the younger stage actors who had earlier featured in the role.

Richard Burton   *Look Back In Anger* (Richardson)   GB, 59

Porthos

The most jovial of Dumas' 'Three Musketeers', good-hearted, large in
stature and a frequent companion of D'Artagnan in his many screen
adventures. The burly frames of Alan Hale and Alan Hale, Jr. filled the

role on several occasions, just as they did for the part of Little John in the Robin Hood spectaculars. In recent years, British actor Frank Finlay has provided an even more swaggering and ebullient Porthos in the two Musketeer films of Richard Lester.

Stanley J. Sandford	*The Iron Mask* (Dwan)	USA, 29
Moroni Olsen	*The Three Musketeers* (Lee)	USA, 35
Russell Hicks	*The Three Musketeers* (Dwan)	USA, 39
Alan Hale	*The Man In The Iron Mask* (Whale)	USA, 39
Gig Young	*The Three Musketeers* (Sidney)	USA, 48
Mel Archer	*Sword Of D'Artagnan* (Boetticher)	USA, 52
Alan Hale, Jr.	*Lady In The Iron Mask* (Murphy)	USA, 52
Gino Cervi	*The Three Musketeers* (Hunebelle)	Fra, 53
Sebastian Cabot	*The Knights Of The Queen* (Bolognini)	It, 54
Bernard Woringer	*The Three Musketeers* (Borderie)	Fra, 61
Mario Petri	*The Secret Mark Of D'Artagnan* (Marcellini)	It/Fra, 62
Livio Lorenzon	*Zorro And The Three Musketeers* (Capuano)	It, 63
Walter Barnes	*Revenge Of The Musketeers* (Tulli)	It, 64
Frank Finlay	*The Three Musketeers* (Lester)	Panama/Spa, 74
Frank Finlay	*The Four Musketeers* (Lester)	Panama/Spa, 75
Alan Hale, Jr.	*The Fifth Musketeer* (Annakin)	Austria, 79

Note: Moroni Olsen repeated his role, as the aged Porthos, in *At Sword's Point* (52), a film in which Alan Hale, Jr. played his son; on the silent screen, George Siegmann featured in *The Three Musketeers* (21) and Martinelli in Henri Berger's two French serials, *The Three Musketeers* (22) and *Twenty Years After* (22).

Presley, Elvis

(1935–1977) The king of 'Rock n' Roll' and the man who started it all back in the 50s with a succession of hits that included 'Heartbreak Hotel', 'Hound Dog', 'It's Now Or Never' and 'All Shook Up'. His film career, which began in 1956 with *Love Me Tender*, spanned fifteen years and included over thirty movies. Denis Sanders' documentary *Elvis: That's The Way It Is* (70) looked at Presley off-stage; John Carpenter's more recent biography featured Kurt Russell.

Kurt Russell	*Elvis — The Movie* (Carpenter)	USA, 79

Purvis, Melvin

Midwest FBI chief who challenged J. Edgar Hoover as a headline hero of the 30s when he shot down John Dillinger in Chicago. His career was brief, however, and after leaving the bureau he eventually committed suicide, supposedly with the very gun that killed Dillinger. He figured in several movies of the 70s which revealed his vain, glory-seeking character to be little different from those of the gangsters he tracked down.

Myron Healy	*Guns Don't Argue* (Karn/Kahn)	USA, 55
Ben Johnson	*Dillinger* (Milius)	USA, 73
Dale Robertson	*The Legend Of Machine Gun Kelly* (Curtis)	USA, 74
Michael Sacks	*The Private Files Of J. Edgar Hoover* (Cohen)	USA, 78
Alan Vint	*The Lady In Red* (Teague)	USA, 79

Note: *The Legend Of Machine Gun Kelly* was originally a TV movie entitled *Melvin Purvis G-Man*; Robertson appeared in a subsequent TV movie, *Kansas City Massacre*, which was not released theatrically.

Pyle, Ernie

(1900–1945) American newspaper correspondent of World War II, much admired by soldiers and civilians for the honesty and warmth of his dispatches from the front line. A Pulitzer Prize winner for his vivid eyewitness accounts, he covered many campaigns in North Africa and Europe before being killed by Japanese machine gun fire on an island near Okinawa. Portrayed on screen by Burgess Meredith in Wellman's *The Story Of G.I. Joe*.

Burgess Meredith	*The Story of G.I. Joe* (Wellman)	USA, 45

Q

Quartermain, Allan

The most famous white hunter of them all and the one on which many subsequent intrepid adventurers have been based. Just two portrayals on screen, both in Rider Haggard's *King Solomon's Mines* in which he leads a search for legendary diamonds in darkest Africa.

Cedric Hardwicke	*King Solomon's Mines*	(Stevenson)	GB, 37
Stewart Granger	*King Solomon's Mines*	(Bennett/Marton)	USA, 50

Note: George Montgomery (as Harry, son of Allan) played Quartermain in Kurt Neumann's 1959 production *Watusi*.

Quatermass, Professor Bernard

Fictional British rocket scientist, first created by Nigel Kneale for BBC TV and then transferred to the movie screen for three above average adventures against beings from outer space. Americanised to the point of rigidity by Brian Donlevy; more accurately played by Andrew Keir in the last, and best in the series, *Quatermass And The Pit*.

Brian Donlevy	*The Quatermass Experiment* (Guest)	GB, 55
Brian Donlevy	*Quatermass II* (Guest)	GB, 57
Andrew Keir	*Quatermass And The Pit* (Ward Baker)	GB, 67

Quilp, Daniel

The fiendish, deformed moneylender in Charles Dickens' 'The Old Curiosity Shop' (1840). Cunning, malicious and permanently leching after the innocent Little Nell, he remains the one Dickensian character who is forever overplayed on screen. The addition of music and lyrics to the only contemporary version of the story, *Mister Quilp*, simply emphasised the problems instead of diminishing them.

Hay Petrie	*The Old Curiosity Shop* (Bentley)	GB, 35
Anthony Newley	*Mister Quilp* (Tuchner)	GB, 75

Note: Thomas Bentley, who directed the 1935 adaptation, filmed *The Old Curiosity Shop* three times, E. Felton (GB, 13) and Pino Conti (GB, 21) appearing as Quilp in his earlier versions.

Greta Garbo performing her exotic temple dance in MGM's *Mata Hari* (1932).

Agatha Christie's spinster sleuth, Miss Marple, played here by the one
and only Margaret Rutherford in *Murder Ahoy* (MGM, 1964).

Miss Christie's other fictional detective, the Belgian Hercule Poirot (Peter Ustinov) investigating in Egypt in *Death On The Nile* (EMI, 1978).

A less subtle crime buster! Ben Johnson as FBI chief Melvin Purvis in *Dillinger* (American International, 1973).

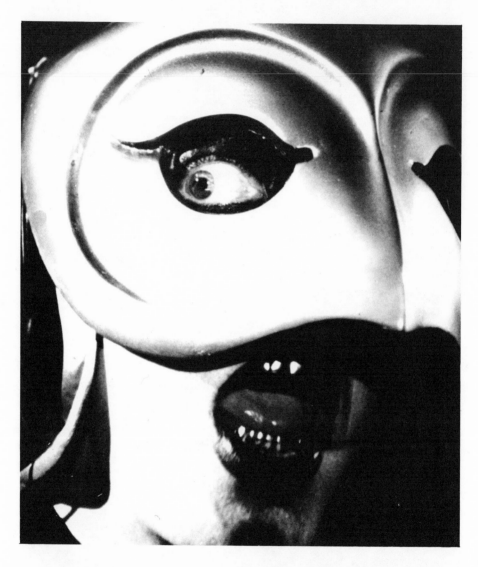

A new look Phantom Of The Opera. William Finley as the disfigured composer in the 1974 rock updating *Phantom Of The Paradise* (Twentieth Century-Fox).

Steve McQueen as long term Devil's Island prisoner, *Papillon* (Columbia, 1973).

President Theodore Roosevelt as portrayed by Brian Keith in John Milius' *The Wind And The Lion* (Columbia/MGM, 1975).

Rudolph Rassendyll (Stewart Granger) and Rupert of Hentzau (James Mason) battle it out at the climax of the 1952 version of *The Prisoner Of Zenda* (MGM).

Charles Laughton repeats his Oscar winning role as Henry VIII in MGM's *Young Bess* (1953).

Superman, 1978 style! Christopher Reeve as the flying man of steel in Richard Donner's *Superman* (Warners).

Tarzan, 30s style. Johnny Weismuller who starred as the Ape Man in a dozen jungle adventures at MGM and RKO.

Kurt Russell in *Elvis — The Movie* (Made for TV, 1979).

Secret agent Violette Szabo (Virginia McKenna) trapped by the Germans in occupied France. A scene from *Carve Her Name With Pride* (Rank, 1958).

The beginning of the end. Paul Newman and Robert Redford prepare to face their last battle in *Butch Cassidy And The Sundance Kid* (Twentieth Century-Fox, 1969).

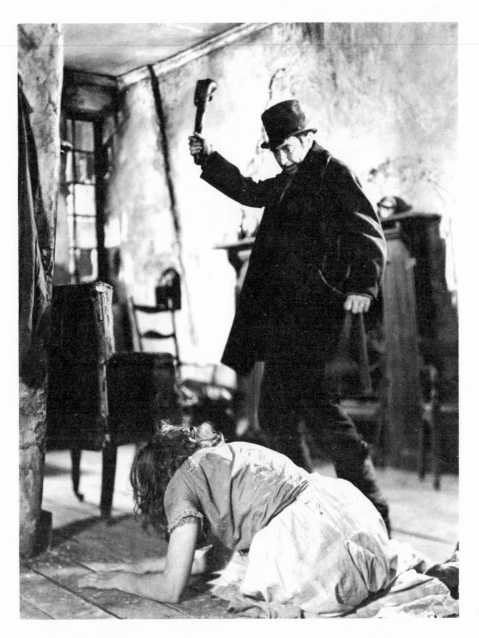

Robert Newton's Bill Sikes batters Nancy to death in David Lean's 1948 classic *Oliver Twist* (Rank).

Preacher Jose Ferrer discovers that the flesh is more attractive than the word in the 1953 production, *Miss Sadie Thompson* (Columbia). Rita Hayworth is the struggling Sadie.

Keir Dullea as the imprisoned Marquis De Sade in Cy Endfield's 1969
film, *De Sade*, for American International.

William Powell as American showman Florenz Ziegfeld in the Oscar-winning movie of 1936, *The Great Ziegfeld* (MGM).

Rudolf Nureyev recreates the famous tango scene in 'The Four Horsemen Of The Apocalypse' in Ken Russell's *Valentino* (United Artists, 1977).

Orson Welles as Cardinal Wolsey in *A Man For All Seasons* (Columbia, 1966).

A bearded Paul Muni in one of his most distinguished portrayals in the 1937 Warner production, *The Life Of Emile Zola*.

R

Raffles

Debonair British jewel thief who steals 'purely for the sport of it all' and lives by his wits and skill in absolute luxury in his expensive rooms in London's Albany. An old-style gentleman hero, personified on screen by Ronald Colman and David Niven, but nowadays somewhat out of fashion, although a TV series starring Anthony Valentine enjoyed recent success in England. Created by Ernest William Hornung in 'The Amateur Cracksman' in 1899.

Ronald Colman	*Raffles* (D'Arrast/Fitzmaurice)	USA, 30
George Barraud	*The Return Of Raffles* (Markham)	GB, 32
David Niven	*Raffles* (Wood)	USA, 40

Note: John Barrymore (USA, 17) and House Peters (USA, 25) both appeared as Raffles on the silent screen.

Raleigh, Sir Walter

(1552–1618) English explorer and courtier, a favourite of Elizabeth I, who fell from favour because of his seduction of one of her maids of honour. The affair formed the basis of the 1955 CinemaScope production, *The Virgin Queen*.

Vincent Price	*The Private Lives Of Elizabeth And Essex* (Curtiz)	USA, 39
Richard Todd	*The Virgin Queen* (Koster)	USA, 55
Edward Everett Horton	*The Story Of Mankind* (Allen)	USA, 57

Raskolnikov

One of the most tormented characters in all fiction, a brilliant young student who meticulously carries out the murder of an old pawnbroker only to find that the memory of the killing haunts him day and night. Dogged by the deceptively patient Inspector Petrovich, he finally confesses and is saved by the love of a young girl. Dostoievsky's original novel, 'Crime And Punishment' was set in 19th century St. Petersburg. Locations have varied in the different screen versions.

Pierre Blanchar	*Crime And Punishment*	(Chenal)	Fra, 35
Peter Lorre	*Crime And Punishment*	(von Sternberg)	
			USA, 35
Hampe Faustman	*Crime And Punishment*	(Faustman)	Swe, 45
Robert Hossein	*Crime And Punishment*	(Lampin)	Fra, 56
Martin Lassalle	*Pickpocket* (Bresson)		Fra, 59
George Hamilton	*Crime And Punishment, USA*	(Sanders)	
			USA, 59
Gueorgui Taratorkine	*Crime And Punishment*	(Kulidjanov)	
			USSR, 70

Note: V. Krivtsov (USSR, 10) and Grigori Khmara (Ger, 23) both appeared in silent screen versions of the novel.

Rasputin

(1871–1916) Notorious Russian peasant monk who acquired great influence over Empress Alexandra in the Russian Imperial Court when he saved her son Alexis several times from near-fatal attacks of haemophilia. The screen has concentrated more on his lecherous traits than on his supposed healing powers and also on his remarkable death, when he was given enough cyanide to kill six men but was still alive when thrown into the River Neva. Film portraits have been variable, although Conrad Veidt, Lionel Barrymore, Christopher Lee and, more recently, Tom Baker, have all revelled in the part.

Conrad Veidt	*Rasputin* (Trotz)		Ger, 32
Lionel Barrymore	*Rasputin And The Empress*	(Boleslawsky)	
			USA, 32
Harry Baur	*Rasputin* (L'Herbier)		Fra, 39
Pierre Brasseur	*Rasputin* (Combret)		It/Fra, 54
Edmund Purdom	*The Nights Of Rasputin*	(Chenal)	
			Fra/It, 60
Christopher Lee	*Rasputin — The Mad Monk*	(Sharp)	GB, 66
Gert Frobe	*I Killed Rasputin* (Hossein)		Fra/It, 67
Wes Carter	*Why Russians Are Revolting* (Sullivan)		USA, 70
Tom Baker	*Nicholas And Alexandra* (Schaffner)		USA, 71

Note: Montagu Love in *Rasputin The Black Monk* (USA, 17), Demetrius Alexis in *The Red Dance* (USA, 28) and Nikolai Malikoff in *Rasputin And The Holy Devil* (Ger, 28) all appeared in the role on the silent screen.

Rassendyll, Rudolph

Noble, self-sacrificing English hero who assumes the guise of his double, the abducted King Rudolf of Ruritania, in order to prevent a take-over of the throne. The central character in Anthony Hope's romantic adventure 'The Prisoner Of Zenda' (1896), never better realised on screen than by Ronald Colman in John Cromwell's definitive 1937 film for Selznick.

Ronald Colman	*The Prisoner Of Zenda*	(Cromwell)	USA, 37
Stewart Granger	*The Prisoner Of Zenda*	(Thorpe)	USA, 52
Peter Sellers	*The Prisoner Of Zenda*	(Quine)	USA, 79

Note: The character was spoofed by Tony Curtis in a duelling episode with Ross Martin in *The Great Race* (65) and by Malcolm McDowall (as Flashman) in his duel with Alan Bates in *Royal Flash* (75).

Rassendyll was played by James K. Hackett (USA, 13), Henry Ainley (GB, 15) and Lewis Stone (USA, 22) in silent versions of *The Prisoner Of Zenda*; by Henry Ainley (GB, 15) and Bert Lytell (USA, 23) in *Rupert Of Hentzau*.

Rembrandt

(1609–1669) Dutch painter who achieved greatness with his series of self-portraits and proved that quality could be synonymous with quantity by providing over 650 oil paintings, 2000 drawings and 300 etchings! As far as films are concerned the quality of performance has been more varied. Laughton's Rembrandt in Korda's film of 1936 was only fitfully impressive; Frans Stelling's performance in the 1978 Dutch production treated the character more as a soap opera figure than an artist of genius.

Charles Laughton	*Rembrandt*	(Korda)	GB, 36
Ewald Balser	*Rembrandt*	(Steinhoff)	Ger, 42
Frans Stelling	*Rembrandt-Feigt 1669*	(Stelling)	Holl, 78

Reuter, Paul Julius

(1816–1899) German-born founder of the famous Reuters News Agency (set up in London in 1851), the first organization to transmit commercial news by telegraph. The subject of the final film biography made by William Dieterle at Warners.

Edward G. Robinson	*A Dispatch From Reuters*	(Dieterle)	USA, 40

Rhodes, Cecil

(1853–1902) British financier and statesman who made a fortune at the Kimberley diamond diggings and succeeded in opening up that part of Africa which later became known as Rhodesia. Prime Minister of Cape

Colony from 1890 to 1896, he was played by Walter Huston in a British screen biography of the mid-thirties.

| Walter Huston | *Rhodes Of Africa* (Viertel) | GB, 36 |
| Wyndham Goldie | *Victoria The Great* (Wilcox) | GB, 37 |

Richard I

(1157–1199) The son of Henry II and Eleanor of Aquitaine; something of a whitewashed historical figure whose feats in the Third Crusade were often over-glamourized and whose character was never quite as noble as inferred in the Robin Hood films. Anthony Hopkins featured as the ambitious Prince Richard in *The Lion In Winter*, Richard Harris as a weary, ageing monarch in *Robin And Marian*.

Henry Wilcoxon	*The Crusades* (DeMille)	USA, 35
Ian Hunter	*The Adventures Of Robin Hood* (Curtiz/Keighley)	USA, 38
Norman Wooland	*Ivanhoe* (Thorpe)	GB, 52
Patrick Barr	*The Story Of Robin Hood And His Merrie Men* (Annakin)	GB, 52
George Sanders	*King Richard And The Crusaders* (Butler)	USA, 54
Patrick Holt	*Men Of Sherwood Forest* (Guest)	GB, 54
Salah Zulficar	*Saladin* (Sebal)	Egy, 63
Anthony Hopkins	*The Lion In Winter* (Harvey)	GB, 68
Frankie Howerd	*Up The Chastity Belt* (Kellett)	GB, 71
Richard Harris	*Robin And Marian* (Lester)	USA, 76

Note: A. Scott Craven in *Ivanhoe* (USA, 13) and Wallace Beery in both *Robin Hood* (USA, 22) and *Richard The Lion-Hearted* (USA, 23) were among the actors who played Richard on the silent screen.

Richard III

(1452–1485) England's last Plantagenet king, a ruthless hunchback who allegedly schemed his way to the throne via several murders including those of the boy princes, Edward and Richard, in the Tower Of London. Powerfully represented by Shakespeare in his 1594 stage play, transferred to the screen by Olivier who duly made his desperate cry, 'A horse! A horse! My kingdom for a horse!' when on the losing end at the Battle of Bosworth.

Basil Rathbone	*Tower Of London* (Lee)	USA, 39
Laurence Olivier	*Richard III* (Olivier)	GB, 55
Vincent Price	*Tower Of London* (Corman)	USA, 62

Note: Frank Benson (GB, 11) and Frederick Warde (USA, 13) both appeared in silent versions of Shakespeare's *Richard III*.

Rice, Archie

Almost as famous a John Osborne creation as Jimmy Porter, a third-rate music hall performer on the skids who drags down all the people around him to his own shabby level. A sordid, pathetic character, especially written for Laurence Olivier who played him with great skill, both on stage (1957) and on screen. The 1975 remake switched the action from the Suez crisis days in Britain to the America of 1944.

| Laurence Olivier | *The Entertainer* (Richardson) | GB, 60 |
| Jack Lemmon | *The Entertainer* (Wrye) | USA, 75 |

Richelieu, Cardinal

(1585–1642) Powerful chief minister to Louis XIII in 17th century France. In the history books, a man largely responsible for the downfall of Protestantism and who greatly strengthened the French monarchy; in the films about the musketeers, always the chief villain, scheming to extend his influence over the weak king and enjoying the physical pleasures of Milady de Winter. Vincent Price and an oversized Charlton Heston are among those who have plotted against D'Artagnan and company. George Arliss appeared in a screen biography of 1935.

Nigel De Brulier	*The Iron Mask* (Dwan)	USA, 29
Osgood Perkins	*Madame DuBarry* (Dieterle)	USA, 34
Nigel De Brulier	*The Three Musketeers* (Lee)	USA, 35
George Arliss	*Cardinal Richelieu* (Lee)	USA, 35
Raymond Massey	*Under The Red Robe* (Seastrom)	GB, 37
Nigel De Brulier	*The Man In The Iron Mask* (Whale)	USA, 39
Miles Mander	*The Three Musketeers* (Dwan)	USA, 39
Aime Clariond	*Monsieur Vincent* (Cloche)	Fra, 47
Vincent Price	*The Three Musketeers* (Sidney)	USA, 48
Paul Cavanaugh	*Sword Of D'Artagnan* (Boetticher)	USA, 52
Renaud-Mary	*The Three Musketeers* (Hunebelle)	Fra, 53
Denis d'Ines	*Mistress DuBarry* (Christian-Jaque)	Fra/It, 54
Daniel Sorano	*The Three Musketeers* (Borderie)	Fra, 61
Rafael Rivelles	*Cyrano And D'Artagnan* (Gance)	Fra, 62
Massimo Serato	*The Secret Mark Of D'Artagnan* (Marcellini)	Fra/It, 62
Christopher Logue	*The Devils* (Russell)	GB, 71
Charlton Heston	*The Three Musketeers* (Lester)	Panama/Spa, 74
Charlton Heston	*The Four Musketeers* (Lester)	Panama/Spa, 75

Note: Silent portrayals of Richelieu included those by Murdoch MacQuarrie in Allan Dwan's *Richelieu* (USA, 14), Nigel De Brulier in the 1921 version of *The Three Musketeers*, Robert B. Mantell in *Under The Red Robe* (USA, 23) and Edward Connelly in *Bardeleys The Magnificent* (USA, 26).

Richthoven, Baron Manfred von

(1882–1918) The most famous German air ace of World War I, noted for his high number of aerial victories (80) and the scourge of the Allies in his deadly red triplane. Roger Corman's 1971 film traced Richthoven's career from 1916 to 1918, alternating his story with that of Roy Brown, the Canadian pilot who eventually shot him down in the last year of the war.

William von Brincken	*Hell's Angels* (Hughes)	USA, 30
Carl Schell	*The Blue Max* (Guillermin)	GB, 66
Ingo Mogendorf	*Darling Lili* (Edwards)	USA, 70
John Phillip Law	*The Red Baron* (Corman)	USA, 71

Note: In *The Red Baron*, Roy Brown was played by Don Stroud.

Rimsky-Korsakov, Nikolai

(1844–1908) Russian composer, best known for his symphonic suites 'Scheherazade' and 'Capriccio Espagnol' and operas based on Russian legends. His native country afforded him a respectful tribute in the early 50s; Hollywood offered *Song Of Scheherazade* and an affair with dance-hall girl Yvonne de Carlo who, according to Universal's scriptwriters, inspired his greatest music. Universal also threw in Eve Arden who gingered up the proceedings by referring to the composer as 'the Russian with two names'.

Jean Pierre Aumont	*Song Of Scheherazade* (Reisch)	USA, 47
David Leonard	*Song Of My Heart* (Glazer)	USA, 48
Grigori Belov	*Rimsky-Korsakov* (Roshal/Kazansky)	
		USSR, 52

Robin Hood

Legendary British outlaw who, according to ancient ballads, stole from the rich to give to the poor during the tyrannical reign of Prince John in 12th century England. As a traditional portrait, Errol Flynn's handsome pre-war swashbuckler will probably never be surpassed; more recently, however, Sean Connery shattered the legend with his ageing outlaw in *Robin And Marian* and brought realism to a character who had previously been reserved solely for escapists and the young in heart.

Errol Flynn	*The Adventures Of Robin Hood* (Curtiz/Keighley)	USA, 38
Russell Hicks	*The Bandit Of Sherwood Forest* (Sherman/Levin)	USA, 46
Jon Hall	*Prince Of Thieves* (Bretherton)	USA, 48
Robert Clarke	*Tales Of Robin Hood* (Tinling)	USA, 51
Harold Warrender	*Ivanhoe* (Thorpe)	GB, 52

Richard Todd	*The Story Of Robin Hood And His Merrie Men*	
	(Annakin)	GB, 52
Don Taylor	*Men Of Sherwood Forest* (Guest)	GB, 54
Richard Greene	*Sword Of Sherwood Forest* (Fisher)	GB, 60
Barrie Ingham	*A Challenge For Robin Hood*	
	(Pennington Richards)	GB, 67
Hugh Paddick	*Up The Chastity Belt* (Kellett)	GB, 71
David Warbeck	*Wolfshead: The Legend Of Robin Hood* (Hough)	
		GB, 73
Brian Bedford	*Robin Hood* (Disney)	USA, 73
Boris Khmielnitski	*Robin Hood* (Tarassov)	USSR, 76
Sean Connery	*Robin And Marian* (Lester)	USA, 76

Note: Cornel Wilde in *The Bandit Of Sherwood Forest* (USA, 46) and John Derek in *Rogues Of Sherwood Forest* (USA, 50) both featured as the son of Robin Hood; June Laverick as his daughter in the misleadingly titled *Son Of Robin Hood* (GB, 58).

Brian Bedford voiced the role in the Disney cartoon; in *Robin And The Seven Hoods*, the gangster updating of the tale, the equivalent role to that of Robin Hood was played by Frank Sinatra (as Robbo).

Douglas Fairbanks was the king of the silent outlaws in Allan Dwan's 1922 spectacular, *Robin Hood*. Robert Frazer (USA, 12), W. Thomas (USA, 13), William Russell (USA, 14) were others who appeared in the part.

Robinson Crusoe

Seventeenth century English squire, shipwrecked for over twenty years on an uninhabited island with only a cat, a dog and finally a young native (Man Friday) for company. A courageous figure in Daniel DeFoe's novel of 1719–20, he has attracted several major film-makers, notably Luis Bunuel whose 1953 Mexican film ranks as perhaps the definitive screen version of the story. The theme was intriguingly revamped into science-fiction terms in *Robinson Crusoe On Mars*; in *Man Friday* Jack Gold told the story from Friday's viewpoint and reversed the roles of master and servant.

Douglas Fairbanks	*Mr. Robinson Crusoe* (Sutherland)	USA, 32
Herbert A. E. Bohme	*Robinson Crusoe* (Fanck)	Ger, 40
Pavel Kadotchnikov	*Robinson Crusoe* (Andrievski)	USSR, 47
Georges Marchal	*Robinson Crusoe* (Musso)	It, 51
Dan O'Herlihy	*The Adventures Of Robinson Crusoe* (Bunuel)	
		Mex, 53
Paul Mantee	*Robinson Crusoe On Mars* (Haskin)	USA, 64
Dick Van Dyke	*Lt. Robinson Crusoe, USN* (Paul)	USA, 66
Hugo Stieglitz	*Robinson Crusoe* (Cardona, Jr)	Mex, 69
Leonid Kuravlev	*The Life And Surprising Adventures Of Robinson*	
	Crusoe (Govorukin)	USSR, 72
Peter O'Toole	*Man Friday* (Gold)	GB, 76

Note: Both the Douglas Fairbanks and Dick Van Dyke performances were in updated variations of DeFoe's story; Robert Z. Leonard (USA, 13), Mario Dani (Fra, 21), Harry C. Myers (USA, 22) and M. A. Wetherell (GB, 27) were among the silent actors who appeared in the role.

Rochester, Edward

The master of Thornfield Hall in Charlotte Bronte's 'Jane Eyre' (1847). A strange, complex character, his moodiness derives from a hopeless marriage to an insane wife, a secret only revealed on the day of his proposed marriage to his young governess. Eventually maimed and blinded amid the blazing walls of his huge mansion. Two notable screen portrayals: Orson Welles and George C. Scott.

Colin Clive	*Jane Eyre*	(Cabanne)	USA, 34
Orson Welles	*Jane Eyre*	(Stevenson)	USA, 44
George C. Scott	*Jane Eyre*	(Delbert Mann)	GB, 71

Note: Tom Conway appeared in the Rochester role in Val Lewton's 1943 horror updating, *I Walked With A Zombie*; Irving Cummings (14), Alan Hale (15), Norman Trevor (21) and the German actor Olaf Fönss (26) were among those who appeared in silent versions.

Rodgers, Richard

(1902–   ) The most durable of all American composers of popular stage music, a man whose melodies (with Lorenz Hart) attracted audiences of the 20s and 30s, and also (with Oscar Hammerstein) those of subsequent decades. His partnership with Hart was the subject of MGM's screen biography, *Words And Music*. Among the Rodgers and Hart shows: 'On Your Toes', 'Babes In Arms', 'The Boys From Syracuse' and 'Pal Joey'; among the Rodgers and Hammerstein musicals: 'Oklahoma', 'South Pacific', 'The King And I', 'The Sound Of Music'.

Tom Drake	*Words And Music*	(Taurog)	USA, 48

Rogers, Will

(1879–1935) American actor and humourist who began as a cowboy rope-twirler in vaudeville and rose, through the Ziegfeld Follies, to become one of America's top movie stars of the early 30s. His charm, wit and cracker-barrel philosophy made him the most successful entertainer of his generation. Killed in a plane crash in 1935, he was played on screen by his look-alike son in Warners' biography of the early 50s.

| A. A. Trimble | *The Great Ziegfeld* (Leonard) | USA, 36 |
| Will Rogers, Jr | *The Story Of Will Rogers* (Curtiz) | USA, 52 |

Note: Lew Harvey featured as Rogers in *Pretty Ladies* (USA, 25).

Romberg, Sigmund

(1887–1951) Hungarian-born composer of light operettas, popular during the 20s and 30s when several of his Broadway hits, 'The Desert Song', 'Maytime', 'The Girl Of The Golden West', 'New Moon', were filmed in Hollywood. Given MGM's lush biography treatment in the 1954 musical *Deep In My Heart*.

| Jose Ferrer | *Deep In My Heart* (Donen) | USA, 54 |

Rome, Tony

Modern private-eye, the creation of novelist Marvin H. Albert. Very much in the laconic Philip Marlowe mould, but minus upturned raincoat and shabby office. Instead, a sailor's cap and a plush houseboat in sunny Miami. Portrayed twice on screen by Frank Sinatra.

| Frank Sinatra | *Tony Rome* (Douglas) | USA, 67 |
| Frank Sinatra | *Lady In Cement* (Douglas) | USA, 68 |

Romeo And Juliet

The immortal star-crossed lovers of William Shakespeare, victims of the tragic family feud between the Montagues and the Capulets in Renaissance Italy. Screen portrayals of the doomed pair have been variable, although the pictorial values of the Castellani and Zeffirelli adaptations frequently compensated for any inadequacy of performance. 'Romeo And Juliet' was first performed on stage in 1596.

Leslie Howard & Norma Shearer	*Romeo And Juliet* (Cukor) USA, 36
Ibrahim Hamouda & Leila Mourad	*Romeo And Juliet* (Selim) Egy, 42
Sapru & Nargis	*Romeo And Juliet* (Hussein) Ind, 47
Laurence Harvey & Susan Shentall	*Romeo And Juliet* (Castellani) GB/It, 54
Meynier & Rosemarie Dexter	*Romeo And Juliet* (Freda) It/Spa, 64
Leonard Whiting & Olivia Hussey	*Romeo And Juliet* (Zeffirelli) GB/It, 68

Note: The musical *West Side Story* (61) updated the Romeo And Juliet theme to contemporary New York and set the tragedy against a feud between two rival street gangs, the Sharks and the Jets. Richard Beymer featured as the Romeo character, Natalie Wood as Juliet.

Silent screen portrayals of the two lovers were given by Sir Godfrey Tearle and Mary Malone (GB, 08), Francis X. Bushman and Beverly Bayne (USA, 16) and Harry Hilliard and Theda Bara (USA, 16).

Rommel, Field Marshal Erwin

(1891–1944) The most famous German soldier of World War II, a man who excelled at every level of command and led the legendary Afrika Korps to decisive victories before being halted by Montgomery at El Alamein. Committed suicide in 1944 after being implicated in the bomb plot against Hitler. James Mason's performance in *The Desert Fox* remains the most distinguished screen portrayal, Erich von Stroheim's in *Five Graves To Cairo* the most melodramatic.

Erich von Stroheim	*Five Graves To Cairo* (Wilder)	USA, 43
James Mason	*The Desert Fox* (Hathaway)	USA, 51
James Mason	*The Desert Rats* (Wise)	USA, 53
Albert Lieven	*Foxhole In Cairo* (Moxey)	GB, 60
Gregory Gay	*Hitler* (Heisler)	USA, 62
Werner Hinz	*The Longest Day* (Wicki/Marton/Annakin)	
		USA, 62
Christopher Plummer	*The Night Of The Generals* (Litvak)	
		Fra/GB, 67
Robert Hossein	*Desert Tanks* (Padget)	Fra/It, 68
Karl Michael Vogler	*Patton* (Schaffner)	USA, 70
Wolfgang Preiss	*Raid On Rommel* (Hathaway)	USA, 71

Roosevelt, Franklin Delano

(1882–1945) The only American President to be re-elected three times, a man who led his country out of the Depression and through World War II despite being crippled by polio. Famous for his fireside radio chats and ringing phrases ('The only thing we have to fear is fear itself'), he has been glimpsed only fleetingly in most screen performances. The one exception is Ralph Bellamy's remarkable portrayal in *Sunrise At Campobello* which relates in detail Roosevelt's inspiring fight against the disease which struck him down in 1921.

Captain Jack Young	*Yankee Doodle Dandy* (Curtiz)	USA, 42
Captain Jack Young	*This Is The Army* (Curtiz)	USA, 43
Godfrey Tearle	*The Beginning Or The End* (Taurog)	USA, 46
Nikolai Cherkasov	*The First Front* (Petrov)	USSR, 49
Ralph Bellamy	*Sunrise At Campobello* (Donehue)	USA, 60

Richard Nelson	*The Pigeon That Took Rome* (Shavelson)	
		USA, 62
Stephen Roberts	*First To Fight* (Nyby)	USA, 67
Stanislav Yaskevich	*The Great Battle* (Ozerov)	
		USSR/Pol/Yug/E.Ger/It, 69
Dan O'Herlihy	*MacArthur* (Sargent)	USA, 77
Howard Da Silva	*The Private Files Of J. Edgar Hoover* (Cohen)	
		USA, 78

Note: In *Sunrise At Campobello*, Greer Garson featured as Eleanor Roosevelt.

Roosevelt, Theodore

(1858–1919) Extrovert American President whose exploits as a Roughrider in the Spanish-American war e.g. in the famous charge up San Juan Hill in Cuba, earned him as much fame as his subsequent years as President when his motto was 'speak softly and carry a big stick'. Character actor Sidney Blackmer appeared several times as Roosevelt in minor roles; Brian Keith developed his bullish personality at length in John Milius' *The Wind And The Lion*, based on a true incident in which Roosevelt sent the marines to Morocco to rescue an American widow and her children, kidnapped by a desert chieftain.

Sidney Blackmer	*This Is My Affair* (Seiter)	USA, 37
Wallis Clark	*Yankee Doodle Dandy* (Curtiz)	USA, 42
Sidney Blackmer	*In Old Oklahoma* (Rogell)	USA, 43
Sidney Blackmer	*Buffalo Bill* (Wellman)	USA, 44
John Merton	*I Wonder Who's Kissing Her Now* (Bacon)	USA, 47
Sidney Blackmer	*My Girl Tisa* (Nugent)	USA, 48
John Alexander	*Fancy Pants* (Marshall)	USA, 50
Edward Cassidy	*The First Travelling Saleslady* (Lubin)	USA, 56
Karl Swenson	*Brighty Of The Grand Canyon* (Foster)	USA, 66
Brian Keith	*The Wind And The Lion* (Milius)	USA, 75

Note: E. J. Radcliffe in *Sundown* (24), Buck Black in *Lights Of Old Broadway* (25) and Frank Hopper in *The Rough Riders* (27) all featured as Roosevelt on the American silent screen.

Rose, Billy

(1899–1966) Brash American showman and nightclub owner, who began his Broadway career producing revues then graduated to long-running hit musicals, e.g. 'Jumbo' (1935) and 'Carmen Jones' (1943). James Caan's screen performance in *Funny Lady* revolved around Rose's marriage to comedienne Fanny Brice.

| James Caan | *Funny Lady* (Ross) | USA, 75 |

Rose-Marie

Melodious belle of a Canadian trading post, loved by both a mountie and a French trapper in the Rudolf Friml/Herbert Stothart stage musical of 1924. The first version of the story was silent; the subsequent versions included substantial story changes and allowed 'Indian Love Call', 'Only A Kiss' and 'The Door Of Her Dreams'.

Jeanette MacDonald	*Rose-Marie*	(Van Dyke)	USA, 36
Ann Blyth	*Rose-Marie*	(LeRoy)	USA, 54

Note: Joan Crawford was the silent Rose-Marie, appearing in Lucien Hubbard's 1928 film for MGM.

Roth, Lillian

(1910–) A former child star who joined Paramount in the 20s and featured in several early musicals (*The Love Parade*, *The Vagabond King*) before losing her battle with alcoholism. Her harrowing experiences and courageous fight back were revealed in a frank autobiography 'I'll Cry Tomorrow', later made into a realistic film by Daniel Mann.

Susan Hayward	*I'll Cry Tomorrow* (Mann)	USA, 55

Note: Susan Hayward sang all her own songs in the film.

Rousseau, Jean Jacques

(1712–1778) French novelist and political theorist who rebelled against the social orders of his time and profoundly influenced the course of the revolution which occurred just a decade after his death. Claude Goretta's 200-minute film covered his last years when he was forced to leave France and live abroad in poverty and near solitude.

François Simon	*The Roads Of Exile* (Goretta)	Fra, 78

Ruggles Of Red Gap

An English gentleman's gentleman, won as a prize in a poker game in Europe and transported by his·'nouveau riche' American master to a new life (and independence) in the Old West. Created in the 1915 play by Harry Leon Wilson; memorably portrayed by Charles Laughton in McCarey's film of 1935.

Charles Laughton	*Ruggles Of Red Gap* (McCarey)	USA, 35
Bob Hope	*Fancy Pants* (Marshall)	USA, 50

Note: Taylor Holmes featured in the 1918 Essanay production and Edward Everett Horton in Paramount's 1923 film. The 1950 Bob Hope movie was a loose remake with Ruggles renamed Humphrey.

Rupert Of Hentzau

A conspirator for the throne of Ruritania in Anthony Hope's 'The Prisoner Of Zenda' and one of the most engaging villains in the swashbuckling genre. Played with charm by Douglas Fairbanks Jr. and suave menace by James Mason, he engages in a climactic duel with hero Rudolf Rassendyll and is always allowed (quite rightly) to escape with his life. Hope must have tired of him, however. In his sequel, 'Rupert Of Hentzau' (1898), filmed only in the silent days, the dashing Rupert at last meets his demise — at the hands of Rassendyll!

Douglas Fairbanks Jr.	*The Prisoner Of Zenda*	(Cromwell)	USA, 37
James Mason	*The Prisoner Of Zenda*	(Thorpe)	USA, 52
Stuart Wilson	*The Prisoner Of Zenda*	(Quine)	USA, 79

Note: Alan Hale (USA, 13), Gerald Ames (GB, 15) and Ramon Novarro (USA, 22) played Rupert in silent versions of *The Prisoner Of Zenda*; Gerald Ames (GB, 15) and Lew Cody (USA, 23) in *Rupert Of Hentzau*.

Russell, Lillian

(1868–1922) Colourful musical star of the Gay Nineties, renowned for her hour-glass figure, feathered hats and legendary exploits off stage, which included the taking and discarding of four husbands. The Fox studio filmed her story in 1940 with Alice Faye as 'Luscious Lillian'. Among her songs: 'Come Down, Ma Evenin' Star', 'After The Ball' and 'Rosie, You Are My Posie'.

Ruth Gillette	*The Great Ziegfeld*	(Leonard)	USA, 36
Alice Faye	*Lillian Russell*	(Cummings)	USA, 40
Louise Allbritton	*Bowery To Broadway*	(Lamont)	USA, 44
Andrea King	*My Wild Irish Rose*	(Butler)	USA, 47

Babe Ruth

(1895–1948) Baseball's most famous player and the greatest hitter of home runs in the history of the game. Just about the perfect athlete — he could run, field, throw and bat — he hit 714 home runs during his spectacular career. Appeared in several silent baseball comedies and light dramas, *Headin' Home* (20), *Babe Comes Home* (26), etc. and as himself in Harold Lloyd's *Speedy* (27) and *Pride of The Yankees* (42).

William Bendix	*The Babe Ruth Story*	(Del Ruth)	USA, 48

S

Sacco And Vanzetti

Italian immigrants to America, well-known for their anarchist activities, who were convicted of the murder of a cashier and guard during a payroll robbery in Massachusetts in April, 1920. Both men vainly protested their innocence but, after seven years of appeals, were executed in the electric chair. Doubts about their guilt remained and, in 1977, both had their names cleared in a special proclamation signed by the Governor of Massachusetts. The 1971 film of Giuliano Montaldo retold their story.

Riccardo Cucciolla (Nicola Sacco)	*Sacco And Vanzetti* (Montaldo)	It, 71
Gian Maria Volonte (Bartolomeo Vanzetti)		

Sade, Marquis De

(1740–1814) Infamous French writer whose cruelty and sexual perversions brought the word sadism into the English language. Spent thirty years of his life in prison, had a quarter of his literary output burned by the police, and died insane. Keir Dullea was the actor chosen to interpret De Sade's mental torment in the Richard Matheson-scripted biography of 1969; tinted orgies in slow motion represented the sexual decadence.

Patrick Magee	*The Persecution and Assassination Of Jean-Paul Marat, as performed by the inmates of the Asylum of Charenton under the direction of the Marquis De Sade* (Brook)	GB, 67
Klaus Kinski	*Marquis De Sade: Justine* (Franco)	W.Ger/It, 68
Michel Piccoli	*The Milky Way* (Bunuel)	Fra/It, 69
Keir Dullea	*De Sade* (Endfield)	USA/W.Ger, 69

Saint, The

Amateur detective (real name Simon Templar), more famous on TV —

through the likeable personality of Roger Moore — than in the movies. A debonair Englishman, he is half-crook, half-detective, and spends most of his time on the Continent and in America, constantly involving himself with villains, police and beautiful women. His nickname is derived from his calling card which shows a stick figure with a halo. First appeared in print in Leslie Charteris' 'Meet The Tiger' in 1929, but did not attract the attention of film-makers until almost a decade later.

Louis Hayward	*The Saint In New York* (Holmes)	USA, 38
George Sanders	*The Saint Strikes Back* (Farrow)	USA, 39
George Sanders	*The Saint In London* (Carstairs)	GB, 39
George Sanders	*The Saint's Double Trouble* (Hively)	USA, 40
George Sanders	*The Saint Takes Over* (Hively)	USA, 40
George Sanders	*The Saint In Palm Springs* (Hively)	USA, 41
Hugh Sinclair	*The Saint's Vacation* (Fenton)	GB, 41
Hugh Sinclair	*The Saint Meets The Tiger* (Stein)	GB, 41
Louis Hayward	*The Saint's Girl Friday* (Friedman)	GB, 53

Salome

The seductive daughter of Herodias who slipped off seven veils whilst dancing for her stepfather, Herod Antipas, and gained the head of John the Baptist as a prize. A minor figure in biblical epics (she was barely glimpsed in *The Greatest Story Ever Told*), but featuring in several film biographies of both the silent and sound cinema.

Rita Hayworth	*Salome* (Dieterle)	USA, 53
Brigid Bazlen	*King Of Kings* (Ray)	USA, 61
Paola Tedesco	*The Gospel According To St. Matthew* (Pasolini)	It/Fra, 64
Donyale Luna	*Salome* (Bene)	It, 72

Note: Theda Bara (18), Nazimova (22) and Diana Allen (23) all starred in American silent productions of *Salome*.

Sand, George

(1804–1876) French writer, as famous for her scandalous love affairs as for her literary accomplishments. Her romance with Polish composer Frederic Chopin has been the subject of several films, notably *A Song To Remember*, a high camp movie with dialogue that only Hollywood at its most flamboyant would have the audacity to deliver, e.g. Sand to Chopin: 'You could make miracles of music in Majorca!'

Lucienne Le Marchand	*Un Amour de Frederic Chopin* (Bolvary)	Fra, 35
Merle Oberon	*A Song To Remember* (Charles Vidor)	USA, 45

Patricia Morison	*Song Without End* (Charles Vidor)	
		USA, 60
Lucia Bose	*Jutrzenka: A Winter In Majorca* (Camino)	
		Spa, 71
Anne Wiazemsky	*Georges Qui?* (Rosier)	Fra, 73
Imogen Claire	*Lisztomania* (Russell)	GB, 75

Note: Dagny Servaes in *Die Lachende Grille* (Ger, 26) and Germaine Laugier in *La Valse de L'Adieu* (Fra, 27) both featured as Sand in European silent productions.

Sansom, Odette

(1912–   ) Undercover agent and radio operator for Peter Churchill in occupied France during World War II. Eventually captured and handed over to the Gestapo, she was tortured but kept alive by the Nazis who believed her to be a relation of Winston Churchill. Awarded a George Cross for bravery after the war, she was the subject of perhaps Anna Neagle's most convincing screen performance.

| Anna Neagle | *Odette*   (Wilcox) | GB, 50 |

Savage, Doc

Pulp fiction superman of the 30s who appeared in 181 stories (mostly written by Kenneth Robeson) but failed to find favour with film-makers until some forty years later, when George Pal produced a tongue-in-cheek account of his adventures. The 'strongest and most intelligent man in the world', he works in conjunction with a personal brains trust called The Amazing Five and aims to conquer crime the world over. First appeared in print in 1933.

| Ron Ely | *Doc Savage — Man Of Bronze*   (Anderson) | USA, 75 |

Sawyer, Tom

Mark Twain's Missouri schoolboy whose adventurous instincts invariably get the better of him and lead him into all kinds of exploits with his pipe-smoking friend, Huckleberry Finn. The pair's visit to a graveyard at midnight, their escape to a tiny island by raft and Tom's encounter with Injun Joe in an underground cavern belong with the immortal moments in American literature. Some decidedly shaky adaptations of Twain's novel have been redeemed by Selznick's classic of 1938 and the sprightly musical of 1973.

| Jackie Coogan | *Tom Sawyer*   (Cromwell) | USA, 30 |
| Jackie Coogan | *Huckleberry Finn*   (Taurog) | USA, 31 |

Billy Cook	*Tom Sawyer, Detective* (Louis King)	USA, 38
Tommy Kelly	*The Adventures Of Tom Sawyer* (Taurog)	
		USA, 38
Roland Demongeot	*Tom Sawyer* (Iacob)	Fra/Rum, 69
Johnny Whitaker	*Tom Sawyer* (Taylor)	USA, 73

Note: Jack Pickford featured as Tom in the silents, *Tom Sawyer* (17) and *Huck And Tom* (18) and Gordon Griffith in *Huckleberry Finn* (20)

Scaramouche

Swashbuckling hero of Rafael Sabatini during the days of the French Revolution. A romantic swordsman, he seeks revenge on the man responsible for the death of his revolutionary friend only to discover that his mortal enemy is his own half-brother. In the now much acclaimed 1952 version, Stewart Granger participates in the longest duel in screen history — $6^1/_2$ minutes — as he fights with Mel Ferrer around the interiors of a lavish French theatre.

Stewart Granger	*Scaramouche* (Sidney)	USA, 52
Gerard Barray	*The Adventures Of Scaramouche* (Isasmendi)	
		Fra/It/Spa, 63
Michael Sarrazin	*The Loves And Times Of Scaramouche* (Castellari)	
		It/Yug, 76

Note: Ramon Novarro played Scaramouche in a lavish silent production by Rex Ingram.

The Scarlet Pimpernel

English dandy who leads a double life during the days of the French Revolution, masquerading as the foppish Sir Percy Blakeney in English high society and, on the other side of the channel, rescuing aristocrats from the terrors of the guillotine. A dashing hero of Baroness Orczy's 1905 novel and several films since the silent days. Definitive screen portrait: Leslie Howard in Alexander Korda's 1934 production.

Leslie Howard	*The Scarlet Pimpernel* (Young)	GB, 34
Barry K. Barnes	*The Return Of The Scarlet Pimpernel* (Schwartz)	
		GB, 38
David Niven	*The Elusive Pimpernel* (Powell/Pressburger)	
		GB, 50

Note: Dustin Farnum starred in a 1917 silent version of *The Scarlet Pimpernel*; Cecil Humphrey in *The Elusive Pimpernel* (GB, 19), Holmes Herbert in *I Will Repay* (GB, 23) and Matheson Lang in *The Triumph Of The Scarlet Pimpernel* (GB, 28) were others who featured in the role.

Schultz, Dutch

New York gangster, in charge of bootlegging in the Bronx and Manhattan in the 20s and 30s, who was also responsible for the murder of Legs Diamond. Met his own death shortly afterwards (1935) when he was shot down 'Godfather style', i.e. over dinner in a New Jersey restaurant, by Alberto Anastasia's executioners from Murder, Inc. Vic Morrow played Schultz in a full-length biography, *Portrait Of A Mobster*, in 1961.

Vic Morrow	*Portrait Of A Mobster* (Pevney)	USA, 61
Vincent Gardenia	*Mad Dog Coll* (Balaban)	USA, 61
John Durren	*Lepke* (Golan)	USA, 75

Schweitzer, Dr. Albert

(1875–1965) French medical missionary, theologian and musician who, in 1913, set up a riverside hospital in the heart of French Equatorial Africa and devoted his life to treating leprosy and being of service to the Africans. Described as the noblest figure of the twentieth century, he has been portrayed just once on celluloid — by Pierre Fresnay in a French biography of the early 50s.

Pierre Fresnay	*The Story Of Albert Schweitzer* (Haguet)	Fra, 52

Note: The leprosy doctor played by Niall MacGinnis in *The Nun's Story* (59) had vague connections with Schweitzer.

Scott, Robert Falcon

(1868–1912) British Antarctic explorer who reached the South Pole on January 18, 1912, just a few weeks after the Norwegian Roald Amundsen. Died with his party when trapped by fierce blizzards on the return journey. Charles Frend's Ealing film chronicled the expedition in detail.

John Mills	*Scott Of The Antarctic* (Frend)	GB, 48

Note: The other members of Scott's ill-fated party were played by Harold Warrender (Dr. Wilson), James Robertson Justice (Taff Evans), Reginald Beckwith (Lt. Bowers) and Derek Bond (Captain Oates).

Scrooge, Ebenezer

Charles Dickens' grasping old skinflint, visited one memorable Christmas Eve by three spirits who show him the error of his ways and change his future life. Along with Fagin, the most coveted of all Dickens

roles although, ironically, it was as an animated character in Richard
Williams' 1972 cartoon that he was most realistically portrayed. Alastair
Sim, who had played the role twenty years earlier, voiced the character
in Williams' film. 'A Christmas Carol' was published in 1843; the first
known film version released in 1901.

Seymour Hicks	*Scrooge* (Edwards)	GB, 35
Reginald Owen	*A Christmas Carol* (Marin)	USA, 38
Alastair Sim	*Scrooge* (Desmond Hurst)	GB, 50
Albert Finney	*Scrooge* (Neame)	GB, 70
Alastair Sim (Voice only)	*A Christmas Carol* (Williams)	GB, 72

Note: Seymour Hicks also played Scrooge in a British silent production
of 1913. Charles Rock (GB, 14) and Rupert Julian in an American
adaptation, *The Right To Be Happy* (16), both featured in the role.

Shaft, John

Black New York private-eye who proved in the 70s that investigating the
activities of racketeers wasn't strictly the prerogative of the white man.
A slick, glossy character who lives high, fights hard and has no illusions
about his limitations: 'I'm not James Bond, just Sam Spade!'

Richard Roundtree	*Shaft* (Parks)	USA, 71
Richard Roundtree	*Shaft's Big Score* (Parks)	USA, 72
Richard Roundtree	*Shaft In Africa* (Guillermin)	USA, 73

Shane

Jack Schaefer's legendary gunfighter who rides into a Wyoming valley,
helps a group of homesteaders in their fight against the cattlemen, then
rides out again as mysteriously as he came. As personified by Alan
Ladd, the most attractive and satisfying hero ever to appear in a
Western and one of the few unrepeatable roles in all cinema. Schaefer's
novel first appeared in print in 1949.

Alan Ladd	*Shane* (Stevens)	USA, 53

Sharp, Becky

Thackeray's famed golddigger from 'Vanity Fair' (1848); an
unprincipled schemer whose sole ambition is to rise as high as she can
in the world, no matter what the cost. Several silent portrayals, but
nothing since 1935 when Miriam Hopkins indulged not only in Becky's
ruthless traits, but also became the first major actress to appear in
three-color Technicolor!

| Myrna Loy | *Vanity Fair* (Franklin) | USA, 32 |
| Miriam Hopkins | *Becky Sharp* (Mamoulian) | USA, 35 |

Note: Helen Gardner (USA, 11), Minnie Madden Fiske (USA, 15) and Mabel Ballin (USA, 23) featured as Becky in silent productions.

She

2,000-year-old ruler of the mountain city of Kuma, an African sorceress of ethereal mystery and beauty who enjoys the luxury of life everlasting by walking into the flame of eternal youth. Known also as Ayesha, she was created by Rider Haggard in his 1887 novel 'She, A History Of Adventure'. Helen Gahagan's 1935 performance remains the most convincing interpretation, Ursula Andress' the most beautiful to look at.

Helen Gahagan	*She* (Pichel/Holden)	USA, 35
Ursula Andress	*She* (Day)	GB, 65
Olinka Berova	*The Vengeance Of She* (Owen)	GB, 68

Note: There were at least five silent versions of *She*, among them a 1908 Edison adaptation in seven scenes. Marguerite Snow (11) and Valeska Suratt (17) featured as Ayesha in subsequent American adaptations, Alice Delysia (16) and Betty Blythe (25) in British versions.

In the 1968 sequel *The Vengeance Of She*, Olinka Berova features as the reincarnation of the ageless queen.

Sheppard, Jack

(1702–1724) The most celebrated thief and escape artist of 18th century London, five times caught and four times escaped. Number five proved to be one too many, however, and although a crowd of 200,000 turned up at Tyburn to witness another possible escape, they were disappointed and Sheppard finished up dangling at the end of a rope, aged 22. Not so in the movie, *Where's Jack?*; Tommy Steele escaped with all the panache of a Tom Jones!

| Tommy Steele | *Where's Jack?* (Clavell) | GB, 69 |

Note: Jonathan Wild, notorious receiver of stolen goods and informer, was played in *Where's Jack?* by Stanley Baker. Wild, too, met his death by hanging, just a year after Sheppard.

The Sheriff Of Nottingham

Robin Hood's chief adversary, a hireling of the scheming Prince John and the most frequent 'loser' of the swashbuckling screen. Peter Finch allowed him a touch of engaging black villainy in Disney's 1952 film; a tired Robert Shaw battled to the death with an ageing Sean Connery in Richard Lester's *Robin And Marian*.

Melville Cooper	*The Adventures Of Robin Hood* (Curtiz/Keighley)	
		USA, 38
Lloyd Corrigan	*The Bandit Of Sherwood Forest* (Sherman/Levin)	
		USA, 46
Tiny Stowe	*Tales Of Robin Hood* (Tinling)	USA, 51
Peter Finch	*The Story Of Robin Hood And His Merrie Men*	
	(Annakin)	GB, 52
Peter Cushing	*Sword Of Sherwood Forest* (Fisher)	GB, 60
John Arnatt	*A Challenge For Robin Hood*	
	(Pennington Richards)	GB, 67
Robert Shaw	*Robin And Marian* (Lester)	USA, 76

Note: Pat Buttram voiced the character in Disney's 1973 cartoon *Robin Hood*; Victor Buono featured as the modern equivalent in the gangster version, *Robin And The Seven Hoods* in 1964.

Alec B. Francis in *Robin Hood* (USA, 12), John Dillon in *Robin Hood And Maid Marian* (USA, 14) and William Lowrey in Allan Dwan's lavish *Robin Hood* of 1922, were among the actors to play the role on the silent screen.

Shomron, General Dan

Commando head of the Israeli Rescue Operation at Entebbe Airport in June, 1976, when Arab guerillas hijacked a plane and held to ransom 250 prisoners. Portrayed on screen three times within eighteen months of the actual event!

Harris Yulin	*Victory At Entebbe* (Chomsky)	USA, 76
Charles Bronson	*Raid On Entebbe* (Kershner)	USA, 76
Arik Lavi	*Entebbe: Operation Thunderbolt* (Golan)	Isr, 77

Note: 'Yonni' Netanyahu, the young colonel who led the assault (and the only soldier killed in the action) was played by Richard Dreyfuss in Marvin Chomsky's film, Stephen Macht in that of Irvin Kershner, and Yehoram Gaon in the 1977 picture.

Shylock

One of Shakespeare's most controversial characters, an avaricious Jewish moneylender who demands his famous 'pound of flesh' when the merchant who has eloped with his daughter fails to repay his debt. On screen, portrayed just once, in robust style by Pierre Brasseur in a French/Italian co-production of 1952. Shakespeare's play 'The Merchant Of Venice' was first performed in 1595.

Pierre Brasseur	*The Merchant Of Venice* (Billon)	Fra/It, 52

Sikes, Bill

The most brutal of all Dickens' creations, a vicious housebreaker who murders his sluttish mistress Nancy before meeting his own death whilst trying to escape over the rooftops of London. William Boyd (later to become famous as Hopalong Cassidy) played the burglar in the 1933 production; the Sikes of Robert Newton in David Lean's film was a last-minute replacement for Robert Donat, the director's first choice for the role.

William Boyd	*Oliver Twist* (Cowen)	USA, 33
Robert Newton	*Oliver Twist* (Lean)	GB, 48
Oliver Reed	*Oliver!* (Reed)	GB, 68

Note: Harry Royston (GB, 12), Mortimer Martine (USA, 12), Hobart Bosworth (USA, 16) and George Siegmann (USA, 22) all played Sikes on the silent screen. G. Raymond Nye featured as the character in the 1921 modernized version. *Oliver Twist Jr.*

Silver, Long John

A pair of crutches, one leg and a parrot screaming 'pieces of eight' brought this roguish pirate to life in Robert Louis Stevenson's classic novel 'Treasure Island' (1883). On screen, just a leer and a roll of Robert Newton's eyeballs were enough to create the same character in a more benevolent but no less effective vein. Wallace Beery, in Victor Fleming's 1934 film, was probably closer to Stevenson's original conception but, in truth, there have been two Long John Silvers, one belonging to Stevenson, one to Newton.

Wallace Beery	*Treasure Island* (Fleming)	USA, 34
Robert Newton	*Treasure Island* (Haskin)	GB, 50
Robert Newton	*Long John Silver* (Haskin)	USA, 54
Boris Andreyev	*Treasure Island* (Fridman)	USSR, 71
Orson Welles	*Treasure Island* (Hough)	GB/Fra,/W.Ger/Spa,72

Note: Addison Rothermel (12) and Charles Ogle (20) were among the actors who portrayed Silver on the silent screen.

Sinbad

Arabian Nights adventurer, a favourite tongue-in-cheek swashbuckler of the 40s and 50s but somewhat overshadowed in more recent years by the terrifying Ray Harryhausen monsters he meets on his travels. Six-armed statues that come to life, sword-fighting skeletons and one-eyed Centaurs tend to remain in the memory longer than Messrs John Phillip Law and Patrick Wayne.

Shemp Howard	*Arabian Nights* (Rawlins)	USA, 42
Douglas Fairbanks, Jr.	*Sinbad The Sailor* (Wallace)	USA, 47
Sebastian Cabot	*Babes In Bagdad* (Ulmer)	USA, 52
Lon Chaney, Jr.	*The Thief Of Damascus* (Jason)	USA, 52
Dale Robertson	*Son Of Sinbad* (Tetzlaff)	USA, 55
Gene Kelly	*The Magic Lamp* (Kelly)	GB, 56
Kerwin Mathews	*The Seventh Voyage Of Sinbad* (Juran)	
		USA, 58
Edward Stolar	*The Magic Voyage Of Sinbad* (Posco)	
		USSR, 62
Guy Williams	*Captain Sinbad* (Haskin)	USA, 63
Toshiro Mifune	*The Lost World Of Sinbad* (Taniguchi)	
		Jap, 63
John Phillip Law	*The Golden Voyage Of Sinbad* (Hessler)	
		GB, 74
Patrick Wayne	*Sinbad And The Eye Of The Tiger*	
	(Wanamaker)	GB, 77

Note: Gene Kelly appeared in the animated Sinbad The Sailor sequence from *The Magic Lamp*. He danced to the music of Rimsky Korsakov.

Sitting Bull

(*c.* 1835–1890) Chief of the Sioux Indians and the man who planned the destruction of Custer and his command at the Little Big Horn in 1876. Did not, as is sometimes believed, take part in the Custer massacre (the attack was led by Crazy Horse and Gaul) but did finish up a decade later as a celebrity of a different kind — as an attraction in Buffalo Bill's Wild West Show. Played twice on screen by J. Carrol Naish.

Chief Thundercloud	*Annie Oakley* (Stevens)	USA, 35
J. Carrol Naish	*Annie Get Your Gun* (Sidney)	USA, 50
Michael Granger	*Fort Vengeance* (Selander)	USA, 53
J. Carrol Naish	*Sitting Bull* (Salkow)	USA, 54
John War Eagle	*Tonka* (Foster)	USA, 58
Michael Pate	*The Great Sioux Massacre* (Salkow)	USA, 65
Frank Kaquitts	*Buffalo Bill And The Indians, or Sitting Bull's*	
	History Lesson (Altman)	USA, 76

Note: Howling Wolf played the Indian chief in the 1936 serial *Custer's Last Stand*.

Smith, Madeleine

(1836–1928) Wealthy Scottish girl, the daughter of a prosperous member of the Scottish gentry, who was tried for the murder of her low-bred suitor in Glasgow during the 1850s. She was acquitted, but doubts about her guilt remained for the rest of her life. David Lean's stylish study of her ill-fated romance and trial remains one of his most serious and underrated films.

Ann Todd	*Madeleine* (Lean)	GB, 50

Smith, Perry and Hickock, Dick

Two young ex-cons who, for no apparent reason, shot a Kansas farmer and his family in November, 1959, and later became the central subjects of Truman Capote's book 'In Cold Blood', which probed into the reasons behind the mystifying slaughter. Richard Brooks' semi-documentary film followed the lives of the two men from the time of the killing to their arrest, appeals and execution in April, 1965.

Robert Blake (Perry Smith) Scott Wilson (Dick Hickock)	*In Cold Blood* (Brooks)	USA, 67

Smith, Stevie

(1902–1971) Depressive British poet and author whose uneventful suburban life and devotion to her maiden aunt were examined in a straight film adaptation of Hugh Whitemore's popular stage play. The film, set almost exclusively in a suburban living room, contains excerpts from Smith's poetic works.

Glenda Jackson	*Stevie* (Enders)	GB, 78

Solo, Napoleon

Smooth-talking American agent for the international organization UNCLE (United Network Command for Law And Enforcement) in its never-ending battle against terrorism and subversion. Accompanied in all his adventures by his Russian sidekick Illya Kuryakin (David McCallum) and permanently under the supervision of benign chief, Mr. Waverly (Leo G. Carroll). All eight film releases were spinoffs from material used in MGM's four-year TV series.

Robert Vaughn	*To Trap A Spy* (Medford)	USA, 65
Robert Vaughn	*The Spy With My Face* (Newland)	USA, 66
Robert Vaughn	*One Of Our Spies Is Missing* (Hallenbeck)	USA, 66
Robert Vaughn	*One Spy Too Many* (Sargent)	USA, 66
Robert Vaughn	*The Spy In The Green Hat* (Sargent)	USA, 67
Robert Vaughn	*The Karate Killers* (Shear)	USA, 67
Robert Vaughn	*The Helicopter Spies* (Sagal)	USA, 68
Robert Vaughn	*How To Steal The World* (Roley)	USA, 68

Sousa, John Philip

(1854–1932) American composer and military bandmaster. Known as The March King, he composed over 100 popular marches including 'Semper Fidelis', 'The Washington Post' and 'Stars And Stripes Forever', all of which were included in Fox's 1952 biography with Clifton Webb.

Clifton Webb	*Stars And Stripes Forever* (Koster)	USA, 52

Spade, Sam

Tough private-eye, as ruthless with females ('When you're slapped you'll take it and like it') as with the hoods who get in his way. The central figure in Dashiell Hammett's 1930 novel 'The Maltese Falcon', he is cynical, mercenary and very different, despite some views to the contrary, to Chandler's subsequent Philip Marlowe. Forever associated with Humphrey Bogart even though Bogie was not the first choice for the role, George Raft having turned the part down in 1941. George Segal played Sam Spade Jr. in the spoof sequel *The Black Bird* in 1975.

Ricardo Cortez	*The Maltese Falcon* (Del Ruth)	USA, 31
Warren William	*Satan Met A Lady* (Dieterle)	USA, 36
Humphrey Bogart	*The Maltese Falcon* (Huston)	USA, 41

Note: In William Dieterle's 1936 version the character was renamed Ted Shayne.

Sparrow, Simon

The hero of Richard Gordon's popular series of comedy 'Doctor' books. Began his screen career in 1954 as a student at St. Swithin's Hospital then continued as a fully-fledged doctor in three subsequent movies. Romantic and anatomical misadventures in all four!

Dirk Bogarde	*Doctor In The House* (Thomas)	GB, 54
Dirk Bogarde	*Doctor At Sea* (Thomas)	GB, 55
Dirk Bogarde	*Doctor At Large* (Thomas)	GB, 57
Dirk Bogarde	*Doctor In Distress* (Thomas)	GB, 63

Note: Sparrow featured in only four of the 'Doctor' movies. Michael Craig starred as Dr. Richard Hare in *Doctor In Love* (60), Leslie Phillips as Gaston Grimsdyke and Simon Burke in the last two in the series *Doctor In Clover* (65) and *Doctor In Trouble* (70).

Spartacus

(d. 71 B.C.) Thracian slave and gladiator who led a rebellion of slaves during the last decades of the tyrannical Roman republic. Finally defeated and killed by Crassus, he was the central figure in Howard Fast's historical novel of 1951, turned into a memorable epic a decade later by Stanley Kubrick.

Massimo Girotti	*Spartacus, The Gladiator*	(Freda)	It, 53
Kirk Douglas	*Spartacus* (Kubrick)		USA, 60

Note: Steve Reeves featured as the *Son of Spartacus*, an Italian film directed in 1962 by Sergio Corbucci.

Spratt, Sir Lancelot

Bombastic head surgeon of Richard Gordon's 'Doctor' books, played to the hilt by James Robertson Justice in the popular film series of the 50s and 60s. A man whose bark is often worse than his bite, although the bark is frequently worth listening to: 'Hang on to your swabs gentlemen. You can cut the patient's throat while he is under an anaesthetic and nobody will mind. But if you leave anything inside you will be in the Sunday papers in no time!'

James Robertson Justice	*Doctor In The House* (Thomas)	GB, 54
James Robertson Justice	*Doctor At Sea* (Thomas)	GB, 55
James Robertson Justice	*Doctor At Large* (Thomas)	GB, 57
James Robertson Justice	*Doctor In Love* (Thomas)	GB, 60
James Robertson Justice	*Doctor In Distress* (Thomas)	GB, 63
James Robertson Justice	*Doctor In Clover* (Thomas)	GB, 65
James Robertson Justice	*Doctor In Trouble* (Thomas)	GB, 70

Note: In *Doctor At Sea* Justice featured not as Sir Lancelot but as his naval equivalent, the blustering Captain Hogg.

Stalin, Josef

(1879–1953) Soviet dictator who took over supreme power after the death of Lenin in 1924 and ruled Russia for the next thirty years. Portrayed on screen most often by M. Gelovani, a Russian actor-director who between 1937 and 1953 made a successful career out of playing this one role.

I. Golshtab	*Lenin In October* (Romm)	USSR, 37
M. Gelovani	*The Man With A Gun* (Yutkevich)	USSR, 38
M. Gelovani	*Great Dawn* (Chiaureli)	USSR, 38
M. Gelovani	*Lenin In 1918* (Romm)	USSR, 39
M. Gelovani	*The Vyborg Side* (Kozintsev/Trauberg)	USSR, 39
M. Gelovani	*Manhood* (Kalatozov)	USSR, 39
M. Gelovani	*Fortress On The Volga* (Ginsburg)	USSR, 42

M. Gelovani	*Defence Of Tsaritsin* (Vasiliev)	USSR, 42
Manart Kippen	*Mission To Moscow* (Curtiz)	USA, 43
M. Gelovani	*The Vow* (Chiaureli)	USSR, 46
M. Gelovani	*Light Over Russia* (Yutkevich)	USSR, 47
M. Gelovani	*The Fall Of Berlin* (Chiaureli)	USSR, 49
A. Dieky	*The Battle Of Stalingrad* (Petrov)	USSR, 50
M. Gelovani	*The Unforgettable Year, 1919* (Chiaureli)	
		USSR, 52
Maurice Manson	*The Girl In The Kremlin* (Birdwell)	USA, 57
A. Kobaladze	*In The October Days* (Vasiliev)	USSR, 58
Buhuti Zakariadze	*The Great Battle* (Ozerov)	
		USSR/Pol/Yug/E.Ger/It, 69
Saul Katz	*Why Russians Are Revolting* (Sullivan)	USA, 70
James Hazeldine	*Nicholas And Alexandra* (Schaffner)	USA, 71

Stanley, Sir Henry Morton

(1841–1904) British explorer and journalist who was commissioned by his newspaper, The New York Herald, to make a hazardous expedition into Central Africa to find David Livingstone. In 1871 he did just that and supposedly uttered the immortal words, 'Dr. Livingstone, I presume'. A suitably determined Spencer Tracy spoke them on screen in Henry King's full scale adventure movie, *Stanley And Livingstone*.

| Hugh McDermott | *David Livingstone* (Fitzpatrick) | GB, 36 |
| Spencer Tracy | *Stanley And Livingstone* (Henry King) | USA, 39 |

Note: Henry Walton featured in the role in M. A. Wetherell's silent film *Livingstone* (GB, 25).

Starr, Belle

(1848–1889) Another of the Wild West's so-called glamorous heroines. In reality no more than a hard-bitten horse stealer from Missouri, but in Hollywood's never-never land, a beauty, first in the shape of Gene Tierney and then in the even more impressive physique of Jane Russell. Belle (real name Myra Belle Shirley) met her death at the hands of a bushwhacker after enjoying violent careers with Cole Younger in Texas and her own rustling gang in Oklahoma. Like Buffalo Bill, she was given legendary acclaim through the newspaper accounts of her exploits.

Gene Tierney	*Belle Starr* (Cummings)	USA, 41
Isabel Jewell	*Badman's Territory* (Whelan)	USA, 46
Isabel Jewell	*Belle Starr's Daughter* (Selander)	USA, 48
Jane Russell	*Montana Belle* (Dwan)	USA, 52
Merry Anders	*Young Jesse James* (Claxton)	USA, 60
Sally Starr	*The Outlaws Is Coming* (Maurer)	USA, 65

Pat Quinn	*Zachariah* (Englund)	USA, 71

Note: Betty Compson featured as Belle Starr in the 1928 silent *Court-Martial*.

Stauffenberg, Colonel Claus von

(1907–1944) Not a name that immediately springs to mind, but a key member of the July plot of 1944 when some German officers attempted to assassinate Hitler and bring to an end World War II. Von Stauffenberg was the man selected to plant the bomb (in a suitcase) next to the Führer during a conference. The bomb exploded but succeeded only in injuring Hitler. The officers in the plot were summarily executed, including von Stauffenberg who was shot in a courtyard. The two German films of 1955 concentrated on the assassination attempt in detail.

Eduard Franz	*The Desert Fox* (Hathaway)	USA, 51
Bernhard Wicki	*Es Geschah Am 20. Juli* (Pabst)	Ger, 55
Wolfgang Preiss	*Der 20 Juli* (Harnack)	Ger, 55
William Sargent	*Hitler* (Heisler)	USA, 62
Gerard Buhr	*The Night Of The Generals* (Litvak)	Fra/GB, 66

Stavisky, Serge Alexandre

(c. 1886–1934) French swindler whose huge bond frauds in Paris in the 30s made sensational headlines and resulted in the exposure of widespread corruption in French government circles. Stavisky's life, motives and suicide were the subject of a 1974 film by Alain Resnais.

Jean-Paul Belmondo	*Stavisky* (Resnais)	Fra/It, 74

Strauss, Johann, Jr.

(1825–1899) Austrian composer-conductor whose beautiful waltzes reflected the romance and gaiety of 19th century Vienna. Fernand Gravet starred in the most lavish account of his life, Horst Buchholz in the most recent and most vulgar. In all film biographies, the music has won, hands down!

Esmond Knight	*Waltzes From Vienna* (Hitchcock)	GB, 34
Anton Walbrook	*Waltztime In Vienna* (Berger)	Ger, 34
Fernand Gravet	*The Great Waltz* (Duvivier)	USA, 38
Kerwin Mathews	*The Waltz King* (Previn)	USA, 63
Horst Buchholz	*The Great Waltz* (Stone)	USA, 72

Note: Johann Strauss, Sr. has been played by Edmund Gwenn in *Waltzes*

From Vienna (34), Anton Walbrook in *Vienna Waltzes* (Austria, 51), Brian Aherne in *The Waltz King* (63) and Nigel Patrick in *The Great Waltz* (72).

Stroud, Robert

The famous 'Birdman Of Alcatraz' who spent most of his adult life in American prisons, using his long solitary confinement to become a renowned world authority on bird-life. One of the most complex of American criminals, he was originally convicted of manslaughter when he killed a man in a fight over a dance-hall girl and was later responsible for killing a prison guard. He died in prison in 1963, aged 76. Burt Lancaster, in a restrained, moving performance, played him on film.

Burt Lancaster	*Birdman Of Alcatraz*	(Frankenheimer)	USA, 62

The Student Prince

Royal hero of the 1924 operetta by Sigmund Romberg, a young German prince who enjoys a fleeting romance with a tavern waitress whilst finishing his education at Heidelberg University. Strictly a hero of his time, but retaining a certain amount of schmaltzy glamour through the Romberg melodies, 'Deep In My Heart', 'Serenade' and 'The Drinking Song'. Edmund Purdom replaced an overweight Mario Lanza in the 1954 version, although Lanza recorded the songs.

Edmund Purdom	*The Student Prince*	(Thorpe)	USA, 54
Christian Wolff	*Alt-Heidelberg*	(Marischka)	Ger, 59

Note: The three silent versions of the story were derived from the non-musical play 'Old Heidelberg' (1902) by Rudolf Bleichman, the source of the Romberg operetta. Wallace Reid in *Old Heidelberg* (USA, 15), Paul Hartmann in *The Student Prince* (Ger, 23) and Ramon Novarro in *The Student Price In Old Heidelberg* (USA, 27) all featured as Prince Karl Heinrich.

Sullivan, John L.

(1858–1918) One of the great heavyweight champions in American boxing history, a man who weighed in at 200lbs and began his career when bare knuckle fighting was still the name of the game. His massive contest with Jim Corbett was the highlight of Raoul Walsh's *Gentleman Jim*; his rise to the top and subsequent fall from grace the subject of a not ineffective biography, *The Great John L.*

George Walsh	*The Bowery*	(Walsh)	USA, 34
Bill Hoolahahn	*Diamond Jim*	(Sutherland)	USA, 35
John Kelly	*My Gal Sal*	(Cummings)	USA, 42

| Ward Bond | *Gentleman Jim* (Walsh) | USA, 42 |
| Greg McClure | *The Great John L.* (Tuttle) | USA, 45 |

The Sundance Kid

Fast-shooting member of Butch Cassidy's outlaw gang, 'The Wild Bunch'. Figured in several routine westerns of the 40s and 50s before reaching heroic stature in the now classic *Butch Cassidy And The Sundance Kid*. Historical photographs reveal Sundance to be far removed from the golden-haired Robert Redford, but his relationship with the non-violent Butch and schoolteacher Etta Place is an intriguing one and was retold with great historical accuracy by George Roy Hill. Sundance, who supposedly died in Bolivia in 1908, was christened Harry Longbaugh.

Arthur Kennedy	*Cheyenne* (Walsh)	USA, 47
Robert Ryan	*Return Of The Badmen* (Enright)	USA, 48
Ian MacDonald	*The Texas Rangers* (Karlson)	USA, 51
William Bishop	*Wyoming Renegades* (Sears)	USA, 55
Scott Brady	*The Maverick Queen* (Kane)	USA, 56
Alan Hale, Jr.	*The Three Outlaws* (Newfield)	USA, 56
Russell Johnson	*Badman's Country* (Sears)	USA, 58
Robert Redford	*Butch Cassidy And The Sundance Kid* (Hill)	USA, 69
Tom Berenger	*Butch And Sundance — The Early Days* (Lester)	USA, 79

Note: John Davis Chandler appeared as The Sundance Kid in *Return Of The Gunfighter*, a TV movie made by James Neilson in 1967.

Superman

The flying strongman from the planet Krypton — an ineffectual newspaper reporter (Clark Kent) by day, a red-caped heroic man of steel by night. The subject of several early film cartoons, two serials, a 50s movie and a TV series, before reaching big budget super-status in Richard Donner's 1978 film. First appeared in print in a comic strip in 'Action Comics' in 1938.

Kirk Alyn	*Superman* (Bennet/Carr)	USA, 48
Kirk Alyn	*Atom Man vs Superman* (Bennet)	USA, 50
George Reeves	*Superman And The Mole Men* (Sholem)	USA, 51
Christopher Reeve	*Superman* (Donner)	GB, 78
Christopher Reeve	*Superman II* (Donner)	GB, 80

Note: Both films starring Kirk Alyn were 15-episode Columbia serials; George Reeves later went on to play Superman in a long-running TV series (53–57).

Lois Lane, girl friend of Clark Kent on The Daily Planet, was played by Noel Neill in the two serials, Phyllis Coates in *Superman And The Mole*

Men, and Margot Kidder in the recent spectaculars starring Christopher Reeve.

Svengali

Sinister Hungarian musician who uses his strange hypnotic powers to transform a beautiful young artist's model into a great singing star. Created by George du Maurier in his 1894 novel 'Trilby' and the central figure in no fewer than seven screen adaptations of the story. Donald Wolfit replaced Robert Newton in the most recent version when the latter walked out halfway through production.

John Barrymore	*Svengali* (Mayo)	USA, 31
Donald Wolfit	*Svengali* (Langley)	GB, 54

Note: Viggo Larsen was the first silent screen Svengali in the Danish film of 1908. Sir Herbert Beerbohm Tree (GB, 14), Wilton Lackaye (USA, 15), Arthur Edmund Carew (USA, 23) and Paul Wegener (Ger, 27) all played the role on the silent screen.

Dr. Syn

18th century vicar, leader of smuggling activities in the small English coastal village of Dymchurch. A creation of novelists Russell Thorndike and William Buchanan ('Christopher Syn'), he has been portrayed three times on screen, Peter Cushing's performance differing from the others in that the character was renamed Dr. Blyss, a cover name for the notorious pirate Captain Clegg.

George Arliss	*Dr. Syn* (Neill)	GB, 38
Peter Cushing	*Captain Clegg* (Scott)	GB, 62
Patrick McGoohan	*Dr. Syn—Alias The Scarecrow* (Neilson)	GB, 63

Szabo, Violette

(1918–1945) Half-English, half-French widow who in 1942 became a Secret Service Agent for the Allies and was parachuted into France. Following several successful missions she was captured by the Gestapo and finally executed in January, 1945, after failing to reveal the identity of her contacts. A courageous heroine whose story is told in R. J. Minney's book 'Carve Her Name With Pride'.

Virginia McKenna	*Carve Her Name With Pride* (Gilbert)	GB, 58

T

Taras Bulba

Heroic figure of the 1835 novel by Nikolai Gogol; a famed, sword-swinging adventurer who joins the Cossacks in their campaign against the Poles in 17th century Ukraine. Mostly portrayed in European and Asian films, Yul Brynner's performance in the 1962 spectacular of J. Lee Thompson being the one exception.

Harry Baur	*Taras Bulba*	(Granovski)	Fra, 36
Vladimir Medar	*Taras Bulba*	(Zaphiratos/Baldi)	Fra/It, 61
Yul Brynner	*Taras Bulba*	(Lee Thompson)	USA, 62

Note: Taras Bulba was played on the silent screen by N. Vassiliev in a Russian version of 1910 and Duvan Torzov in Vladimir Strizhevski's German adaptation of 1923.

Tarzan

Possibly the world's best-known fictional hero, the son of an English nobleman who is abandoned in Africa and raised by apes who teach him their language. Hence the famous jungle call, 'aaah-eee-aaah!' The first screen Tarzan, Elmo Lincoln, appeared just four years after the publication of Edgar Rice Burroughs' 'Tarzan Of The Apes' in 1914; Johnny Weismuller, who worked his way through a dozen loincloths, played Tarzan more times than any other actor.

Johnny Weismuller	*Tarzan The Ape Man*	(Van Dyke)	USA, 32
Buster Crabbe	*Tarzan The Fearless*	(Hill)	USA, 33
Johnny Weismuller	*Tarzan And His Mate*	(Gibbons)	USA, 34
Herman Brix	*The New Adventures Of Tarzan*	(Kull)	USA, 35
Johnny Weismuller	*Tarzan Escapes*	(Thorpe)	USA, 36
Herman Brix	*Tarzan And The Green Goddess*	(Kull)	USA, 38
Glenn Morris	*Tarzan's Revenge*	(Lederman)	USA, 38
Johnny Weismuller	*Tarzan Finds A Son*	(Thorpe)	USA, 39
Johnny Weismuller	*Tarzan's Secret Treasure*	(Thorpe)	USA, 41
Johnny Weismuller	*Tarzan's New York Adventure*	(Thorpe)	
			USA, 42

Johnny Weismuller	*Tarzan Triumphs* (Thiele)	USA, 43
Johnny Weismuller	*Tarzan's Desert Mystery* (Thiele)	USA, 43
Johnny Weismuller	*Tarzan And The Amazons* (Neumann)	USA, 45
Johnny Weismuller	*Tarzan And The Leopard Woman* (Neumann)	
		USA, 46
Johnny Weismuller	*Tarzan And The Huntress* (Neumann)	USA, 47
Johnny Weismuller	*Tarzan And The Mermaids* (Florey)	USA, 48
Lex Barker	*Tarzan's Magic Fountain* (Sholem)	USA, 49
Lex Barker	*Tarzan And The Slave Girl* (Sholem)	USA, 50
Lex Barker	*Tarzan's Peril* (Haskin)	USA, 51
Lex Barker	*Tarzan's Savage Fury* (Endfield)	USA, 52
Lex Barker	*Tarzan And The She-Devil* (Neumann)	USA, 53
Gordon Scott	*Tarzan's Hidden Jungle* (Schuster)	USA, 55
Gordon Scott	*Tarzan And The Lost Safari* (Humberstone)	
		GB, 57
Gordon Scott	*Tarzan's Fight For Life* (Humberstone)	
		USA, 58
Gordon Scott	*Tarzan's Greatest Adventure* (Guillermin)	
		GB, 59
Denny Miller	*Tarzan The Ape Man* (Newman)	USA, 59
Gordon Scott	*Tarzan The Magnificent* (Day)	GB, 60
Jock Mahoney	*Tarzan Goes To India* (Guillermin)	GB, 62
Jock Mahoney	*Tarzan's Three Challenges* (Day)	USA, 63
Mike Henry	*Tarzan And The Valley Of Gold* (Day)	
		USA/Swi, 66
Mike Henry	*Tarzan And The Great River* (Day)	USA, 67
Mike Henry	*Tarzan And The Jungle Boy* (Day) USA/Swi, 68	
Ron Ely	*Tarzan's Jungle Rebellion* (Witney)	USA, 70
Ron Ely	*Tarzan's Deadly Silence* (Friend/Dobkin)	
		USA, 70

Note: Herman Brix, who played Tarzan twice in the 30s, subsequently changed his name to Bruce Bennett.

Elmo Lincoln played the Ape Man three times on the silent screen — in *Tarzan Of The Apes* (USA, 18), *The Romance Of Tarzan* (USA, 18) and the 15-episode serial *The Adventures Of Tarzan* (USA, 21).

Gene Pollar (20), P. Dempsey Tabler (20), James Pierce (27) and Frank Merrill (28) were other silent Tarzans.

Tauber, Richard

(1892–1948) Austrian-born opera singer who established himself as one of the leading tenors of the pre-war period, first in Mozart opera and then in light opera by Lehar. Appeared in several British musicals of the 30s, e.g. *Blossom Time*, *Hearts Desire*, *Land Without Music*.

Rudolf Schock	*The Richard Tauber Story* (Morischka)	Aus, 53

Tchaikovsky, Peter Ilyich

(1840–1893) Russian composer of many of the world's most melodic symphonies and ballets. His homosexual problems, coupled with the demands of his nymphomaniac wife, led, not surprisingly, to a life full of torment and anguish. They also helped create 'Romeo And Juliet', 'Swan Lake', 'The Sleeping Beauty' and 'The Nutcracker Suite'. Talankin's overblown 191-minute Russian film treated the composer with due reverence; Ken Russell's vivid *The Music Lovers* cast aside the solemnity and opted for the torment!

Frank Sundstrom	*Song Of My Heart* (Glazer)	USA, 48
Innokenti Smoktunovsky	*Tchaikovsky* (Talankin)	USSR/USA, 70
Richard Chamberlain	*The Music Lovers* (Russell)	GB, 71

Thalberg, Irving G.

(1899–1936) American film producer, long known as the boy wonder, who graduated to legendary status at MGM after an apprenticeship at Universal. Robert Evans' minor portrait in *Man Of A Thousand Faces* showed Thalberg during his years at Universal with Lon Chaney; Robert De Niro's performance as Monroe Stahr (a prototype for Thalberg) in *The Last Tycoon* revealed him in full command of a major studio. An arrogant, ruthless yet brilliant man, Thalberg encouraged MGM to pursue a literary trend in their movies of the 30s.

Robert Evans	*Man Of A Thousand Faces* (Pevney)	USA, 57
Robert De Niro	*The Last Tycoon* (Kazan)	USA, 76

Note: Louis B. Mayer, boss of MGM during Thalberg's period as production head, has been played on screen by Jack Kruschen in Alex Segal's *Harlow* (65), Martin Balsam (as Everett Redman) in Gordon Douglas' *Harlow* (65) and Allen Garfield in *Gable And Lombard* (76).

Thaw, Harry K.

A man who earned himself a place in the annals of American crime when he walked into the Madison Square Garden dining theatre on a June night in 1906 and, in full view of everybody, put three bullets through the head of architect Stanford White. The events leading up to the murder, i.e. White's supposed liaison with Thaw's wife, Evelyn Nesbitt, were reconstructed in Fleischer's *The Girl In The Red Velvet Swing*. Thaw, a millionaire, was found to be insane, but was eventually released from prison and lived for another 25 years.

Farley Granger	*The Girl In The Red Velvet Swing* (Fleischer)
	USA, 55

The Thief Of Bagdad

Magical Arabian Nights figure of adventure and romance who has enjoyed encounters with Oriental villains, giants, dragons, winged horses, etc., ever since Douglas Fairbanks turned him into one of the most famous heroes of the silent screen.

Sabu	*The Thief Of Bagdad*		
		(Powell/Berger/Whelan)	GB, 40
Steve Reeves	*The Thief Of Bagdad*	(Lubin)	Fra/It, 61
Kabir Bedi	*The Thief Of Bagdad*	(Donner)	GB, 79

Note: Fairbanks' silent version, directed by Raoul Walsh, was released by United Artists in 1924.

Thompson, Sadie

South Seas island prostitute, converted to religion by a repressed missionary, who quickly resorts to her former way of life when the missionary himself seduces her. First created by Somerset Maugham in his 1921 short story 'Rain'; updated into a song-and-dance trollop in the 1953 film of Curtis Bernhardt.

Joan Crawford	*Rain* (Milestone)		USA, 32
Rita Hayworth	*Miss Sadie Thompson*	(Bernhardt)	USA, 53

Note: Gloria Swanson played Sadie in the 1928 film of Raoul Walsh; the Rev. Alfred Davidson, the fire and brimstone preacher who succumbs to the pleasures of the flesh has been played by Lionel Barrymore (28), Walter Huston (32) and Jose Ferrer (53).

Thumb, Tom

Five-inch hero of an old 16th century nursery tale, turned into a woodland musical figure in the 1958 fantasy of George Pal, who combined ingenious puppet and animation techniques with the film's live-action sequences. The film marked one of the last appearances of the acrobatic Russ Tamblyn in an MGM musical role.

Russ Tamblyn	*Tom Thumb*	(Pal)	GB, 58
Titoyo	*Tom Thumb*	(Boisrond)	Fra, 72

Three Men In A Boat

Or, in other words, Harris, George and J., Jerome K. Jerome's trio of British incompetents who attempt a peaceful boating holiday on the Thames only to find themselves involved in a series of unmitigated disasters with tents, rain, girls and the Hampton Court Maze. Jerome's special brand of literary humour has yet to be satisfactorily transferred to the screen despite three attempts by British film-makers.

Harris

William Austin	*Three Men In A Boat*	(Cutts)	GB, 33
Jimmy Edwards	*Three Men In A Boat*	(Annakin)	GB, 56

George

Edmond Breon	*Three Men In A Boat*	(Cutts)	GB, 33
Laurence Harvey	*Three Men In A Boat*	(Annakin)	GB, 56

J

Billy Milton	*Three Men In A Boat*	(Cutts)	GB, 33
David Tomlinson	*Three Men In A Boat*	(Annakin)	GB, 56

Note: Manning Haynes (Harris), Johnny Butt (George) and Lionelle Howard (J) featured in Challis Sanderson's 1920 British silent version.

Tibbetts, Colonel Paul

(1915–) The man who trained and commanded the specialist crew who dropped the atomic bombs on Hiroshima and Nagasaki in August, 1945. His own plane dropped the bomb 'Little Boy' on Hiroshima. The full story of the training of the crew and the mission itself is recounted in the Norman Panama/Melvin Frank production *Above And Beyond*.

Barry Nelson	*The Beginning Or The End?*	(Taurog)	USA, 47
Robert Taylor	*Above And Beyond*	(Panama/Frank)	USA, 53

Tibbs, Virgil

The best-known black cop in films, first brought to life on screen in the Oscar-winning *In The Heat Of The Night*, a tale of two detectives, one white, one black, reluctantly working in harness to solve a murder in the Deep South. Other film cases, involving prostitution and drug-running, set in San Francisco. A creation of novelist John Ball.

Sidney Poitier	*In The Heat Of The Night*	(Jewison)	USA, 67
Sidney Poitier	*They Call Me MISTER Tibbs*	(Douglas)	USA, 70
Sidney Poitier	*The Organization*	(Medford)	USA, 71

Topaze

Mild mannered, scrupulously honest French provincial schoolteacher who is used as a front by a corrupt city official, suddenly sees the error of his ways and rises to undreamed of heights as the biggest swindler of them all! The central character in Marcel Pagnol's satirical stage play of

1928; portrayed on five occasions on screen, each time memorably.

Louis Jouvet	*Topaze* (Gasnier)	Fra, 33
John Barrymore	*Topaze* (d'Arrast)	USA, 33
Arnaudy	*Topaze* (Pagnol)	Fra, 36
Fernandel	*Topaze* (Pagnol)	Fra, 50
Peter Sellers	*Mr. Topaze* (Sellers)	GB, 60

Topper, Cosmo

Unassuming hero of Thorne Smith's novels, a timid, henpecked little banker who suddenly finds himself plagued by a couple of ghosts determined to liberate him from his nagging wife and humdrum career. During the three films made about the character the ghosts changed frequently, but Roland Young was always the long-suffering Topper.

Roland Young	*Topper* (McLeod)	USA, 37
Roland Young	*Topper Takes A Trip* (McLeod)	USA, 39
Roland Young	*Topper Returns* (Del Ruth)	USA, 41

Toulouse-Lautrec, Henri

(1864–1901) Parisian artist and lithographer whose stunted growth caused him to be a figure of ridicule for most of his adult life and who found solace only amongst the whores and dancers of Montmartre. His lonely, alcoholic life and brilliant skill as a painter were recreated with affection by John Huston in the biography *Moulin Rouge*.

Jose Ferrer	*Moulin Rouge* (Huston)	GB, 52
Jerry Bergen	*Lust For Life* (Minnelli)	USA, 56

Tracy, Dick

The first comic strip detective hero, conceived by Chester Gould in 1931 and brought to the screen in 1937 in the Republic serial *Dick Tracy*. Tough and square-jawed, he is remembered for two key phrases: 'Little crimes lead to big crimes' and 'Crime does not pay'.

Ralph Byrd	*Dick Tracy* (Taylor/James)	USA, 37
Ralph Byrd	*Dick Tracy Returns* (Witney/English)	USA, 38
Ralph Byrd	*Dick Tracy's G-Men* (Witney/English)	USA, 39
Ralph Byrd	*Dick Tracy vs. Crime, Inc.* (Witney/English)	USA, 41
Morgan Conway	*Dick Tracy* (Berke)	USA, 45
Morgan Conway	*Dick Tracy vs. Cueball* (Douglas)	USA, 46
Ralph Byrd	*Dick Tracy's Dilemma* (Rawlins)	USA, 47

| Ralph Byrd | *Dick Tracy Meets Gruesome* (Rawlins) | USA, 47 |

Note: The first four Ralph Byrd films on the above list are all serials, the remaining four all features.

Trapp, Maria von

The world-famous children's governess who taught her charges to sing, wed their stern father Captain von Trapp and finally escaped with them from a Nazi-dominated Austria to America. Portrayed on screen in two German films long before Julie Andrews set the hills alive with 'The Sound Of Music' in 1965.

Ruth Leuwerik	*The Trapp Family* (Liebeneiner)	Ger, 56
Ruth Leuwerik	*The Trapp Family In America* (Liebeneiner)	Ger, 58
Julie Andrews	*The Sound Of Music* (Wise)	USA, 65

Note: Hans Holt played Captain von Trapp in the two German pictures, Christopher Plummer in the 1965 musical.

Trilby

George du Maurier's tragic heroine of his novel 'Trilby', an artist's model and habituee of the Latin Quarter in Paris who falls under the influence of the musician Svengali and is hypnotised into becoming a great singer. When her mentor dies suddenly of a heart attack her voice dies also. A romantic, helpless character (full name Trilby O'Ferral), she has attracted actresses from Germany, Denmark, Britain and America.

| Marian Marsh | *Svengali* (Mayo) | USA, 31 |
| Hildegarde Neff | *Svengali* (Langley) | GB, 54 |

Note: Oda Alstrup (Den, 08), Viva Birkett (GB, 14), Clara Kimball Young (USA, 15), Andree Lafayette (USA, 23) and Anita Dorris (Ger, 27) all played the role on the silent screen.

Trotsky, Leon

(1877–1940) Influential communist leader and a top member of Lenin's Bolshevik government; expelled after Lenin's death because of ideological differences with Stalin. Screen portraits have been surprisingly few although his final weeks in exile in Mexico, where he was assassinated in 1940, were examined in some detail in Joseph Losey's film of 1972.

| D. F. Barry | *Why Russians Are Revolting* (Sullivan) | USA, 70 |
| Brian Cox | *Nicholas And Alexandra* (Schaffner) | USA, 71 |

Richard Burton	*The Assassination Of Trotsky* (Losey)	
		Fra/It/GB, 72
Yves Peneau	*Stavisky* (Resnais)	Fra/It, 74

Truman, Harry S.

(1884–1972) American President who proved to be a much tougher cookie than most people bargained for when he succeeded to the Presidency on the death of Franklin Roosevelt in April, 1945. Famous for his 'The buck stops here' remark, he was honoured with a one man performance by James Whitmore in the 1975 film, *Give 'Em Hell, Harry!* Truman made the decision to use the atomic bomb to end the war against Japan, an event depicted in *The Beginning Or The End?*

Art Baker	*The Beginning Or The End?* (Taurog)	USA, 46
James Whitmore	*Give 'Em Hell, Harry!* (Binder)	USA, 75
Ed Flanders	*MacArthur* (Sargent)	USA, 77

Note: In *Alias Jesse James*, a small boy is shown playing 'The Missouri Waltz' on the James family's piano. When Bob Hope asks the youngster his name, he replies, 'Harry Truman, sir.'

Turpin, Dick

(1706–1739) Famed highwayman of 18th century England. In real life, no more than a common horse thief and housebreaker who was hanged for murder on the gallows at York; in legend, the man who rode his gallant steed Black Bess from London to York in a single night. A hero figure in all the several movies made about his adventures.

Victor McLaglen	*Dick Turpin* (Stafford/Hanbury)	GB, 33
Louis Hayward	*Dick Turpin's Ride* (Murphy)	USA, 51
Philip Friend	*Dick Turpin — Highwayman* (Paltenghi)	GB, 56
David Weston	*The Legend Of Young Dick Turpin* (Neilson)	
		GB, 65

Note: Turpin was also a popular screen figure in the silent days. Among the actors who played him were Percy Moran in four British films of 1912; Matheson Lang in the 1922 British production, *Dick Turpin's Ride To York*; and Tom Mix in John Blystone's *Dick Turpin* (USA, 25).

Tutankhamen

(*c.* 1371–*c.* 1352 B.C.) Egyptian Pharaoh, aged just nineteen years when he died, whose magnificent tomb was discovered at Thebes by Lord Carnarvon and Howard Carter in November, 1922. The discovery gave rise to the famous horror tale, *The Mummy*, first filmed with Boris Karloff in 1932. It was also the background to a recent movie about a Pharaoh's curse and a young girl who sees visions of the boy king during her tour of the Tutankhamen exhibition in London.

Seif El Din	*A Story Of Tutankhamen* (Scott)	GB, 73

Twain, Mark

(1835–1910) American novelist and humourist (real name, Samuel Clemens) who earned worldwide fame for creating 'Tom Sawyer' and 'Huckleberry Finn' and satirizing established institutions and traditions. A former Mississippi riverboat pilot, he adapted his pen name from a well-known river call ('mark twain' meaning 'by the mark of two fathoms'). He drew on his boyhood experiences along the Mississippi for many of his literary characters and was afforded a respectful 130-minute Warner Bros tribute in 1944.

Fredric March	*The Adventures Of Mark Twain* (Rapper)	USA, 44

Note: Ronald Adam appeared as Samuel Clemens in the 1954 version of Twain's story, *The Million Pound Note*; Karl Formes in *A Connecticut Yankee At King Arthur's Court* (21), Leslie King in *Broadway Broke* (23) and Charles Gerson in *The Pony Express* (25) all featured briefly as the author on the silent screen.

Twist, Oliver

Workhouse orphan boy led into a life of crime by a gang of thieves in 19th century London. The central figure in Charles Dickens' novel of 1837–39. Not the easiest character to play on screen, his 'whiter than white' character being generally overshadowed by those of Fagin, Bill Sikes and co.

Dickie Moore	*Oliver Twist* (Cowen)	USA, 33
John Howard Davis	*Oliver Twist* (Lean)	GB, 48
Mark Lester	*Oliver!* (Reed)	GB, 68

Note: Ivy Millais (GB, 12), Miss Vinnie Burns (USA, 12), Marie Doro (USA, 16) and Jackie Coogan (USA, 22) all played Oliver Twist on the silent screen. Harold Goodwin featured in the 1921 modernized version *Oliver Twist Jr.*

U

Uncle Remus

Whimsical black storyteller (created by Joel Chandler Harris), noted for his tales of the adventures of Brer Rabbit. Just one screen interpretation — by James Baskett in Disney's *Song Of The South*, a live-action/animated production featuring three cartoon Brer Rabbit stories — 'The Tar Baby', 'The Briar Patch' and 'The Laughing Place'. Harris' tales of the Deep South were first collected together in 1880 in the book 'Uncle Remus, His Songs And Sayings'.

James Baskett	*Song Of The South*	(Foster)	USA, 46

Usher, Roderick

Edgar Allan Poe's decaying nobleman who determines that the madness that has plagued his family for generations shall at last come to an end with the deaths of his sister and himself in their crumbling mansion. A role hammed to perfection by Vincent Price in Roger Corman's 1960 film, *The House Of Usher*.

Kay Tendeter	*The Fall Of The House Of Usher*	(Barnett)	GB, 50
Vincent Price	*The House Of Usher*	(Corman)	USA, 60

Note: Melville Webber and Jean Debucourt (in a French film by Jean Epstein) both featured as Usher in silent films released in 1928.

V

Valachi, Joseph

Not the most important member of the Cosa Nostra, but one of the few Mafia members to break the organization's code of silence. An enforcer, numbers runner and narcotics peddler for the Luciano 'Family', he turned informer in 1959 when sentenced to 15 years in Atlanta for violation of the narcotics laws. He died of a heart attack in 1971 in a Texas prison. His life was portrayed by Charles Bronson in Terence Young's film *The Valachi Papers* (also known as *Cosa Nostra*).

| Charles Bronson | *The Valachi Papers* (Young) | Fra/It, 72 |

Valentino, Rudolph

(1895–1926) *The* romantic movie star of the early 20s, a 'Sheik of the Silver Screen' who caused female fainting fits and male boredom with his amorous escapades in a series of famous silent films: *The Four Horsemen Of The Apocalypse* (21), *The Sheik* (21), *Blood And Sand* (22), etc. His life on and off the screen has been the subject of two film biographies, the first starring look-alike Anthony Dexter, the second featuring Rudolf Nureyev and directed in flamboyant style by Ken Russell.

Anthony Dexter	*Valentino* (Allen)	USA, 51
Rudolf Nureyev	*Valentino* (Russell)	GB, 77
Matt Collins	*The World's Greatest Lover* (Gene Wilder)	USA, 77

Valjean, Jean

One of literature's most pitiable victims, a French peasant who escapes from a living hell (over twenty years imprisonment for stealing a loaf of bread) only to spend the rest of his life eluding his fanatical pursuer Inspector Javert. The leading figure in Victor Hugo's scathing indictment of injustice in 19th century France, 'Les Miserables' (1862).

| Harry Baur | *Les Miserables* (Bernard) | Fra, 34 |
| Fredric March | *Les Miserables* (Boleslawski) | USA, 35 |

Domingo Soler	*Les Misérables* (Rivero)	Mex, 44
Gino Cervi	*Les Misérables* (Freda)	It, 46
T. S. Baliah	*Ezhai Padum Padu* (Ramanath)	Ind, 50
Michael Rennie	*Les Misérables* (Milestone)	USA, 52
Sohrab Modi	*Kundan* (Modi)	Ind, 55
Jean Gabin	*Les Misérables* (Le Chanois)	Fra/It, 58
Richard Jordan	*Les Misérables* (Glenn Jordan)	GB, 79

Note: Henry Krauss featured as Valjean in Albert Capellani's 1913 French version; William Farnum in Frank Lloyd's 1917 adaptation and Gabriel Gabrio in Henri Fescourt's film of 1925. Earlier versions of the story were released in France in 1909 and America in 1910.

Vance, Philo

Debonair private detective of S. S. Van Dine, first introduced to the reading public in 1926 ('The Benson Murder Case') and to the screen three years later. The epitome of the elegant dilettante-sleuth, he was best represented on film by the polished characterisations of William Powell who played him on four occasions. During Powell's heyday he featured in at least one classic crime film, Michael Curtiz's *The Kennel Murder Case* (33).

William Powell	*The Canary Murder Case* (St. Clair)	USA, 29
William Powell	*The Greene Murder Case* (Tuttle)	USA, 29
Basil Rathbone	*The Bishop Murder Case* (Grinde/Burton)	
		USA, 30
William Powell	*The Benson Murder Case* (Tuttle)	USA, 30
William Powell	*The Kennel Murder Case* (Curtiz)	USA, 33
Warren William	*The Dragon Murder Case* (Humberstone)	
		USA, 34
Paul Lukas	*The Casino Murder Case* (Marin)	USA, 35
Edmund Lowe	*The Garden Murder Case* (Marin)	USA, 36
Wilfrid Hyde White	*The Scarab Murder Case* (Hankinson)	GB, 36
Grant Richards	*Night Of Mystery* (Dupont)	USA, 37
Warren William	*The Gracie Allen Murder Case* (Green)	
		USA, 39
James Stephenson	*Calling Philo Vance* (Clemens)	USA, 40
William Wright	*Philo Vance Returns* (Beaudine)	USA, 47
Alan Curtis	*Philo Vance's Gamble* (Wrangell)	USA, 47
Alan Curtis	*Philo Vance's Secret Mission* (LeBorg)	USA, 47

Van Gogh, Vincent

(1853–1890) Tormented Dutch artist, a pioneer of Expressionism, whose tortured, depressed life, first as a Methodist preacher and finally as a painter among the Provencal landscapes at Arles, was faithfully recreated by Vincente Minnelli in *Lust For Life*. Much of the film was shot in the actual places where Van Gogh lived and worked.

Kirk Douglas	*Lust For Life* (Minnelli)	USA, 56

Van Helsing, Professor

Count Dracula's deadliest foe, a vampire hunter with all the necessary tricks of the trade needed to rid the world of the bloodsucking tyrant of Transylvania. The two actors most associated with holding a trembling crucifix in front of bared fangs and driving a stake through Dracula's heart, are Edward Van Sloan and Peter Cushing. But despite their determination and noble intentions the count has steadfastly refused to die.

Edward Van Sloan	*Dracula* (Browning)	USA, 31
Edward Van Sloan	*Dracula's Daughter* (Hillyard)	USA, 36
Peter Cushing	*Dracula* (Fisher)	GB, 58
Peter Cushing	*Brides Of Dracula* (Fisher)	GB, 60
Herbert Lom	*El Conde Dracula* (Franco)	Spa, 70
Peter Cushing	*Dracula A.D. 1972* (Gibson)	GB, 72
Peter Cushing	*The Satanic Rites Of Dracula* (Gibson)	GB, 73
Nigel Davenport	*Dracula* (Cohen)	USA, 73
Peter Cushing	*The Legend Of The Seven Golden Vampires* (Baker)	GB/Hong Kong, 74
Walter Ladengast	*Nosferatu — The Vampyre* (Herzog)	W.Ger, 79
Laurence Olivier	*Dracula* (Badham)	USA, 79

Verloc

Anarchist villain of Joseph Conrad's 1907 novel 'The Secret Agent'. He operates with his fellow conspirators in the back streets of London where he plans to overthrow the forces of law and order and is eventually murdered by his wife. In Hitchcock's 1936 adaptation *Sabotage*, the character was brought up to date and turned into the manager of a small cinema. The net result was the same, however, a knife in the back from Sylvia Sidney!

Oscar Homolka	*Sabotage* (Hitchcock)	GB, 36

Victoria, Queen

(1819–1901) British monarch and Empress of India who reigned for most of the 19th century and whose life inspired two Anna Neagle film biographies of the late 30s. Only an occasional, minor character on the modern screen, but portrayed in some depth in the post-war period —

by Romy Schneider in *The Young Victoria* and Irene Dunne in *The Mudlark*, a unique movie about a London orphan who smuggles himself into Windsor Castle and persuades the ageing queen to emerge from her lengthy seclusion after the death of her husband, Prince Albert.

Margaret Mann	*Disraeli* (Green)	USA, 29
Madeleine Ozeray	*La Guerre Des Valses* (Berger)	Ger/Fra, 33
Hanna Waag	*Waltz Time In Vienna* (Berger)	Ger, 34
Pamela Stanley	*David Livingstone* (Fitzpatrick)	GB, 36
Anna Neagle	*Victoria The Great* (Wilcox)	GB, 37
Anna Neagle	*Sixty Glorious Years* (Wilcox)	GB, 38
Pamela Stanley	*Marigold* (Bentley)	GB, 38
Gaby Morlay	*Entente Cordiale* (L'Herbier)	Fra, 38
Fay Compton	*The Prime Minister* (Dickinson)	GB, 41
Evelyn Beresford	*Annie Get Your Gun* (Sidney)	USA, 50
Irene Dunne	*The Mudlark* (Negulesco)	GB, 50
Helena Pickard	*The Lady With The Lamp* (Wilcox)	GB, 51
Muriel Aked	*The Story Of Gilbert And Sullivan* (Gilliat)	GB, 53
Sybil Thorndike	*Melba* (Milestone)	GB, 53
Anna Neagle	*Lilacs In The Spring* (Wilcox)	GB, 54
Romy Schneider	*The Young Victoria* (Marischka)	Ger, 55
Mollie Maureen	*The Private Life Of Sherlock Holmes* (Billy Wilder)	GB, 70
Susan Field	*The Adventures Of Sherlock Holmes' Smarter Brother* (Gene Wilder)	USA, 75

Villa, Pancho

(1877–1923) Mexican revolutionary leader, for some a ruthless bandit, for others a noble champion of the people. Unlike Zapata, who was also active in the 1910 revolution, he survived the conflict only to be brought down by an assassin's bullet in 1923. Recent portrayals have been of heroic stature, i.e. Yul Brynner in *Villa Rides!* and Telly Savalas in *Pancho Villa*; Wallace Beery's more fiery portrait in the pre-war *Viva Villa!* allowed Villa a higher degree of sadism and cruelty.

Wallace Beery	*Viva Villa!* (Conway)	USA, 34
Domingo Soler	*Let's Go With Pancho Villa* (de Fuentes)	Mex, 36
Leo Carrillo	*Pancho Villa Returns* (Contreras)	Mex, 50
Alan Reed	*Viva Zapata!* (Kazan)	USA, 52
Rodolfo Hoyos	*Villa!* (Clark)	USA, 58
Pedro Armendariz	*This Was Pancho Villa* (Rodrigues)	Mex, 59
Pedro Armendariz	*Pancho Villa And Valentina* (Rodrigues)	Mex, 60
Yul Brynner	*Villa Rides!* (Kulik)	USA, 68
Eraclio Zepeda	*Reed: Insurgent Mexico* (Leduc)	Mex, 71
Telly Savalas	*Pancho Villa* (Martin)	Spa, 72

Voltaire

(1694–1778) French satirist and novelist whose literary works and crusading ideas helped foster the French Revolution of 1789. A constant source of irritation to the political and religious establishment figures of his time, he was the 'embodiment of 18th century enlightenment'. Just one screen biography to date and a half-hearted one at that, John Adolfi's 1933 film with George Arliss.

George Arliss	*Voltaire* (Adolfi)	USA, 33
Maurice Schutz	*Le Diable Boiteux* (Guitry)	Fra, 48
Jacques de Feraudy	*Versailles* (Guitry)	Fra, 54

W

Wagner, Richard

(1813–1883) Fiercely nationalistic German composer whose sweeping dramatic works — 'Tannhäuser', 'Tristan und Isolde', 'Nibelungen' — revolutionized the world of opera and whose egotism and emotional instability earned him a notoriety that went side by side with his fame as a musician. The subject of a low budget biography by William Dieterle, he has also featured prominently in films about his patron, Ludwig II of Bavaria.

Paul Bildt	*Ludwig II* (Kautner)	Ger, 55
Alan Badel	*Magic Fire* (Dieterle)	USA, 56
Lyndon Brook	*Song Without End* (Charles Vidor)	USA, 60
Gerhard Marz	*Ludwig—Requiem For A Virgin King* (Syberberg)	
		W.Ger, 72
Trevor Howard	*Ludwig* (Visconti)	It/Fra/W.Ger, 73
Paul Nicholas	*Lisztomania* (Russell)	GB, 75

Wallis, Sir Barnes Nevill

(1887–   ) The most famous of the World War II boffins, an English aircraft designer whose invention of a revolutionary bouncing bomb enabled the RAF to destroy the vital Ruhr dams in Germany. Portrayed in some depth by Michael Redgrave in the 1955 film *The Dam Busters*.

Michael Redgrave	*The Dam Busters* (Anderson)	GB, 55

Watson, Dr.

Famed chronicler of the adventures of Sherlock Holmes and, unquestionably, one of the most difficult characters to play convincingly on screen. Generally emerges as a bluff, likeable buffoon, e.g. Nigel Bruce, if only to accentuate the brilliance of his famous partner. Colin Blakely's younger Watson in *The Private Life Of Sherlock Holmes* and James Mason's more mature doctor in the recent *Murder By Decree* stand perhaps as the most believable interpretations.

H. Reeves Smith	*The Return Of Sherlock Holmes*	
	(Dean/Brook)	USA, 29
Ian Fleming	*The Sleeping Cardinal* (Hiscott)	GB, 31
Athole Stewart	*The Speckled Band* (Raymond)	GB, 31
Fred Lloyd	*The Hound Of The Baskervilles*	
	(Gundrey)	GB, 32
Ian Fleming	*The Missing Rembrandt* (Hiscott)	GB, 32
Ian Hunter	*The Sign Of Four* (Cutts)	GB, 32
Reginald Owen	*Sherlock Holmes* (Howard)	USA, 32
Warburton Gamble	*A Study In Scarlet* (Marin)	USA, 33
Ian Fleming	*The Triumph Of Sherlock Holmes* (Hiscott)	
		GB, 35
Fritz Odemar	*Der Hund Von Baskerville* (Lamac)	Ger, 37
Ian Fleming	*Silver Blaze* (Bentley)	GB, 37
Heinz Ruhmann	*The Man Who Was Sherlock Holmes* (Hartl)	
		Ger, 37
Nigel Bruce	*The Hound Of The Baskervilles* (Lanfield)	
		USA, 39
Nigel Bruce	*The Adventures Of Sherlock Holmes* (Werker)	
		USA, 39
Nigel Bruce	*Sherlock Holmes And The Voice Of Terror*	
	(Rawlins)	USA, 42
Nigel Bruce	*Sherlock Holmes And The Secret Weapon* (Neill)	
		USA, 42
Nigel Bruce	*Sherlock Holmes In Washington* (Neill)	USA, 43
Nigel Bruce	*Sherlock Holmes Faces Death* (Neill)	USA, 43
Nigel Bruce	*Spider Woman* (Neill)	USA, 44
Nigel Bruce	*The Scarlet Claw* (Neill)	USA, 44
Nigel Bruce	*The Pearl Of Death* (Neill)	USA, 44
Nigel Bruce	*The House Of Fear* (Neill)	USA, 45
Nigel Bruce	*The Woman In Green* (Neill)	USA, 45
Nigel Bruce	*Pursuit To Algiers* (Neill)	USA, 45
Nigel Bruce	*Terror By Night* (Neill)	USA, 46
Nigel Bruce	*Dressed To Kill* (Neill)	USA, 46
Campbell Singer	*The Man With The Twisted Lip* (Grey)	GB, 51
Andre Morell	*The Hound Of The Baskervilles* (Fisher)	
		GB, 59
Thorley Walters	*Sherlock Holmes And The Deadly Necklace*	
	(Fisher)	W.Ger, 62
Donald Houston	*A Study In Terror* (Hill)	GB, 65
Colin Blakely	*The Private Life Of Sherlock Holmes*	
	(Billy Wilder)	GB, 70
Vaclav Voska	*Sherlock Holmes' Desire* (Skalsky)	Czech, 71
Thorley Walters	*The Adventures Of Sherlock Holmes' Smarter*	
	Brother (Gene Wilder)	USA, 75
Robert Duvall	*The Seven-Per-Cent Solution* (Ross)	USA, 76
Dudley Moore	*The Hound Of The Baskervilles* (Morrissey)	
		GB, 78
James Mason	*Murder By Decree* (Clark)	GB, 79

Note: Reginald Owen remains the only actor to play both Holmes and Watson on screen; Joanne Woodward featured as the psychiatrist Dr. Watson in *They Might Be Giants* (71); Bernard Fox in *The Hound Of The Baskervilles* (72) and Patrick MacNee in *Sherlock Holmes In New York* (77) starred as the doctor in made-for-TV movies.

Chief among the silent screen Watsons were those of Arthur M. Cullin in *The Valley Of Fear* (GB, 16), Hubert Willis in the Stoll series of the 20s, Roland Young in *Sherlock Holmes* (USA, 22) and Georges Seroff in *Der Hund Von Baskerville* (Ger, 29).

Wellington, Duke Of

(1769–1852) English general and statesman, victor over Napoleon at Waterloo and Prime Minister from 1828–30. For film-makers, a less appealing figure than Bonaparte and warranting only one full-length biography by Victor Saville in 1935. Christopher Plummer's suave, witty Wellington in Bondarchuk's *Waterloo* went some way to redressing the balance in 1970.

Humberstone Wright	*Congress Dances* (Charell)	Ger, 31
C. Aubrey Smith	*The House Of Rothschild* (Werker)	USA, 34
William Faversham	*Becky Sharp* (Mamoulian)	USA, 35
George Arliss	*The Iron Duke* (Saville)	GB, 35
Matthew Boulton	*The Firefly* (Leonard)	USA, 37
James Dale	*Victoria The Great* (Wilcox)	GB, 37
C. Aubrey Smith	*Sixty Glorious Years* (Wilcox)	GB, 38
Torin Thatcher	*The Miracle* (Rapper)	USA, 59
Christopher Plummer	*Waterloo* (Bondarchuk)	It/USSR, 70
John Neville	*The Adventures Of Gerard* (Skolimowski)	
		GB/It/Swi, 70
Laurence Olivier	*Lady Caroline Lamb* (Bolt)	GB/It, 72

The Werewolf

A reluctant member of the horror scene, just any old John Doe during the daylight hours, but a hairy faced, long toothed killer when the moon is full. Supposedly derived from Greek superstition, he made his first sound screen appearance in 1935 when botanist Henry Hull was bitten by a werewolf while searching for a mysterious flower in Tibet. Since then, college boys, young girls, even politicians (*The Werewolf Of Washington*) have had the bite put on them, been changed into werewolves and despatched by the traditional silver bullet. Lon Chaney gave the definitive portrayal in the 1941 production *The Wolf Man*. He subsequently played the role on another five occasions.

Henry Hull	*The Werewolf Of London* (Walker)	USA, 35
Lon Chaney, Jr.	*The Wolf Man* (Waggner)	USA, 41
Lon Chaney, Jr.	*Frankenstein Meets The Wolf Man* (Neill)	USA, 43

Matt Willis	*The Return Of The Vampire* (Landers)	USA, 43
Nina Foch	*Cry Of The Werewolf* (Levin)	USA, 44
Lon Chaney, Jr.	*House Of Frankenstein* (Kenton)	USA, 44
Lon Chaney, Jr.	*House Of Dracula* (Kenton)	USA, 45
June Lockhart	*She-Wolf Of London* (Yarbrough)	USA, 46
Lon Chaney, Jr.	*Abbott & Costello Meet Frankenstein*	
	(Barton)	USA, 48
Steven Ritch	*The Werewolf* (Sears)	USA, 56
Michael Landon	*I Was A Teenage Werewolf* (Fowler, Jr.)	USA, 57
Lon Chaney, Jr.	*Face Of The Screaming Werewolf* (Warren)	Mex, 60
Oliver Reed	*Curse Of The Werewolf* (Fisher)	GB, 61
Curt Lowens	*Werewolf In a Girl's Dormitory* (Benson)	It, 62
Ursula Howells	*Dr. Terror's House Of Horrors* (Francis)	GB, 64
Paul Naschy	*Frankenstein's Bloody Terror* (Equiluz)	Spa, 68
Paul Naschy	*Las Noches Del Hombre* (Gover)	Spa, 68
Paul Naschy	*Shadow Of The Werewolf* (Klimovsky)	
		Spa/W.Ger, 70
Paul Naschy	*The Fury Of The Wolf Man* (Zabalazar)	Spa, 70
Paul Naschy	*Doctor Jekyll And The Werewolf* (Klimovsky)	Spa, 71
Paul Naschy	*Curse Of The Devil* (Alonzo)	Spa/Mex, 73
Dean Stockwell	*The Werewolf Of Washington* (Ginsberg)	USA, 73
Kerwin Mathews	*The Boy Who Cried Werewolf* (Juran)	USA, 73
David Rintoul	*Legend Of The Werewolf* (Francis)	GB, 74
Michael Gambon	*The Beast Must Die* (Annett)	GB, 74

White, Pearl

(1889–1938) Silent movie queen who was tied screaming to railway tracks, flung from cliff tops and generally manhandled in several silent serials during the ten-year period, 1914–23: *The Exploits Of Elaine* (14), *The Perils Of Pauline* (14), *The Fatal Ring* (17), etc. A former stunt girl, she was played on screen in a loose, much fictionalised biography, by Betty Hutton.

| Betty Hutton | *The Perils Of Pauline* (Marshall) | USA, 47 |

Who, Dr.

Absent-minded scientist/inventor of The Tardis, a telephone box time machine which journeys through several galaxies, bringing new adventures wherever it lands. A popular TV character, created for the BBC by Terry Nation and played on the small screen by William Hartnell, Patrick Troughton, Jon Pertwee, Tom Baker, etc. Peter Cushing has been the Doctor's sole interpreter in the movies.

| Peter Cushing | *Dr. Who And The Daleks* (Flemyng) | GB, 65 |
| Peter Cushing | *Daleks—Invasion Earth 2150 A.D.* (Flemyng) | GB, 66 |

Wilde, Oscar

(1854–1900) The wittiest author of his generation, noted for his brilliant epigrams and sophisticated writings ('The Importance Of Being Earnest', 'The Picture Of Dorian Gray'), and notorious for his homosexual association with Lord Alfred Douglas. The affair caused headlines in the 1890s when Douglas' father, The Marquis of Queensbury, accused Wilde of sodomy and perversion and was the focal point of both 1960 screen biographies. Ken Hughes' version emerged as the most successful of the two, not least for the performance of Peter Finch who movingly brought out both the wit and moral decay of the writer. Wilde died in exile in Paris in 1900.

Robert Morley	*Oscar Wilde* (Ratoff)	GB, 60
Peter Finch	*The Trials Of Oscar Wilde* (Hughes)	GB, 60
John De Marco	*The Best House In London* (Saville)	GB, 69

Wilson, Thomas Woodrow

(1856–1924) A former schoolmaster who brought dignity, courage and a quiet honesty to his eight-year term as the 28th President of the United States. Zanuck's 154-minute tribute with Alexander Knox playing the President, covered Wilson's entire political life, from his years at Princeton University to when he took America into World War I and helped found the League Of Nations. Despite its unimaginative approach, the film remains the most detailed chronicle of a Presidential career ever put on celluloid.

Alexander Knox	*Wilson* (Henry King)	USA, 44
Earl Lee	*The Story Of Will Rogers* (Curtiz)	USA, 52
L. Korsakov	*The Unforgettable Year — 1919* (Chiaureli)	USSR, 52

The Wizard Of Oz

Or, in other words, a phoney, a sham wizard to whom Dorothy, along with The Scarecrow, The Tinman and The Cowardly Lion, travels for help after a cyclone has transported her from Kansas to the magical land of Oz. Frank Morgan portrayed him in the Judy Garland classic, Graham Matters in the Australian updated rock film, and Richard Pryor (as a failed politician) in the all-black musical *The Wiz*.

Frank Morgan	*The Wizard Of Oz* (Fleming)	USA, 39
Graham Matters	*Oz* (Lofven)	Austral, 76
Richard Pryor	*The Wiz* (Lumet)	USA, 78

Note: Charles Murray appeared as the Wizard in Larry Semon's little-known silent production of 1925.

The other major characters in this famous Frank Baum story, first published in 1900, have been played as follows:

Dorothy

Dorothy Dwan	*The Wizard Of Oz* (Semon)	USA, 25
Judy Garland	*The Wizard Of Oz* (Fleming)	USA, 39
Joy Dunstan	*Oz* (Lofven)	Austral, 76
Diana Ross	*The Wiz* (Lumet)	USA, 78

Note: Liza Minnelli voiced the character of Dorothy in Hal Sutherland's full-length animated feature, *Journey Back To Oz* in 1972.

The Scarecrow

Larry Semon	*The Wizard Of Oz* (Semon)	USA, 25
Ray Bolger	*The Wizard Of Oz* (Fleming)	USA, 39
Bruce Spence	*Oz* (Lofven)	Austral, 76
Michael Jackson	*The Wiz* (Lumet)	USA, 78

Note: Mickey Rooney voiced The Scarecrow in the cartoon, *Journey Back To Oz* (72); in the Australian rock movie the character was renamed Surfie.

The Tinman

Oliver Hardy	*The Wizard Of Oz* (Semon)	USA, 25
Jack Haley	*The Wizard Of Oz* (Fleming)	USA, 39
Michael Carmen	*Oz* (Lofven)	Austral, 76
Nipsey Russell	*The Wiz* (Lumet)	USA, 78

Note: Danny Thomas voiced The Tinman in *Journey Back To Oz*; in the Australian movie the character was renamed Mechanic.

The Cowardly Lion

Bert Lahr	*The Wizard Of Oz* (Fleming)	USA, 39
Gary Waddell	*Oz* (Lofven)	Austral, 76
Ted Ross	*The Wiz* (Lumet)	USA, 78

Note: Milton Berle voiced the character in *Journey Back To Oz*; The Cowardly Lion did not appear in the 1925 silent version and was renamed Bikie in the Australian movie of 1976.

Wolsey, Cardinal Thomas

(1471–1530) 16th century English cardinal and Lord Chancellor, for a period all powerful, but finally a humiliated figure when he failed to secure the Pope's agreement to Henry VIII's divorce from Catherine of Aragon. Orson Welles made him a figure of decay and frustrated ambition in *A Man For All Seasons*; Anthony Quayle a pathetic and ineffectual character in *Anne Of The Thousand Days*.

Percy Marmont	*The Pearls Of The Crown* (Guitry-Jaque)	
		Fra, 37
D. A. Clarke-Smith	*The Sword And The Rose* (Annakin)	GB, 53
Orson Welles	*A Man For All Seasons* (Zinnemann)	GB, 66
Anthony Quayle	*Anne Of The Thousand Days* (Jarrott)	GB, 69
Terry Scott	*Carry On Henry* (Thomas)	GB, 71
John Bryans	*Henry VIII And His Six Wives* (Hussein)	GB, 72

Note: Herbert Tree in *Henry VIII* (GB, 11), Hal Reid in *Cardinal Wolsey* (USA, 12) and Arthur Forrest in *When Knighthood Was In Flower* (USA, 22) were among the actors who played Wolsey in the silent era.

Y

Yamamoto, Admiral Isoroku

(1884–1943). Japanese naval strategist and commander who planned the attack on Pearl Harbour in December, 1941, and then quickly suffered reversals at the hands of the Americans in the Pacific, i.e. at the Battle of Midway. Eventually killed when shot down by American aircraft in 1943; played many times on screen by Japanese actor Toshiro Mifune.

James T. Goto	*The Gallant Hours* (Montgomery)	USA, 60
Toshiro Mifune	*I Bombed Pearl Harbour* (Matsubayashi)	Jap, 60
Toshiro Mifune	*Admiral Yamamoto* (Maruyama)	Jap, 68
Shogo Shimada	*Gateway To Glory* (Murayama)	Jap, 69
Toshiro Mifune	*The Militarists* (Horikawa)	Jap, 70
Soh Yamamura	*Tora! Tora! Tora!* (Fleischer)	USA/Jap, 70
Toshiro Mifune	*Midway* (Smight)	USA, 76

York, Alvin C.

Deeply religious and pacifist Tennessee farmer who was obliged to go against his beliefs in World War I and finished up being acclaimed 'the greatest civilian soldier of the war'. His heroic exploits reached almost unbelievable proportions when he killed 25 of the enemy and captured 132 prisoners single-handed. Howard Hawks' film, which won Gary Cooper an Oscar, was an adaptation of York's diaries.

| Gary Cooper | *Sergeant York* (Hawks) | USA, 41 |

Younger, Cole

(1844–1916) The most notorious of the three Younger brothers. A rider with Quantrill in the American Civil War and later with the Jesse James gang, he was a casualty of the ill-fated raid on the bank of Northfield (1876) and spent his next 25 years in jail, reputedly with 17 bullets still resting harmlessly in his body. Generally a second string western character but examined at length in Philip Kaufman's *The Great Northfield Minnesota Raid*.

Glenn Strange	*Days Of Jesse James* (Kane)	USA, 39
Dennis Morgan	*Bad Men Of Missouri* (Enright)	USA, 41
Steve Brodie	*Return Of The Badmen* (Enright)	USA, 48
Wayne Morris	*The Younger Brothers* (Marin)	USA, 49
James Best	*Kansas Raiders* (Enright)	USA, 50
Bruce Bennett	*The Great Missouri Raid* (Douglas)	USA, 51
Bruce Cabot	*Best Of The Badmen* (Russell)	USA, 51
Jim Davis	*Woman They Almost Lynched* (Dwan)	USA, 53
Sam Keller	*Jesse James' Women* (Barry)	USA, 54
Alan Hale, Jr.	*The True Story of Jesse James* (Ray)	USA, 56
Myron Healy	*Hell's Crossroads* (Andreon)	USA, 57
Frank Lovejoy	*Cole Younger, Gunfighter* (Springsteen)	USA, 58
Willard Parker	*Young Jesse James* (Claxton)	USA, 60
Bruce Sedley	*The Outlaws Is Coming* (Maurer)	USA, 65
Cliff Robertson	*The Great Northfield Minnesota Raid* (Kaufman)	USA, 72

Z

Zapata, Emiliano

(*c.* 1879–1919) Mexican revolutionary who joined with Pancho Villa to overthrow the Diaz regime in 1911. An idealised but excitingly cinematic biography by Elia Kazan (script by John Steinbeck) followed Zapata from his years as a bandit outlaw and general, to his short term as President and subsequent assassination by the military. Brando's Zapata stands high amongst his finest work.

Marlon Brando	*Viva Zapata!* (Kazan)	USA, 52
Tony Davis	*Guns Of The Magnificent Seven* (Wendkos)	USA, 69

Note: The Tony Davis performance was of Zapata as a child.

Zaroff, Count

Richard Connell's bizarre sadist, a fanatical big game hunter who becomes bored with killing animals and turns to hunting humans instead. Operates from his own private island and chooses his victims from those shipwrecked on the rocky coasts. There have been many variations of the role down the years — with several changes of name — but Leslie Banks' original performance remains the authoritative portrayal.

Leslie Banks	*The Most Dangerous Game* (Schoedsack/Pichel)	USA, 32
Edgar Barrier	*A Game Of Death* (Wise)	USA, 46
Trevor Howard	*Run For The Sun* (Roy Boulting)	USA, 56

Note: Both *Johnny Allegro* (49) and *Kill Or Be Killed* (50) were loose adaptations of the Zaroff story; *To Kill A Clown* (72), based on a novel by Algis Budrys, featured Alan Alda as a crippled Vietnam veteran who hunts down a young couple on an island off the New England coast.

Ziegfeld, Florenz

(1869–1932) The most celebrated of all American showmenimpresarios, producer of such Broadway shows as 'Sally', 'Rio Rita' and 'Show Boat', but best-known for his lavish series of Follies 'glorifying the American girl'. Appropriately enough, the subject of the first three hour Hollywood musical biography, the Oscar-winning *The Great Ziegfeld*, produced by MGM in 1936.

William Powell	*The Great Ziegfeld* (Leonard)	USA, 36
William Powell	*Ziegfeld Follies* (Minnelli)	USA, 45
Eddie Kane	*The Jolson Story* (Green)	USA, 46
William Forrest	*I'll See You In My Dreams* (Curtiz)	USA, 52
William Forrest	*The Eddie Cantor Story* (Green)	USA, 53
Wilton Graff	*The I Don't Care Girl* (Bacon)	USA, 53
Paul Henreid	*Deep In My Heart* (Donen)	USA, 54
Walter Woolf King	*The Helen Morgan Story* (Curtiz)	USA, 57
Walter Pidgeon	*Funny Girl* (Wyler)	USA, 68
Paul Stewart	*W. C. Fields And Me* (Hiller)	USA, 76

Note: Bernard Randall in *Polly Of The Follies* (22) and Bertram Marburgh (as Lew Kline) in *An Affair Of The Follies* (27) both featured as Ziegfeld on the silent screen.

Zola, Emile

(1840–1902) 19th century novelist, regarded by many as the French Charles Dickens in his never-ending quest for social reform and for his compassionate portraits of the lower classes. 'L'Assommoir', 'Nana' and 'Therese Raquin' are among those of his novels filmed; the Oscar-winning *The Life Of Emile Zola* retold his life, Hollywood style, in 1937. Zola figures prominently in the films made about the famous Dreyfus case.

Heinrich George	*The Dreyfus Case* (Oswald)	Ger, 30
George Merritt	*Dreyfus* (Kraemer/Rosmer)	GB, 31
Paul Muni	*The Life Of Emile Zola* (Dieterle)	USA, 37
Emlyn Williams	*I Accuse!* (Jose Ferrer)	GB, 58

Index